D1650638

Adrian Gilbert is the b̲_____ ̲he
Quest for a Secret Tradition and *Signs in the Sky,* and
co-author of *The Orion Mystery, The Mayan Prophecies*
and *The Holy Kingdom.*

For more information about Adrian Gilbert and his
books visit his website at: www.adriangilbert.co.uk

For Sophia, who was lost and is found

Angel showing St John the City of New Jerusalem.
From *Iconum Biblicarum*, Strasbourg, 1630.

THE NEW JERUSALEM

Adrian Gilbert

CORGI BOOKS

THE NEW JERUSALEM
A CORGI BOOK : 0 552 14848 2

Originally published in Great Britain by Bantam Press,
a division of Transworld Publishers

PRINTING HISTORY
Bantam Press edition published 2002
Corgi edition published 2003

1 3 5 7 9 10 8 6 4 2

Copyright © Adrian Gilbert 2002

All photographs are by the author unless individually credited.

The right of Adrian Gilbert to be identified as the author of this
work has been asserted in accordance with sections 77 and 78 of
the Copyright Designs and Patents Act 1988.

Set in 10/12pt Sabon by
Falcon Oast Graphic Art Ltd.

Corgi Books are published by Transworld Publishers,
61–63 Uxbridge Road, London W5 5SA,
a division of The Random House Group Ltd,
in Australia by Random House Australia (Pty) Ltd,
20 Alfred Street, Milsons Point, Sydney, NSW 2061, Australia,
in New Zealand by Random House New Zealand Ltd,
18 Poland Road, Glenfield, Auckland 10, New Zealand
and in South Africa by Random House (Pty) Ltd,
Endulini, 5a Jubilee Road, Parktown 2193, South Africa

Printed in Great Britain by
Cox & Wyman Ltd, Reading, Berkshire.

CONTENTS

LIST OF PLATES

LIST OF ILLUSTRATIONS

ACKNOWLEDGEMENTS

I would like to thank the following organizations and individuals for their help in bringing this work to fruition: the staff of the British Library, who do such sterling work on behalf of scholars worldwide; the staff of the British Museum, who continue to maintain to the highest standards the finest collection of antiquities in the world; the staff of the Library of the Royal Society for their help and friendliness; the staff and librarians of the United Grand Lodge of England, ever helpful even to non-masons such as myself; the officers of the British Israel World Federation, especially Michael Clark, for their willingness to supply information; the College of Arms and in particular the Windsor Herald of Arms for advice on the arms of William Gilbert; the Lord Mayor and Corporation of London for the use of the Guildhall Library and the supply of important pictures; the Bishop of London and the Dean and Chapter of St Paul's Cathedral, who look after this national treasure so well; the staff of the National Portrait Gallery for reorganizing the Tudor and Stuart collections in such a wonderfully evocative way.

I should also like to thank the following publishers for permission to reproduce quotations from their books: Gothic Image, who publish John Michell's *New Light on the Ancient Mysteries of Glastonbury*, and Thames & Hudson, who now publish his remarkable book *City of Revelation* under its revised title *Dimensions of Paradise*, as well as Joscelyn Godwin's biography of Robert Fludd and Margaret Whiney's biography of Wren; Oxford University Press for quotes from *Francis Bacon*; Frank Cass & Co., publishers of *The Posthumous Works of Robert Hooke*; Penguin Books, publishers of Lewis Thorpe's translation of Geoffrey of Monmouth's *History of the Kings of Britain*; The Arden Shakespeare for the quote from *The Second Part of King Henry VI*; Random House, publishers of *The Hiram Key* by Christopher Knight and Robert Lomas, and also *The Rosicrucian Enlightenment* and other books by the late Dame Frances Yates; Macmillan for the quote from Anne Savage's translation of the *Anglo-Saxon Chronicles*; Phanes Press for quotations from Joscelyn Godwin's translation of *Atalanta Fugiens*; Harvill Press, publishers of *Freemasonry* by Alexander Piatigorsky.

I give grateful acknowledgement to John Michell, Professor Keith Critchlow, the late Dame Jeanette Jackson and other key members, past and present, of RILKO. They were the pioneers in the study of sacred architecture and I have but built on their work. I have a further debt of gratitude to my wife, Dee, who puts up with so much; to Michael Ives, who keeps my computers running even when they don't want to; to 'angel' Donna McNeely for encouragement at a difficult time in the project; and to my agent Bill Hamilton of A.M. Heath, and my American agent Elizabeth Joyce, who help me maintain enthusiasm in my work.

I would also like to thank Sally Gaminara and Simon Thorogood who commissioned the book, Gillian Bromley who edited it, and all the other staff of Transworld who have worked so hard to make this book a success. Finally thanks are due to my friend and former colleague Robert Bauval, who first put me on to the esoteric connection between St Paul's Cathedral and the Dome of the Rock, thereby reviving my interest in London as a hermetic city.

PREFACE

On 2 September 1666 a chance spark from a baker's oven ignited the premises above. Within minutes the immediate neighbourhood of Pudding Lane, just north of the Thames near to London Bridge, was engulfed in flames. The fire raged for five days before it was eventually brought under control, and by then virtually the whole of the City of London had been destroyed. Though, miraculously, only nine people are known to have died in the conflagration, 373 acres of land within the walls and 63 acres outside were laid bare. Serious fires that destroyed whole towns were not, of course, unknown events at a time when most houses were built of wood. For example, in 1694 a fire destroyed a large part of Warwick, and in 1731 almost the whole of Blandford Forum in Dorset was reduced to ashes. Nevertheless, because London, England's capital city, was so much larger than these provincial towns, the Great Fire of 1666 was on a completely different scale. In all over thirteen thousand houses and ninety parish churches were destroyed. Old St Paul's Cathedral, which prior to the fire had been one of the largest and most spectacular buildings in Europe, was completely gutted. After careful consideration, the authorities were left with no choice but to demolish what remained of the great Gothic edifice and to start again from scratch.

Almost from the start there was a sense that the fire was God's handiwork. England had already suffered much turmoil during the seventeenth century, including civil war – the first major internal strife to afflict the island of Britain since the ending of the Wars of the Roses in 1485. The ten-year rule of Oliver Cromwell between 1649 and 1658 had brought little joy to the citizens of London who, like it or not, were required to live like Puritans. It is therefore not surprising that they rejoiced when in 1660 Charles II was restored to the throne, the theatres were reopened and a sense of normality returned. But then the Great Plague of 1665 drew attention to the appalling mess that was Old London, its streets open sewers. The destruction of the city the following year seemed providential in that it provided an opportunity to clear away the un-satisfactory legacy of the past and start again from scratch.

King Charles II took an active interest in the rebuild-ing of London, which provided him with an ideal opportunity to act as a monarch should in the role of benevolent father to his people. He was, despite his later reputation as a womanizer, a much better king than is generally acknowledged. One can only imagine what would have happened had James, duke of York (later King James II), been the elder brother. Almost certainly the restored monarchy would not have taken root again so easily, and it is quite possible that England would have plunged back into civil war. Indeed, Britain's enduring return to monarchical rule is largely attributable to the political maturity of Charles II. This had much to do with his own experience of life, which bred in him a pragmatism rare in any man, still less a monarch living in the seventeenth century – and much to do also with the fact that he was surrounded by a closely knit circle of exceptionally able men. How these men came by their wisdom, and how they put their stamp on the new London that they built after the fire, will be the subject of later chapters. Suffice it to say here that they were men of vision who looked upon city planning as a means of doing God's work.

PROLOGUE

Then came one of the seven angels who had the seven bowls full of the seven last plagues, and spoke to me, saying, 'Come, I will show you the Bride, the wife of the Lamb.' And in the spirit he carried me away to a great, high mountain, and showed me the holy city Jerusalem coming down out of heaven from God, having the glory of God, its radiance like a most rare jewel, like a jasper, clear as crystal.

It had a great high wall, with twelve gates, and at the gates twelve angels, and on the gates the names of the twelve tribes of the sons of Israel were inscribed; on the east three gates, on the north three gates, on the south three gates, and on the west three gates.

And the wall of the city had twelve foundations, and on them the twelve names of the twelve apostles of the Lamb.

Rev. 21: 9–14

Within the souls of men there has always been a yearning for a lost and nearly forgotten golden age, a time when justice ruled and peace prevailed, a time of brotherhood, of sharing and of temperance. For the Israelites the golden age was that of Solomon: a mighty king of the tenth century BC who inherited a united kingdom of Israel from his father David and raised it to even greater levels of prosperity and abundance. An astute tactician who outsmarted rivals and enemies alike, he was respected above all for his wisdom, which found its highest expression in the building of the first great Temple of Jerusalem. Alas, this golden age could not last, for as soon as Solomon died the kingdom of Israel split in two. Civil war and the growth of power-ful enemies without laid the little country open to attack, and before long its cities lay in ruins. The Jews were enslaved and could only bewail the destruction of Jerusalem – a lament that still echoes around the precincts of where Solomon's Temple once stood.

Yet, if the Bible is to be believed, the history and mission of the Israelites were not solely those of the Jews. Following the division of Solomon's kingdom, the two southernmost tribes (Benjamin and Judah) became the kingdom of Judah, while the northern ten of the original twelve tribes formed a separate kingdom of their own which in the Bible is called variously Israel, Samaria (after its capital city) or Ephraim (after its leading tribe). This northern kingdom lasted until only *c.*722 BC when Samaria was sacked by the Assyrians and the people of northern Israel, the so-called 'lost tribes', were forcibly transported to new homes on the south-eastern fringes of the Caspian Sea. In their place were planted certain tribes of Medes who became the much-reviled Samaritans of Jesus' time. Nobody knows for certain exactly what happened to the lost tribes of Israel, for at this juncture they dis-appear from the Bible narrative. However, it is prophesied in the Bible that one day the identity of their descendants would become known and that they would

24

be reunited with their brethren from Judah in a single kingdom, ruled over by a descendant of King David.

Strange as it may at first seem, there is a long tradition that the lost tribes of Israel escaped from captivity and, migrating ever westwards, eventually settled in Britain. Whether or not this migration actually happened or is merely a myth, the idea undoubtedly had a profound effect upon the development of Britain as a world power. More specifically, there is clear evidence that this esoteric undercurrent linking Britain with Israel influenced intellectual circles in the sixteenth century and was one of the chief motivating factors behind the English Reformation.

It is my contention that in the seventeenth century an attempt was made to rebuild London as the New Jerusalem. This idea resonates in William Blake's words to the hymn 'Jerusalem', now in effect the alternative national anthem of England, which are based on a very real belief: that Christian Britain was identifiable as the successor state of ancient Israel. Blake lived at a critical time (1757–1827) in the history of Britain. It is clear from his writings that, witnessing the beginnings of an industrial revolution that was to reshape the world, he was appalled at the human cost of industrialization as more and more people were sucked into the capital from the surrounding countryside to tend its 'satanic mills'. He was keenly aware of the paradox between the London he saw around him and the archetypal city of New Jerusalem described at the end of the book of Revelation. Yet for all this he seems to have believed in Britain's destiny as the latter-day Israel. The verse we know as 'Jerusalem' was an affirmation of his faith and hope that the New Jerusalem would fare better than the old. Though he had misgivings about industrialism he believed, rightly as it turned out, that London was destined to become the most influential city in the world. How this came about – how, for a time at least, London became the New Jerusalem – is the subject of this book.

My interest in the subject of city planning was first aroused in the early 1970s by the books of John Michell, and in particular by his cult bestseller *City of Revelation*.[1] In this book he suggested that the design of Glastonbury Abbey in Somerset was based upon an archetypal model known as the 'New Jerusalem'. This is described in graphic detail towards the end of Revelation, the last book of the Bible. The New Jerusalem would in many ways emulate the Garden of Eden, the archetypal paradise into which Adam and Eve were placed at the beginning of the book of Genesis. According to St John the Divine, the author of Revelation, it was to be a futuristic city with twelve gateways, one for each of the twelve tribes of Israel. It would have no need for the sun, for it would be permanently lit by the radiance of God. At its centre would grow the Tree of Life, bearing twelve fruits, one for each month of the year, and from it would spring a river of pure water.

This description is heavy with cosmic symbolism. In ancient times the cosmos was widely depicted as a celestial city with God at its centre. As the city was a microcosm of the macrocosm, so it should ideally be built according to plans based upon the ratios of the orbits of the planets and have twelve gates, representative of the twelve signs of the zodiac. The building of New Jerusalem at the start of the New Age would be the necessary prelude to God's putting the world to rights. As John Michell puts it in another of his books:

St John in Revelation followed the Essene tradition with his depiction of the New Jerusalem as a city with twelve gates, corresponding to the twelve tribes of Israel and to other twelve-fold systems. His visionary city, like Plato's twelve-tribe city-state of Magnesia, was an image of the traditional cosmology, the numerically codified model of God's creation which has inspired all the examples of twelve-tribe, zodiacally ordered nations throughout history. In Jewish mysticism, the regathering of Israel's twelve tribes at Jerusalem is the essential prelude to the restoration of divine government, as in the days of King Solomon. Jesus's mission was entirely to his own Jewish people, his intention being to make them worthy of their twelve-tribe inheritance and thus to expedite the Millennium.[2]

John Michell found evidence that led him to believe that the pattern of the New Jerusalem was not just a theoretical schema but had been used during the middle ages as a blueprint for church design. His work focused mainly on Glastonbury, a town famously associated with legends concerning Joseph of Arimathea, the Holy Grail and King Arthur. In 1976 I made my own study of certain churches in the City of London, focusing on the area around St Paul's Cathedral. What I was looking for was evidence that these churches had been aligned in some way that might suggest that they had been put up according to a master plan similar to that which had been found by John Michell at Glastonbury. To my surprise I found clear signs that, consciously or unconsciously, the builders did seem to have been guided by such a plan. The most immediately perceptible indication of this plan was the fact that the main axis of St Paul's runs straight through the old church of the Knights Templar which was about half a mile from the cathedral. Visiting this church, which lies within the precincts of the Inns of Court at Temple Bar, I found something else which at the time I did not understand. Almost uniquely among old churches in Britain, the Temple Church consisted of two parts. The nave of the church, which at the time of the Templars seems to have had a special function, was circular in shape, its roof supported by six free-standing pillars. It was empty of embellishments except for eight sculpted effigies of knights, three of whom were identified as medieval earls of Pembroke. Emerging eastwards from this round nave there was a rectangular extension that made up the main body of the building. At the far eastern end of this there stood the high altar and it was apparent that it was in this part of the church that services were held.

The reasons for this curious design were not hard to understand. The Knights Templar were warriors whose order originally had its headquarters in Jerusalem, and they would naturally have looked upon that city's Church of the Holy Sepulchre, which similarly had a round nave in the western end (containing the empty tomb of Jesus Christ) attached to a rectangular choir, as their model. This was clear enough; but there did seem to be something else about this design that was perhaps more esoteric. I bought a copy of the guide book and from this it became clear that the church as a whole and not just its round nave was constructed to a very definite geometrical plan. Even a cursory analysis of its ground plan revealed that it was based on a pattern called the *vesica piscis* or 'dish of fish'.

Returning to the map of London, I found that the line linking the Temple Church with St Paul's, if continued eastwards, ran through the little Church of St Mary Axe. I also discovered that if a circle were drawn using the crossing of St Paul's Cathedral as its centre and the distance from this to the Temple Church as a radius, then its circumference would pass through not only St Mary Axe but also St John's Clerkenwell. This was very interesting, as this latter church was built around 1145, and though all that remains of the building today is the crypt it had once been the centre of a large priory: the English headquarters of the Knights Hospitaller or Order of St John of Jerusalem.

Like the Temple Church, St John's Clerkenwell also had a circular nave in emulation of the Church of the Holy Sepulchre in Jerusalem. And there was a further symbolic link between these two churches: not only were they both round churches and the same distance away from St Paul's Cathedral, but the angle between the radii linking them to that building was exactly 60°. Moreover, the line linking St John's Clerkenwell with St Paul's Cathedral, if continued, would pass through

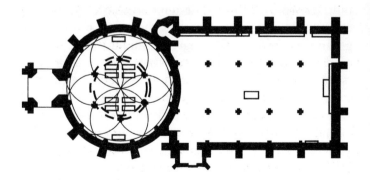

Fig. 1. Plan of the Temple Church, London.

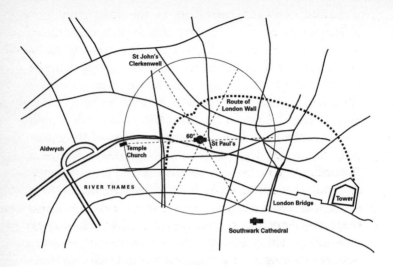

Fig. 2. The area around St Paul's, showing alignments
and angles.

Southwark Cathedral on the south bank of the River
Thames.

I could not know if these alignments were intentional
or merely coincidental, but they certainly seemed
indicative of some grand design that embraced the City
of London. True, in themselves they were not much to
go on; but from these meagre beginnings I could begin
to see that there could have been some underlying
pattern linking St Paul's with at least some of the out-
lying churches of Old London. Looking for a cosmic
connection, I thought that St Paul's might have been
intended to represent the sun at the centre of a zodiac
marked out by important churches, as part of a
medieval vision of London as the cosmic city: an image
of heaven on earth. It seemed likely (though I couldn't
prove it) that the many other churches around St Paul's

were intended to represent what medieval astronomers called the 'fixed stars'. During the seventeenth century and earlier their pointed spires would have dominated the skyline in a veritable galaxy. But though I made some attempt to correlate particular churches with specific stars (for example, the churches of St Mary-le-Strand and St Clement Danes with two of the stars in the constellation of Pegasus), I could not easily correlate the area around St Paul's with the zodiac. Accordingly I rather lost interest in the whole subject and put this research to one side to concentrate on other matters. Later, however, I was to discover that there was much more to the plan than this simple correlation with stars, and that there were overlays of patterns belonging to different periods of London's history.

Further investigation revealed that the curious alignment of St Paul's Cathedral with the apparently insignificant Temple Church that had first caught my attention was a fairly recent phenomenon. Prior to the rebuilding of St Paul's Cathedral after the Great Fire by Christopher Wren the direction of its axis had not been aligned with the Temple Church at all. It was he who had changed the axis of the nave, and I felt certain that he must have done so for some particular purpose. As the change was clearly intentional, it led me to look again at the city's development in the late seventeenth century and to investigate more closely the activities and allegiances of the leading figures of the period. At the same time I also became interested in the way that the ideas of Francis Bacon had influenced the re-construction of London. I began to suspect that a decision had been taken immediately after (if not even before) the Great Fire of 1666 that London should be rebuilt as a model city of the type he describes in his utopia *The New Atlantis*. The fulfilment of these researches was, at that time, still far in the future. Nearly twenty years were to pass before I would find the key that would reveal the secrets of London as a cosmic city – two decades during which I was able to be involved in many different adventures and projects.

The present work explores several different esoteric traditions which have had an impact on the development of London. These traditions, linking the city with ancient Troy, with King Arthur, with Freemasonry and with the movement we know as Rosicrucianism, are woven together in a tangled web of symbolism. In this book I have tried to untangle this web, to analyse how these traditions have contributed as sources of inspiration, and to show how they have been blended together to make the city we know today.

CHAPTER ONE

LEGENDS OF NEW TROY

London is a very ancient city. For its founding we have to look far back into the mists of time, to an age long before the adventurous Saxons arrived in their keels on the coast of Kent and made southern Britain their home. Apart from a brief period in Saxon times when Winchester rose to pre-eminence, it has nearly always been England's capital city. According to modern historians and archaeologists, it was the Romans who first built the City of London soon after their conquest of Britain which began in AD 43. Though this conflicts with tradition, it is certainly true that they made it their financial and commercial centre for some four centuries, until their final retreat from Britain in AD 410. Yet their choice of London as their business centre is strange, for according to the Roman historian Tacitus, London did not rank as a Roman *colonia* – a garrison town, built to Roman specifications and where Roman law held sway. Although Tacitus himself never visited Britain, it is fair to assume that he knew what he was talking about, as he was married to the daughter of Agricola, a renowned general who spent much time in Britain. Moreover, the Romans already had two *coloniae* in the south-east of England, Camulodunum (now Colchester) and Verulamium (now St Albans), both of which housed large numbers of veterans from the Roman legions as settlers. The choice of these two places for colonization was not accidental. In 55 BC Julius Caesar had invaded Britain and seized a stronghold or *oppidum* of his opponent, a British king called Caswallon. Although Caesar later retreated back to Gaul, this stronghold would thereafter have been regarded by the Romans as their own by right of conquest. In the opinion of many historians this *oppidum* was a town that later became the *colonia* of Verulamium. Similarly, it was in the vicinity of Colchester that in AD 43 the legions of Claudius won another decisive battle against the Britons. As part of a peace treaty, the local king had to cede land to Claudius, and the colonial city of Camulodunum was founded on the remains of whatever *oppidum* may have already been there. London, by contrast, was not a Roman *colonia* as such; but it seems to have enjoyed a position of pre-eminence right from the start of the Roman occupation of south-east England. It can only have enjoyed this special status because it was already a thriving trading city before the Romans arrived in Britain.

For modern readers it may come as something of a surprise to hear that the city of London pre-dates the Roman invasion. Yet there is nothing new in claiming this; indeed, it was the common opinion among ancient historians writing before about 1700. They repeat a legendary history of the founding of London – one recorded by the twelfth-century chronicler Geoffrey of Monmouth in his *History of the Kings of Britain*, but to be found in many other ancient sources also. This states that London was founded centuries before the coming of the Romans by a Trojan prince named Brwt (Brutus in Latin), after whom was named the island of Britain.[1]

> Once he had divided up his kingdom, Brutus decided to build a capital. In pursuit of this plan, he visited every part of the land in search of a suitable spot. He came at length to the River Thames, walked up and down its banks and so chose a site suited to his purpose. There then he built his city and called it Troia Nova. It was known by this name for long ages after, but finally by a corruption of the word it came to be called Trinovantum.[2]

According to these legends, Brutus was a great-grandson of the Aeneas who had escaped from Troy at the time of its ruin to find sanctuary in Italy.[3] Brutus is said to have brought with him to Britain an invasion force of Trojan émigrés from Greece where, following the destruction of Troy, they had been kept as slaves until, under Brutus' leadership, they rebelled and escaped by ship. Brutus and his followers are said eventually to have made their way to Britain, where he founded his 'New Troy' on the north bank of the Thames.

According to these same legends of origin, around 60 BC a king of Britain called Lud (Lloyd) rebuilt this city of Trinovantum and gave it a curtain wall for its defence. During his reign the city was renamed Kaer Lud, from which is said to be derived its Latin name of Londinium and hence the modern name London.[4] Lud's name is also memorialized in that of Ludgate, the main western entrance to the City of London near to which, according to Geoffrey of Monmouth, he was buried. Not long afterwards, in 54 BC, Julius Caesar invaded Britain for the second time. Although in his account of this campaign, his *Commentarii de bello gallica*, he does not mention London, he nevertheless records that the tribe local to this area was called the Trinovantes. It is not unreasonable to assume that they derived their name from that of the main city of southeast England – Trinovantum – but that name itself may have an origin linked only indirectly to the home city of its supposed founder.

Traditionally the name Troy is derived from that of an eponymous ancestor of the Trojans named Tros. However, the city in what is now Anatolian Turkey

Fig. 3. The triangle land of Troy.

generally referred to as Troy was actually called Ilium; properly speaking, the name Troy, or rather 'the Troad', belonged to the province of which Ilium was the capital. This province, located on the southern fringe of the Dardanelles, forms the north-westerly corner of Anatolia and its most noticeable feature is that it has the shape of an equilateral triangle. It therefore seems likely that the name Troad (or Troy) was not really derived from that of an ancestor, real or imagined, but simply meant 'Triangle land'.

Now, in his *De bello gallica* Caesar states that the island of Britain was also triangular, though irregular in shape. He gives the dimensions of this triangle as 475 miles by 665 miles by 760 miles. A scale drawing of this triangle reveals that while it bears little relationship to the actual geography of Britain, the shape has symbolic meaning (see the appendix). This is extremely important, as it suggests that in the ancient world Britain, like Troy itself, was regarded as a triangle land. As the Britons believed they were descended from Trojan exiles, this would explain the name 'New Troy' or Trinovantum as signifying the whole triangular island; the pre-Roman city of London may have been called by this name because it was the capital of the triangular island of Britain in just the same way as the original Troy (really Ilium) took its name from that of the Troad, the land over which it presided.[5]

This traditional history of the founding of London is treated with extreme scepticism by modern historians, who in general are steadfast in their opinion that before the Romans came to Britain the islanders were incapable of building cities. Yet Caesar himself writes that

37

The population [of Britain] was very large, the ground thickly studded with homesteads, closely resembling those of the Gauls, and the cattle very numerous. For money they use either bronze, or gold coins, or iron ingots of fixed weights. Tin is found inland, and small quantities of iron near the coast; the copper that they use is imported. There is timber of every kind, as in Gaul, except beech and fir.[6]

Though the Britons might have learnt about the use of money from the continental Gauls, we have here Caesar's own account that they had gold coins before even he arrived in Britain. In fact, hoards of pre-Roman coins – gold, silver and bronze – have been found in the London area. In this context it is worth remembering that the Greek historians Herodotus and Xenophanes attributed the invention of coinage to the Lydians, whose kingdom in Asia Minor was a near neighbour of ancient Troy. Many of the coins found in the London area feature a helmeted head – rather as our coins today carry the image of the reigning sovereign – and the helmets so depicted are not Roman but of a distinctly Greek or Trojan type. Caesar also records how the Britons excelled at chariot warfare, something which had long since gone out of fashion on the continent of Europe but which is described in detail in the *Iliad*, Homer's account of the Trojan war.

That the pre-Roman Britons were skilful artisans is revealed by the numerous objects on display in the British Museum. The bracelets worn by the nobility are not that dissimilar from others on display from eastern Turkey. The ornamentation on shields and other objects is in no way inferior and neither is the quality of their bronze weaponry: swords, spears and arrowheads. Looking at these objects one gets the over-all impression of an advanced iron age society possessing all the knowledge and skills needed for civilized life. Though not conclusive evidence, these few artefacts alone would suggest that it would be wise to retain an open mind on claims of Trojan origins for the ancient Britons. Further research is likely to prove that there is a substrate of truth underneath the myth.

Up until very recently – three hundred years ago at the most – the identification of London with New Troy was regarded as fact by everyone who mattered. One of the few surviving traces of this belief is to be found in the so-called 'troy measures'. These measures were not named after ancient Troy in Anatolia but rather 'New Troy' or London. Up until their abolition in 1879 troy measures were the legal standards used in Britain, probably having their origins in the fixed weights remarked upon by Caesar in 54 BC. The 'troy ounce' of 480 grains was not abolished with the rest and remains even today a legal measure for weighing gold, silver, platinum and precious stones.

Archaeological evidence also suggests that even if pre-Roman London was not quite the advanced city described by Geoffrey of Monmouth, its foundation must pre-date at least the Claudian invasion of AD 43. The Romans themselves recorded that in AD 60, just seventeen years after their invasion began, Queen Boadicea ('Victoria') led an uprising against their rule. During this rebellion some seventy thousand Romans and their sympathizers were killed and London was burnt to the ground. Archaeological investigations carried out at various places, such as the site of St Swithin's Church in Cannon Street, have revealed the presence of a burnt layer that must be linked with

Boadicea's uprising.[7] As St Swithin's is quite a long way from the Forum at Leadenhall Market, the indications are that even in AD 60 London was a considerable city – by far the largest in Britain. Furthermore, during the building of London's first underground sewers in 1840 the remains of massive walls were found in nearby Bush Lane. Because modern archaeologists give no credence to the idea that London had a pre-Roman history, it has been assumed that these walls belonged to a Roman 'governor's palace'. However, as we have seen, at least in the early period of occupation the centre of Roman power in Britain was not London but Camulodunum (Colchester), where many veterans from the Roman army had settled. Here, so Tacitus tells us, there was a local senate house, a statue of Victory and a new temple to the 'divine Claudius'. It follows that if a Roman governor had a palace anywhere at this time, it would most likely have been in Camulodunum. In any case, the foundations found in Bush Lane were deeper than the layer of burning that must date to AD 60. This would suggest that the 'palace' dates back to a period before ever there was a Roman 'governor' to live in it. What seems most likely is that this building did not belong to a Roman ruler at all but rather to a pre-Roman British king.

Certainly Geoffrey of Monmouth records that King Lud 'was famous for his town-planning activities. In addition to building the walls of Trinovantum he girded it round with many towers. He also ordered the citizens of Trinovantum to construct their homes and buildings in such a style that no other city in the most far-flung of kingdoms could boast of *palaces more fair*' (italics added).[8] Now, while Geoffrey is by no means always a reliable source and is frequently guilty of hyperbole, one cannot but feel that there is a core of truth to what he is saying here and that the 'governor's palace' found at Bush Lane may actually predate the Roman invasion and have belonged to the kings of Britain.

Immediately to the north of this 'governor's palace' there once stood a strange menhir called the 'London Stone'. The top part of this menhir can today be viewed through a grille in the wall of the Overseas Chinese Bank Corporation, whose building now stands on the site of St Swithin's Church, destroyed during the Blitz. William Camden (1551–1623) and other historians record that distances on milestones throughout Britain were measured in relationship to this stone. The London Stone should therefore be regarded as the central omphalos or 'navel-stone' not just of London but of the kingdom of Britain as a whole. The proximity of this important stone to the 'palace', and the fact that it is not mentioned anywhere in Roman records, support the conclusion that the palace was not built for any Roman governor but was indeed the residence of the pre-Roman kings of Britain – maybe even King Lud himself.

Further archaeological evidence that London was already a great city before the Claudian invasion has come to light more recently. In 1999 archaeologists from the Museum of London carried out extensive excavations at Fenchurch Street near Leadenhall Market. Here they found the remains of 'part of the largest Roman shopping centre in the whole of northern Europe'. An article published about this find in the London *Evening Standard* reported that the team of seventeen archaeologists had found 'the remains of the earliest Roman buildings in London'.[9] It went on: 'What looks like layers of bright red and brown earth,

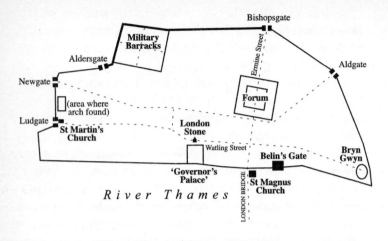

Fig. 4. Roman London.

the archaeologists say, would have been the city's earliest buildings, razed to the ground by Queen Boadicea in AD 60.' What the article did not explain was how, given that the Romans did not even begin their conquest of Britain until AD 43, there could have been such a large and flourishing market, of the magnificence they describe, at the time of Boadicea's rebellion in AD 60. Seventeen years is hardly long enough to have built the 'largest shopping centre in northern Europe', especially at a time when the conquest of Britain was very far from complete. Curiously, this article was accompanied by a photograph of one of the archaeologists holding aloft a piece of pottery. This picture was accompanied by the caption: 'Leslie Dunwoody with a Roman amphora, dated 30 AD, found at the building site in Fenchurch Street.' Since this amphora apparently pre-dates the Roman invasion by thirteen years, it would suggest that the marketplace, and therefore the city of

42

London, was in existence at least a dozen years before the Claudian invasion.

Indeed, evidence of London's great antiquity had been found by the archaeologists of the Museum of London a few months earlier, when they had discovered the remains of what they described as a 'triumphal arch', 'mausoleum' or 'big defensive structure'.[10] The massive foundations for this structure, which they estimated as having been about 30 metres long by 15 metres wide, were found during building work being carried out next to the Old Bailey law courts at the western extremity of the old City of London. This site is only a short distance away from Ludgate, where until 1760 the western gate of the City of London stood. The medieval Ludgate was rebuilt several times, once in 1215 and again in 1586. Excavations carried out at Ludgate itself have not revealed remains of any earlier 'Roman' gateway on the site. However, given the new evidence that has come to light, it would appear that today's archaeologists may have stumbled upon the remains of the original western gate of the city – the gateway attributed to King Lud – which, even if no older than the Roman period, certainly pre-dates the medieval gateway on the site of what is now called Ludgate. What seems to have happened is that the original gateway was demolished (probably so that the stones could be used for building) during Saxon times, and then later, when the walls of London with their gates were restored, was rebuilt on a different site a couple of hundred yards further south – presumably so that it would be directly opposite the entrance to St Paul's Cathedral.

Fragments of the old Roman walls, built of flint and ragstones, still exist and can be viewed in the gardens of the Museum of London. That the wall was rebuilt in Roman times is evidenced by the remains of tombstones that have been found embedded in it. The most spectacular of these is a memorial to the Roman procurator Julius Classicianus, which was found embedded in the wall of a turret to the east of the City wall near Tower Hill. It carries an inscription that in translation reads: 'To the spirits of the departed and to Gaius Julius Alpinus Classicianus of the Fabian voting tribe . . . Procurator of the Province of Britain. Julia Pacata daughter of Indus, his unhappy wife had this built.' During Roman imperial times, a procurator was a financial manager as opposed to a military commander. His job was to look after the investments of the emperor and other important Romans in Britain, as well as superintending the gathering of taxes. Classicianus is a known individual, mentioned in Tacitus' *Annals* as being sent to Britain in the aftermath of Boadicea's rebellion:

> Still the savage British tribesmen were disinclined for peace, especially as the newly arrived imperial agent [procurator] Gaius Julius Alpinus Classicianus, successor to Catus Decianus, was on bad terms with Suetonius [the imperial governor of Roman forces in Britain], and allowed his personal animosities to damage the national interests. For he passed round advice to wait for a new governor who would be kind to those who surrendered, without an enemy's bitterness or a conqueror's arrogance. Classicianus also reported to Rome that there was no prospect of ending the war unless a successor was appointed to Suetonius, whose failures he attributed to perversity – and his successes to luck.[11]

Suetonius was recalled to Rome, where in AD 66 he became a consul. He was replaced as governor in Britain by Publius Petronius Turpilianus, who reached the accommodation with the Britons that Tacitus describes as 'peace with honour'. Classicianus must have lived in London for his widow to have built a tomb for him there. One must assume that his mausoleum stood in the east of the city, fairly close to the Tower of London, where fragments of it were later found. That Classicianus' monument was used as building material for the city's walls indicates that these must have been rebuilt some time later. Archaeologists suggest a date of around AD 200, though it may have been earlier.

Situated close to Ludgate Circus is the church of St Martin's-within-Ludgate (see plate 4). Though the building was largely reconstructed following the fire of 1666, this is one of the oldest religious foundations in London. That it was once a Brittano-Roman shrine is evidenced by the finding there in 1669 of a tombstone featuring a relief of a Roman soldier. He wears a tunic with a military belt and has a long cloak draped over his shoulder; in his right hand he holds a centurion's staff, and in his left he clutches what looks like a scroll (see plate 5). In translation, the inscription on the stone reads: 'To the spirits of the departed and to Vivius Marcianus of the 2nd Legion Augusta, Janceana Martina his most devoted wife set up this memorial.' Given this lady's surname, 'Martina', it is tempting to think that she may have been a Christian and that this church was named after her family rather than St Martin, who came from Gaul. This Janceana may also have been related to another woman with the same surname, Claudia Martina, part of whose funerary monument (a six-sided pedestal) has also been recovered from the western Ludgate cemetery. In translation the inscription on this pedestal, which would probably have once supported her statue, reads: 'To the spirits of the departed and to Claudia Martina, aged 19, Amencletus, slave of the province, set this up to his most devoted wife, she lies here.'

Punctuating the walls of Roman London were (at least) four more gates, facing approximately in the cardinal directions. According to Geoffrey, the southern gateway to the City of London was originally built by another pre-Roman British king called Belinus or 'Belin'. As this gateway faced on to the River Thames it was primarily a dock, but it seems also to have functioned as a mausoleum:

> In the town of Trinovantum Belinus caused to be constructed a gateway of extraordinary workmanship, which in his time the citizens called Billingsgate, from his own name. On the top of it he built a tower which rose to a remarkable height; and down below at its foot he added a water-gate which was convenient for those going on board their ships . . . Finally, when his last day dawned and carried him away from this life, his body was cremated and the ash enclosed in a golden urn. This urn the citizens placed with extraordinary skill on the very top of the tower in Trinovantum which I have just described.[12]

The cremation of the dead and the placing of the ashes of the deceased in an urn is an old British custom that goes back to the stone age. Such funerary urns are frequently found buried in the chalk downlands of Wiltshire and Dorset, and examples can be seen in the

British Museum. Although the placing of Belinus' ashes on the top of a gateway might seem very strange, we should not dismiss such a legend out of hand. There seems to have been a strong tradition that if the remains of a warrior were placed on or near a gateway his spirit would go on protecting the city against invaders.

Old Billingsgate was until recently the site of a fish market, which is how we remember it today. However, it is clear that throughout most of the history of London, Billingsgate dock was the principal port for bringing in many types of goods, not just fish, to Leadenhall Market. Near to Billingsgate is the site of Old London Bridge. Again, it was thought until recently that the Romans were the first to bridge the Thames here. However, during the period of great drought in the late 1990s, when the river was at a very low level, wooden bridge-piles dating from before this time were found. This is further evidence that the city of London pre-dates the Roman invasion of AD 43.

London Bridge, which until the opening of Westminster Bridge in 1750 was the only fixed crossing of the Thames at London, has been built and rebuilt many times. The present-day bridge is some 60 yards to the west of the original site; Old London Bridge was aligned with Fish Street. Next to what was then the northern pier of the bridge, at the bottom of Fish Street, stands the Church of St Magnus. Though nobody knows for certain who founded this church, it is assumed that it is named after the patron saint of the Orkneys, who was assassinated in 1115, at a time when the Orkney Islands still had close ties with Norway. Accordingly, close to the altar and standing in-congruously in this Wren church, there is a fairly modern, brightly painted effigy of St Magnus as a

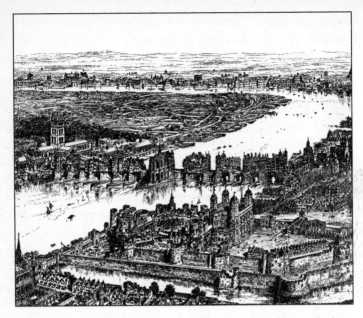

Fig. 5. Artist's impression of Old London Bridge, with the Tower of London in the foreground. By H.W. Brewer.

Viking warrior. Romantic as this attachment between London Bridge and the Orkneys may seem, in point of fact there is probably little real connection. A church stood on the site of St Magnus' centuries before the martyrdom of this hero of Orkney, whose home lay to the north even of Scotland. The real patron of the Church of St Magnus, London Bridge, is almost certainly Magnus Maximus, a British emperor who in AD 383 usurped the western Roman empire. Though his attempt ultimately ended in failure (he was executed in 388), in Britain he was regarded as a Christian saint. In the medieval Welsh Triads he is credited not only with building churches but with founding the archbishopric of London. It seems very likely, therefore, that it was he who endowed a church on the north side of London Bridge, perhaps intending that one day it would serve as his mausoleum. In the event, his rebellion having failed, Magnus Maximus was beheaded at Apulia in Italy. It seems unlikely that his remains were brought back for burial in Britain.

The eastern entrance to the Roman city of London was Aldgate. This guarded the access to the main road leading eastwards to Camulodunum. Near to it stood another pre-Roman foundation: the Bryn Gwyn. Today this eastern area of the city is covered by the walls, towers and other structures that make up the largely medieval Tower of London. Yet the Bryn Gwyn, or 'White Hill', on which now stands the Norman keep called the 'White Tower', was in pre-Roman times a holy place. Here, according to tradition, was the burial mound of Brutus where later was placed the head of Bran the Blessed. According to the legends contained in the *Mabinogion*, the medieval stories of ancient Wales, Bran, the son of King Lleir, was a giant. However, what was most remarkable about him was that even after he died (in Ireland) and was decapitated, his head continued to speak. It was brought back to Britain and buried on the Bryn Gwyn. The head prophesied that as long as it remained there the island of Britain would be protected from invasion. It was later disinterred – with ultimately calamitous consequences – on the orders of King Arthur, who felt it to be invaliant to rely on supernatural powers of protection rather than force of arms. Today the legend of Bran, whose name means 'crow' in Welsh, lives on in the ravens who guard the Tower of London. The Welsh for raven is *cigfran*, from *cig* meaning 'meat' and *fran*, a variant on *bran*. It is said today that as long as the ravens remain in the Tower, England will be safe from invasion. They are well looked after by the Yeomen of the Guard, but just to make sure that they don't escape and bring about England's downfall, their flight feathers are clipped.

Memories of the Tower's prehistoric origins are preserved in the name of another of its structures, the Broad Arrow Tower, in which many prisoners were held in Tudor times prior to their execution. The name of this tower comes from the symbol known as the 'broad arrow', or symbol of Awen, the muse, which even today is used as a logo on government property and by the Ordnance Survey. According to the later bards of Wales, in druidic times this symbol, drawn with three lines /l\, represented the vowels OIU (or OIW) that made up the unutterable name of God: 'The symbol of God's Name from the beginning was /l\, afterwards O I V, and now O I W; and from the quality of this symbol proceed every form and sign of voice, and sound, and name, and condition.'[13] The shape of the broad arrow is said to derive from three rays of sunlight, or rather shadows cast at different times of day by an upright stone. However, it could not have escaped the notice of the Druids that /l\ is similar in shape to the footprint made by a bird such as the crow or raven. The naming of the Broad Arrow Tower is therefore probably connected with the same legends to do with ravens and Bran the Blessed.

Two further gates pierced the northern walls of the City of London. The first of these, Bishopsgate, is probably the older of the two. It aligns with the road leading north from Old London Bridge via the central market area of Leadenhall. This was the gate leading on to Ermine Street, the main road running up the east of England to York and thence north to Hadrian's Wall.

The second was Aldersgate. This was further west along the north wall and close to a Roman fort built at the time of the Emperor Hadrian in *c.*AD 120. This gate seems to be a later addition, although it guards the approaches from Verulamium, which as we have seen was an important Roman city.

The final gate in the circuit of the walls before returning was Newgate. This is something of a misnomer, as it is clearly very old and indeed was probably built at the same time as Ludgate. No doubt, like Ludgate itself, it was built as a replacement for the 'old Ludgate' whose remains have recently been excavated near the Old Bailey. For centuries Newgate functioned not only as a gateway but as a gaol. It was close to the north-west corner of the city, giving access to the main road leading to Oxford: Oxford Street. Until 1783 condemned criminals would be taken from Newgate Prison to be paraded along Oxford Street on their way to execution at Tyburn – now Marble Arch. Later the gallows was transferred to Newgate Prison itself, which thereby earned a fearsome reputation as a place of death. The gaol itself was a sombre and forbidding building, whose name still sends a tingle down the spine.

During later periods of London's history other gates were added as the need for better access became more important than defence. Eventually almost the whole city wall was demolished so that new roads and railways could better penetrate to the heart of the capital.

The Romans finally withdrew from (or were pushed out of) Britain in AD 410. From that time onwards the Saxons, who already had some settlements in East Anglia, began invading Britain in increasing numbers. The most famous Briton leading the resistance to these incursions was, of course, King Arthur. He is most closely associated with Wales and the west country, but he would also have had a court in London.[14] Quite possibly the story of King Arthur drawing a sword from a stone is connected with a real ritual that once took place involving the London Stone.

According to Geoffrey of Monmouth, King Arthur was succeeded as Pendragon (literally 'head dragon', or commander-in-chief) of Britain by a string of rulers, including 'Malgo' – Maelgwyn, king of Gwynedd. The last few kings of Britain in Geoffrey's account were said to have been descended from this powerful ruler from north Wales. The history of these times (the sixth to eighth centuries) is very confused, but it is clear that the last but one of these kings was called Cadwallon. He is one of the few non-Saxon rulers to be noted by name in the *Anglo-Saxon Chronicle*, a year-by-year diary of important events that was compiled during the reign of King Alfred the Great of Wessex (c.AD 890). For the year AD 633 there is the following entry: 'Edwin, the king [of Northumbria], was killed by Cadwallon and Penda [king of Mercia] at Hatfield Chase on October 14th . . . Afterwards Cadwallon and Penda went and ravaged all the land of Northumbria.'[15]

As we would expect, Geoffrey of Monmouth has much more to say about this British king, whose body, he tells us, was embalmed after death and placed inside a golden statue:

Finally, after forty-eight years, Cadwallo [*sic*], this most noble and most powerful King of the Britons, become infirm with old age and illness, departed this life on the fifteenth day after the Kalends of December. The Britons embalmed his body with balsam and aromatic herbs and placed it inside a bronze statue which, with extraordinary skill, they had cast to the exact measure of his stature. They mounted this statue, fully armed, on a bronze horse of striking beauty, and erected it on top of the West Gate of London [Ludgate], in memory of the victory which I have told you and as a source of terror to the Saxons. Underneath they built a church in honour of St Martin, and there divine services are celebrated for Cadwallo himself and for others who die in the faith.[16]

Thus, like his remote ancestor King Lud, Cadwallon was apparently buried at Ludgate. He was the last Welsh king to succeed in asserting his authority over England. His son King Cadwallader, though he ravaged Kent, faced a period of plague and starvation, and was eventually forced by these circumstances to abandon Britain altogether and cross to Brittany, taking with him a large number of people. Cadwallader died at Rome in AD 689 and was buried there. From that time onwards the Saxon kingdoms of Kent, East Anglia, Sussex, Mercia, Northumbria and Wessex steadily grew in power at the expense of a central authority based in London. With this transfer of power to regional centres, such as Winchester, London went into a steep decline. Large areas of the city became derelict and its centre of gravity shifted out of the walled enclosure of the old Romano-British city westwards to the Aldwych ('Old Town' in Anglo-Saxon), situated in the area where today the large Aldwych roundabout regulates traffic from the Strand, Kingsway, Waterloo Bridge and Fleet Street.

However, by the time of King Edgar (d. 975) the uni-fication of the Saxon kingdoms of Wessex, Kent and

Fig. 6. Artist's impression of the Ludgate area, showing old
St Paul's Cathedral. By H.W. Brewer.

Mercia had shifted the centre of political power back to London. During his reign and for some while after there lived one of the most important figures in English ecclesiastical history: St Dunstan. This prelate, who rose to become archbishop of Canterbury, was born in Somerset in the environs of Glastonbury. His fortunes varied under various Saxon kings. During the reign of Aethelstan (r. 925–39) his learning brought charges of black magic and he was forced to go into exile. Recalled under Athelstan's successor Edmund (r. 939–46), he became an important counsellor to the king and was made abbot of Glastonbury, which under his guiding hand became a great centre of learning. To a large extent the fame enjoyed by that abbey town ever since is a result of his activities. When Edmund died and was succeeded by Eadred (r. 946–55), Dunstan effectively took over the running of the kingdom, until Eadred's successor, Eadwig (r. 955–9), forced him back into temporary exile. He was once more recalled when Edgar (r. 959–75) took the throne and appointed Dunstan first as bishop of London and later archbishop of Canterbury. In gratitude Dunstan had a memorial chapel to King Edgar built at Glastonbury, the foundations of which were rediscovered by Frederick Bligh Bond in the early part of the twentieth century. Dunstan built this chapel close to where he believed Joseph of Arimathea had built an earlier church; within a few centuries it would grow to become the largest and richest monastery in England.

Dunstan was not only active in Somerset; he was also largely responsible for establishing or re-establishing a number of churches in London. Indeed, so important and far-reaching was his work in bringing about a Christian revival in England that after his death he was canonized, and his fame in the middle ages was only slightly less than that of St Thomas à Becket.

King Edward the Confessor (r. 1042–66) took over the kingdom in 1042 after a period of political turbulence that had seen Danish kings on the throne of England. In many ways his reign marks a watershed in English history, for it was he who established the cult of kingship in the way we know it today. He built a new abbey at Westminster, where there had long stood a church dedicated to St Peter on the site of a Roman (or probably pre-Roman) temple to Apollo. This Benedictine abbey very quickly rose to become the most splendid in the land, its neighbouring palace the centre of political power. As a result even today Parliament meets in the Palace of Westminster, and the great church of Westminster Abbey was for centuries the preferred place of burial for English kings and queens. It is still the place where they are crowned, and here resides the coronation chair which until very recently (1996) contained the 'Stone of Destiny'. More will be said about this curious relic later.

Edward the Confessor died in 1066 and was briefly succeeded by Harold II Godwinson. His defeat at the Battle of Hastings ushered in the Norman dynasty. Almost immediately Duke William of Normandy – now King William I of England – set about an ambitious programme of castle-building. The most important of these fortifications was the Tower of London, which he built on top of the Bryn Gwyn. In the time of the Druids, before the Romans came to Britain, this mound would have been the *gorsedd* of the area, where the king would sit in court and, as well as administering justice, witness competitions of song and poetry. According to druidic law all such activities had to be conducted in the open, where the eye of God, the sun, could watch proceedings. William must have known of the symbolic importance of the Bryn Gwyn, for by appropriating it for his castle he was making a statement about his control over not just London but all of England.

The Tower of London, which in William I's day consisted only of a keep, was to become one of the most feared places in England. Within the curtain walls of what grew into a self-contained village, political prisoners were often kept for many years; from it, less fortunate individuals would be taken out on to Tower Green to have their heads struck off. Even today the Tower of London continues to be the stronghold of London, and up until Oliver Cromwell's time it functioned as a royal palace too. Within its guarded precincts are kept the royal regalia: the crown, sceptre, orb and other jewels used in coronation ceremonies for the kings and queens of the United Kingdom.

William the Conqueror was succeeded by his second son, William II or 'Rufus'. There followed two more Norman kings, Henry I and Stephen, before the first of the Plantagenets, Henry II, came to the throne in 1154. It was around this time that Geoffrey of Monmouth translated the Welsh chronicles into Latin as the *Historia Regnum Britanniae* – the work we know as *The History of the Kings of Britain*. Besides sparking off interest in the legend of King Arthur, this book revealed to Londoners the great antiquity of their city. As London developed through the middle ages, so elements of its ancient history as New Troy were incorporated into its familiar street furniture. The London Stone continued to be an object of fascination right up until 1742 when, as part of a general

Fig. 7. Artist's impression of old Westminster. By H.W. Brewer.

road-widening scheme that led to the demolition of London's gates, its top was cut off and removed from the centre of Cannon Street to the nearby church of St Swithin's. Prior to that time it was a prominent landmark in London, not just because it was a traffic hazard (many a cartwheel was broken in collision with it) but because of its enormous antiquity.

In 1450 a squire from Kent called Jack Cade led a peasants' revolt against corrupt rule by the aristocracy. Cade claimed to be secretly descended from the late Edmund Mortimer, earl of March and Ulster, whose line was believed to be extinct. Edmund's father, Roger Mortimer, was a direct descendant of Edward III through his second son, the Duke of Clarence, and had been declared heir apparent by his cousin, Richard II. If Cade's lineage could have been proved then he would have had a claim not just on the extensive lands of the Mortimers but on the throne of England itself (see plate 6).

William Shakespeare, who knew the streets of London well, had great fun relating the story of Jack Cade's rebellion in *The Second Part of King Henry VI*. In Act IV scene 6 Cade arrives at the London Stone and strikes it with his staff (in other versions of the story he used his sword) before delivering a little speech to the surrounding mob of his supporters:

> *Cade.* Now is Mortimer lord of this city. And here, sitting upon London Stone, I charge and command that, of the city's cost, the pissing-conduit run nothing but claret wine this first year of our reign. And henceforward it shall be treason for any that calls me other than Mortimer.

While Shakespeare pours scorn on Jack Cade's claim

to be a genuine descendant of Edmund Mortimer (it would have been dangerous to say otherwise), he clearly knew all about the London Stone and the idea of its being the omphalos or navel-stone of England. As such it functions as Cade's throne, the seat of his authority. Such allusions would not have been wasted on a Tudor audience, who loved nothing more than mysterious, ancient traditions.

Another favourite story of medieval Londoners was that of the giants Gog and Magog. Today there are figures representing these giants preserved at the Guildhall in London, but few people seem to know why they are there. Once more we have to go back to Geoffrey of Monmouth's book, in which there is a story of how, when Brutus and his Trojans arrived in Britain, they found the island sparsely inhabited by a race of giants. One of these, called Gogmagog, wrestled with a Trojan hero called Corineus and was eventually thrown to his death from a cliff-top called in consequence 'Gogmagog's Leap'. In the 1811 translation into English of the *Brut Tysilio*, a Welsh version of the chronicles translated by the Revd Peter Roberts, there is a footnote suggesting that Gogmagog is a corrupted form of Cawr-Madog, meaning 'Madog the great' or 'Madog the giant' in Welsh. It would appear that Geoffrey, or some other monk, confused Cawr-Madog with Gog of Magog, the name of a war leader who the Bible prophesies will lead an invasion of the Holy Land at the end of the age (Ezek. 28: 2–11; Rev. 20: 8). In another version of the Gogmagog tale, the *Recuyell des histoires de Troye*, Gog and Magog are two separate giants. In this story they are not killed but brought back as slaves by Brutus to his city of New Troy. Here they were to be employed as gatekeepers, opening and closing the great gates of the palace.

The story of Gog and Magog, the paired giants who worked the gates of London, was very popular in the middle ages and effigies of them were placed on the city gates at least as early as the reign of Henry VI. These were destroyed in the Great Fire of 1666, but so popular were they that new ones were made in 1708 and installed at the Guildhall. This pair of statues was destroyed in 1940 during the Blitz, the third great fire of London, when the roof and much of the interior furnishings of the Guildhall were burnt. A new pair of statues was carved to replace them when the Guildhall was repaired after the war.

Another pair of giants, also probably intended to represent Gog and Magog, was part of a clock put up in 1671 on the roof of the Church of St Dunstan-in-the-West, an ancient church close to the western end of Fleet Street. To mark the hours the giants would wield their clubs and strike a bell. When this church was demolished in 1829 the Marquess of Hertford bought the clock, with its Ionic temple exterior and twin giants hammering out the time, and had it moved to Regent's Park. A century later, in 1935, the clock was bought by Lord Rothermere, owner of the *Daily Mail*, and moved back to Fleet Street. Today the giants can be seen hammering their bell outside the nineteenth-century Church of St Dunstan that was built to replace the one knocked down in 1829 (see plate 8). This is thoroughly appropriate, for opposite the church are some of the few wooden houses that survived the Great Fire – visible remnants of a London that passed away that fateful day in 1666.

The church of St Dunstan-in-the-West is also close to a large Victorian figure of a dragon supporting the arms of London: the red cross of St George on a white background with a small *gladius* or Roman sword emblazoned in the chief dexter quarter of the shield (see plate 7). The presence of this sword refers to another legend: that when Julius Caesar made his first attempt at the conquest of Britain in 55 BC, he lost his sword in hand-to-hand fighting with Nennius, the brother of King Caswallon, in a battle on the beach where the Romans landed. Caesar was driven off and the Britons brought this sword back to London in triumph. A few days later Nennius died from the wounds he had received in the fight, and both he and the sword were buried near the north gate (either Aldersgate or Bishopsgate) of the City of London. Later Caesar's sword was incorporated, with the cross of St George and the motto *Domine dirige nos*, 'Lord lead us', into the arms of London. The shield with its dragon supporter stands on a small traffic island at the western end of Fleet Street, on the spot once occupied by the Temple Bar – another gateway, of later construction than Ludgate, which controlled the passage of traffic into and out of the City of London. It was a tradition that when the sovereign entered the City of London he would be met by the mayor at the gate and be presented with the Sword of the City. This he would take but immediately return, showing thereby his respect for the traditions and customs of London.

During the middle ages London prospered as never before. To a large extent it was a city dominated by churches and monasteries. By the end of the twelfth century there were at least 120 churches in the City of London alone, which means there must have been one on practically every street corner. Just as today every bank and financial institution in the world seeks to have a foothold in the City, so then did all the various religious orders and societies. By the time of the dissolution of the monasteries in the 1530s London boasted at least nineteen major monastic institutions and many smaller houses. South-west of St Paul's the enormous monastery of Blackfriars dominated that stretch of the north bank of the Thames. East of Newgate was Greyfriars Monastery, built by the popular Franciscans whose vows of poverty did not prevent them from building the largest church in London after St Paul's Cathedral. At the dissolution, the main building of this monastery was turned into Christ's Hospital School. The church was partly destroyed, but its chancery became Christ Church parish church. Not to be outdone, the Whitefriars or Carmelites built a monastery close to the Temple, south of what is now Fleet Street. Today the site is occupied by the offices of several newspapers. The Brown or Austin friars built their priory in the east of the City. Following the dissolution of the monasteries, part of their church was given over for Protestant worship to foreigners, principally the Dutch. Today the rebuilt church on this site is known as the Dutch Church Austin Friars.

The many other monasteries in addition to all of these included the Priory of St Bartholomew the Great (which established St Bartholomew's Hospital) and the Priory of St Mary Overy at Southwark, both of which were Augustinian. There was the Abbey of St Clare of the Minories, known as East Minster, which stood close to the Tower of London and which derived its full name from the order of St Clare nuns resident there called the Sorores Minores or Lesser Sisters. They were affiliated to the Greyfriars or Franciscans. Also near to the Tower were the church and monastic building of the 'Crutched' or Crossed Friars, a mendicant order whose members wore a habit with a red cross on the back and each carried an iron cross in his hand. Today nothing remains of their house, which was in the vicinity of Fenchurch Street Station. To these may be added many other religious houses, either founded through the beneficence of some great aristocrat or planted as a branch house by one or another of the established orders. Thus by the time Henry VIII came on to the throne the City of London was to all intents and purposes a religious fiefdom. There was little that went on in the city that did not involve the church, either directly or through one or another of its religious orders. Even prostitution was to some extent controlled by the church, for the 'stews', the brothels of the south bank (in the vicinity of the new Tate Modern), were owned by the Bishops of Winchester – and con-sequently in Shakespeare's time the women who worked there were known as 'Winchester Geese'.

This situation could not continue for ever. Over the course of the sixteenth and seventeenth centuries England went through a series of revolutions, religious and secular, that brought about a new Age of Enlightenment. The forces behind this transformation were multifarious, but at the heart of the changes lay a growing conviction among the English that their country had a special destiny; that it was a 'New Israel'. Under this impulse the old traditional belief that London was a 'New Troy' was discarded in favour of a new utopianism. The intellectuals of the period rewrote the history books, removing all references to Troy. Brutus, the Trojans and Trinovantum, Gog and Magog, King Lud, King Belin and Bran the Blessed were all consigned to the dustbin of mythology. In place of these old legends and traditions London was to be given a fresh identity.

CHAPTER TWO

QUEEN ELIZABETH AND THE DESTINY OF ENGLAND

The British empire, which was to reach its apogee under Queen Victoria, owed its origins to another queen of England: Elizabeth I. An extraordinary woman who for a time dominated the political stage of Europe as well as Britain, she combined intelligence, education and wit with a strong sense of self-preservation and a will of steel. She was, in fact, a thoroughly modern monarch who enjoyed the company of scholars, adventurers and even heretics, provided what they had to say was interesting and did not threaten her kingdom. It is no accident, therefore, that it was during her reign that forces were unleashed which were to propel first Britain and later the rest of Europe into a new age of scientific rationalism.

Yet she was a complex figure whose motives were often difficult to fathom, even in her own time. There can be no doubting that she enjoyed power and the exercise of sovereignty; but, unlike most monarchs of her age, she did not regard these as satisfying in themselves. Elizabeth was a woman of vision. Her ambition was to serve her country in the pursuit of a greater cause: its transformation from a small state on the

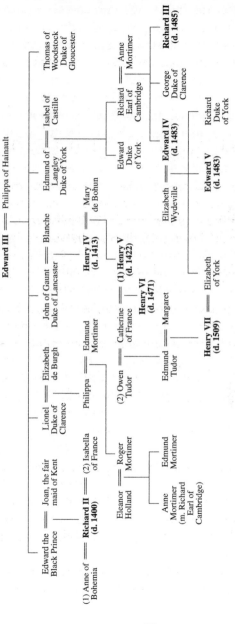

Fig. 8. The lineage of Henry VII.

periphery of Europe into God's chosen vehicle for the redemption of first its own people and then the rest of the world. To this end she was prepared to make sacrifices herself and expected others to do likewise.

Elizabeth I was the second daughter of King Henry VIII, whom she idolized. Today we take a fairly jaundiced view of Henry, focusing on his authoritarianism and multiple marriages. His showdown with his Lord Chancellor, Thomas More, which ultimately led to the latter's execution, has left an indelible stain on his own reputation, as did the execution of notable churchmen such as John Fisher, bishop of Rochester, and Richard Whiting, abbot of Glastonbury. Yet though Henry was undoubtedly a bully, and a spendthrift to boot – his despoliation of England's abbeys owed more to his need for money than anything else – he was no man's fool. He believed in the need for a reformation of the English church not just because he desired to replace the pope as its head but because its power posed a constant challenge to his own authority as monarch.

Henry VIII's father was Henry VII, who acceded to the throne of England at the end of the Wars of the Roses. These wars had had their origin several generations earlier, when King Richard II had been illegally deposed by Henry IV (Bolingbroke). They began in earnest when the latter's 'Lancastrian' grandson, Henry VI, was expelled from the throne by a 'Yorkist' claimant, Edward IV. To bolster his claim to the throne, Edward ordered his heralds to draw up his family tree. This was published on a roll, some 18 feet long, which today resides in the Lancashire record office. Going back through the centuries, it made the astonishing claim that Edward was descended

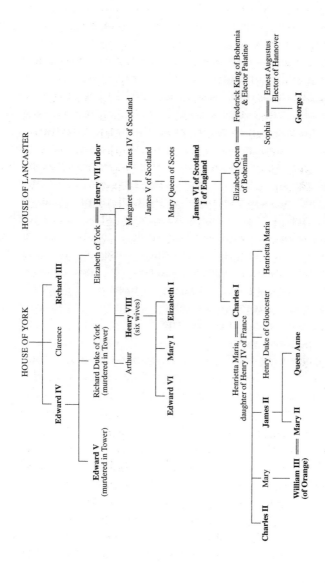

Fig. 9. The family tree of the House of Tudor, showing links to the House of Stuart.

from Jehoshaphat and the ancient kings of Israel.

When Edward IV died he was succeeded by his young son, Edward V, with his uncle Richard, duke of Gloucester, acting as regent. Not long thereafter Edward, along with his younger brother, was murdered in the Tower of London. Gloucester, who was almost certainly guilty of plotting the boys' murders, then took the throne himself as King Richard III. The suspicion that Richard had organized the murder of the two boys made his rule unpopular from the start and turned public support in favour of his rival, Henry, earl of Richmond. Their forces met at the Battle of Bosworth and Richmond, the last surviving Lancastrian of any note, became King Henry VII. To cement his position he married Richard's niece, Elizabeth Woodville, ending the Wars of the Roses by bringing together, under one roof as it were, the contending houses of York and Lancaster. This uniting of the red rose of Lancaster with the white rose of York was symbolized by the hybrid Tudor rose. More concretely, the unity of the two houses was incarnated in the form of Henry VII's children, most especially Henry VIII, his second son who, following the death of his elder brother Arthur, was to inherit the throne. Meanwhile Henry VII's eldest daughter, Margaret, married James IV of Scotland – a union which in due course was to have profound consequences for both kingdoms.

Henry VIII had royal Welsh blood running in his veins and could trace his lineage back to the pre-Christian, pre-Saxon and indeed pre-Roman kings of Britain. His father, Henry VII, was not only a Lancastrian but the grandson of Owen Tudor, a Welsh nobleman who had secretly married Catherine of France, the widow of Henry V. Owen Tudor, who was beheaded at Hereford by the Yorkists in 1461, traced his lineage back to Ednyfed Fychan, the steward of Llewellyn the Great, and Ednyfed's wife Gwenllian. She was a direct descendant of Owen son of Hywell Dda, the famous prince of Dyfed who lived in the tenth century at the time of King Athelstan of England. The ancestry of Owen son of Hywell Dda is listed in the Black Book of Carmarthen, today among the documents making up the Harleian 3859 collection in the British Library, which traces the line of these Welsh kings and princes back to such legendary kings of the dark ages as Arthur, Maelgwyn of Gwynedd, Cadvan and Cadwallader, and beyond these to such figures as Magnus Maximus, who usurped the Roman empire in AD 383, Constantine the Great, who turned the Roman empire Christian in AD 325, and Beli Mawr (Belin the Great), who ruled Britain c.100–80 BC. Other lists go back to Brutus, the eponymous founder of Britain, who as we saw in chapter 1 was, according to the legends of London, of royal Trojan descent, being the great-grandson of Aeneas, the founding father of Rome. These names had a resonance for Tudor audiences, for they are all mentioned in Geoffrey of Monmouth's famous *History of the Kings of Britain*, which four centuries after its publication in AD 1136 was still regarded as a faithful rendition of early British history. More to the point, Geoffrey's book repeated an ancient prophecy that one day the original inhabitants of Britain, that is to say the Welsh, would regain control of the island of Britain from the Saxon English.

Henry VII was acutely aware of his pedigree and that he was the first Welsh king to sit on the throne of Britain since the time of Cadwallader the Blessed, who died at Rome in AD 689. In his mind at least, it was clear that in taking over the throne of England he was fulfilling Geoffrey's prophecy. Accordingly, like Edward IV before him, he ordered his heralds to research his genealogy carefully and to draw up lists of his ancestors as far back as they could be traced. This was done and the results were published.

Henry VII was not the only one to see such a connection between his dynasty and Cadwallader. In a piece entitled 'The Periods of Oral Tradition and Chronology', which gives an outline chronology of British/Welsh history and which was republished in the Iolo MSS of 1848, there appears the following passage:

> From the time of the Emperor Arthur to that of Cadwalader [sic] the Blessed, one hundred and sixty years; and Cadwalader was the last king of Britain descended from the primitive royal lineage of the Island, until it was restored in the person of Henry VII, who is the present king, whom may God defend; Amen . . .
>
> . . . And the result is, – that from the first arrival of the Cimbri [Welsh] in this Island, according to well digested tradition and chronology, to the time of Howel the Good [Hywell Dda, prince of Dyfed], a period of no less than two thousand five hundred and seven years has elapsed; and from the time of Howell the Good to this present year of the coronation of King Henry VII, the son of Edmond, the son of Owen Tudor, (all of them being genuine Britons of the primitive royal lineage) five hundred and forty-five years. So that from the first arrival of the primitive Britons in the Island, to the present year [1485], three thousand and fifty-two years have intervened.[1]

Clearly the Tudors had reason to be pleased with such a long and illustrious ancestry, reaching back into the mists of time; but there were also other conclusions to be drawn from their family tree. In several of their ancestral lists there is mention of one Anna, 'a blood relative of the Virgin Mary', as having married into the royal house of Britain. If this were true, then it would mean that Tudor blood was not only royal but derived in part from the Holy Family itself. This secret holy lineage was connected with the central myth of the 'Matter of Britain', the legend of Joseph of Arimathea bringing the Holy Grail to the island shortly after the crucifixion.[2]

Henry VIII, like almost all his subjects, was well aware of these legends and must also have known about the traditions linking him to the family of the Virgin Mary. Moreover, as a grandson of Edward IV (through his mother, Elizabeth of York) he inherited the Yorkist family tree that went back to the kings of Israel as well as the Welsh one going back to Brutus. He would also have known of the tradition that the pre-Augustinian British church had been founded by Joseph of Arimathea, even before Rome was converted to Christianity. The conviction that this was so, that in its original form the British church owed no allegiance to Rome, no doubt gave him the confidence to defy the pope and to declare himself head of the Church of England. As Dame Frances Yates, late Reader in the History of the Renaissance at London University, put it:

The glorification of the Tudor monarchy as a religious imperial institution rested on the fact that the Tudor reform had dispensed with the Pope and made the monarch supreme in both church and state. This basic political fact was draped in the mystique of 'ancient British monarchy', with its Arthurian associations, represented by the Tudors in their capacity as an ancient British line, of supposed Arthurian descent, returning to power and supporting a pure British Church, defended by a religious chivalry from the evil powers (evil according to this point of view) of Hispano-Papal attempts at universal domination.[3]

This was certainly the approach taken by Henry VIII, who, building on his father's work in tracing the lineage back to King Arthur and beyond, stressed the importance of King Arthur's Round Table.

The Round Table of King Arthur has a mystical meaning far beyond and above its function as a simple piece of dining furniture. It represents, symbolically, the table of the Last Supper at which Jesus Christ ate the Passover meal with his twelve apostles, chosen in symbolic re-creation of the original twelve sons of Israel. Thus, as the old covenant between God and humanity was channelled through the family of Israel, so the new covenant was to be manifested through Christ's 'sons': his apostles. There is a cosmic dimension to this arrangement as well, for each apostle/son of Israel represents a different sign of the zodiac and therefore a different destiny. In the book of Revelation the city of New Jerusalem, which would one day be made manifest on earth, would have twelve gateways. Each of the twelve apostles, like the twelve sons of Israel, was linked to a different gateway. Their twelve unique destinies imply twelve different pathways through life, all leading to the same goal of unity with God, but approaching from different directions. King Arthur's Round Table, therefore, is connected with the vision of the New Jerusalem as the city of grace with twelve gateways. Banquets held at the table were not just orgies of self-indulgence but sacraments connected with the mystery of the Holy Grail.

The Plantagenets – and after them the Tudors – inherited and used an ancient round table, thereby associating themselves more deeply with this mystery. This table, 18 feet in diameter, today hangs in the Great Hall of Winchester Castle (see plate 9). Its provenance is unknown but recently, using dendrochronology, it has been dated to 1290. If this is correct then it probably comes from Wales, for around that time in Glamorgan bardic festivals associated with a 'system of the Round Table' were being celebrated each year. However, the Tudors probably believed that it was the very table used by King Arthur himself some seven hundred years previously.

Henry VIII instructed that the Round Table be repainted in green and white: the colours of Wales. The table is divided into twenty-five segments or place settings: two places for each sign of the zodiac, plus an extra one for the king, who represents the sun. The number of twenty-four knights plus the sovereign is also that of the Order of the Garter, founded in the fourteenth century. It seems likely, therefore, that at one time the Garter knights sat around this very table. At the centre of the table Henry had painted the emblem of the red and white Tudor rose. This would have had a dual meaning for the banqueting knights of his era. First, the rose was an ancient symbol of discretion; so its presence at the heart of the table served as a symbolic reminder that everything discussed there was to be kept secret. Secondly, because it was a Tudor rose, it emphasized the important role of Henry's own dynasty at the centre of the contemporary Arthurian myth. All this we can read as part of Henry's advertising campaign, promulgating the message that, just as the illustrious Arthur had been the British church's shield against the incursions of not just the pagan Saxons but also the vainglorious Romans, so now he, as Arthur's successor, would now protect it from Roman Catholic diktat.

Henry's daughter and successor Elizabeth was even more anti-Catholic than her father. As far as she was concerned the pope was not God's duly appointed legate but a latter-day Caesar whose influence needed to be banished for ever from her realm. She shared Henry's conviction that the Tudor lineage went back to kings who ruled over Britain from before the time of the Romans. She would have known that according to Geoffrey of Monmouth, whose *Historia Regnum Britanniae* of 1136 was still highly regarded in her time, London was originally called Trinovantum or 'New Troy',[4] and that King Lud (or Llud) had been buried near to the western gate of the city which was thereafter named Porthllud in Welsh, Ludgate in English.

Ludgate was rebuilt over and over again in the course of London's long history. The last time was in 1586, during the reign of Queen Elizabeth. She clearly knew all about the story of King Lud, for when she had Ludgate rebuilt a statue of her was placed in a niche over the gate facing down towards Fleet Street, while in niches on the other side of the gate were placed statues of King Lud and his sons: Androgeus (Avarwy) and Tenvantius (Teneufan). The implication of the symbolism is clear. Just as these illustrious ancestors of hers built up the walls of London and defended the city from the depredations of the Romans, so she was now its Protestant guardian against Philip II of Spain and his spiritual overlord the pope. The statues of Elizabeth and her supposed ancestors graced Ludgate for nearly two hundred years. Then, in 1760, as part of a road widening scheme, the gateway was demolished and the statues removed. Today Elizabeth's is to be found in Fleet Street, in a niche above the entrance to the Church of St Dunstan-in-the-West, while those of King Lud and his two sons moulder quietly under the porch of the same church (see plates 10 and 11).

Elizabeth was adamant that the British church was not, in its original foundation, a satellite of Rome. In her reply to a letter from five Roman Catholic bishops who begged her to see sense and come back to the Catholic faith, she pulled no punches:

> As to your entreaty for us to listen to you, we waive it; yet do return to you this our answer. Our realm and subjects have been long wanderers, walking astray, while they were under the tuition of Romish pastors, who advised them to own a wolf for their head (in lieu of a careful shepherd), whose inventions, heresies and schisms be so numerous, that the flock of Christ have fed on poisonous shrubs for want of wholesome pastures. And whereas you hit us and our subjects in the teeth, that the Romish Church first planted the Catholic faith within our realms, the records and chronicles of our realms testify the contrary; and your own Romish idolatry maketh you liars: witness the ancient monument of Gildas; unto which both foreign and domestic have gone in pilgrimage there to offer. This author testifieth Joseph of Arimathea to be the first preacher of the Word of God within our realms.

Long after that when Austin [St Augustine] came from
Rome, this our realm had bishops and priests therein,
as is well known to the wise and learned of our realm
by woeful experience, how your church entered therein
by blood; they being martyrs for Christ, and put to
death, because they denied Rome's usurped authority.[5]

There are many references in Welsh histories to how
the converted Saxons, in the name of the Augustinian
church, set about destroying the earlier churches of
Britain. In the savage wars of the sixth century church
buildings were often burnt down and any priests or
monks resident either slain or enslaved. According to
The Anglo-Saxon Chronicle, the greatest such
atrocity happened in AD 604. In the record for this year,
it says:

Aethelferth [Saxon king of Northumbria] led his army
to Chester, and there killed countless Welsh; and so the
prophecy of Augustine was fulfilled, when he said, 'If
the Welsh will not be at peace with us [viz. his Roman
church mission], they shall perish at the hands of the
Saxons.' There also two hundred priests were killed,
when they went there in order to pray for the Welsh
forces.[6]

In her defence of English independence from the
church of Rome Elizabeth refers to the writings of a
monk called Gildas, who in the sixth century wrote a
famous history of his times entitled *De excidio et
conquestu britanniae* – 'concerning the destruction and
invasion of Britain'. St Augustine came to Canterbury
in AD 597 to convert the pagan Saxons, but as Gildas
attests, there was already in existence at that time a

native British church. He says that Christianity was brought to Britain in the later part of the reign of Tiberius Caesar. Tiberius died in AD 37, so this means AD 36–7 at the latest. Gildas himself makes no mention of Joseph of Arimathea, but in Elizabeth's day the story of how he brought the Grail to Britain was common knowledge among storytellers and historians alike. For example, the legend of how Joseph converted Arviragus, a king of Britain who ruled at the time of the Claudian invasion, is told in the mid-fifteenth-century *Hardynge's Chronicle*. Composed in the form of rhyming couplets, this was based on earlier sources; as Hardynge had been employed by first Henry V and then his son Henry VI, one can assume Queen Elizabeth would have had his work in her library.[7] Clearly Elizabeth felt that she had ammunition enough to resist the claims of Roman sovereignty over both the Church of England and, perhaps more importantly, her throne. Yet if Elizabeth had read Gildas then she would have found other reasons for resisting Rome's claims of supremacy in church matters.

Gildas' book is composed very much in the style of Jeremiah's Lamentations, and it is clear that he saw himself as having a similar role in the affairs of his country as that prophet had at the time of the fall of Jerusalem. Throughout his work he compares Britain with Israel as he admonishes and chastises his compatriots for their cowardice in resisting invaders. Thus he writes:

I saw moreover in my own time, as that prophet [Jeremiah] also had complained, that the city [Jerusalem] had sat down lone and widowed, which before was full of people; that the queen of nations and

79

the princess of provinces (i.e. the church), had been made tributary; that the gold was obscured, and the most excellent colour (which is the brightness of God's word) changed; that the sons of Sion (i.e. of holy mother church), once famous and clothed in the finest gold, grovelled in dung; and what added intolerably to the weight of grief of that illustrious man [Jeremiah], and to mine, though but an abject whilst he had mourned them in their happy and prosperous condition, 'Her Nazarites were fairer than snow, more ruddy than old ivory, more beautiful than the sapphire' [Lam. 4: 7]. These and many other passages in the ancient Scriptures I regarded as a kind of mirror of human life, and I turned also to the New [Testament], wherein I read more clearly what perhaps to me before was dark, for the darkness deaf, and truth shed her steady light – I read therein that the Lord had said, 'I came not but to the lost sheep of the house of Israel' [Matt. 15: 24] and on the other hand, 'But the children of this kingdom shall be cast out into outer darkness, there shall be weeping and gnashing of teeth' [Matt. 8: 12].[8]

Gildas continues in like vein for several more pages, quoting extracts from the scriptures and using these to illustrate the similarity of the predicament of his own times – Britain under invasion by the Saxons – with the earlier plight of Israel, first at the time of the destruction of Jerusalem by the Babylonians and later under the Roman repression at the time of Jesus. The asides in parentheses, associating what he is saying with the church, are probably interpolations put in by later scribes. Read without these, it is clear he is not always writing allegorically but is interpreting events directly in the light of prophecy. If God punished the Israelites of old, he asks his compatriots, what better could they expect?

> If God's peculiar people, chosen from all the people of
> the world, the royal seed, and holy nation, to whom he
> said, 'My first begotten Israel,' its priests, prophets and
> kings, throughout many ages, his servant and apostle,
> and the members of his primitive church, were not
> spared when they deviated from the right path, what
> will he do to the darkness of this our age, in which,
> besides all the huge and heinous sins, which it has in
> common with all the wicked of the world committed, is
> found an innate, indelible, and irremediable load of
> folly and inconstancy?[9]

Yet it is clear from Gildas' testament that he regarded
Britain as something more than a country whose kingdom, in its destruction at the hands of invaders,
somewhat resembled ancient Israel. In his diatribe he
seems to be hinting that, either by adoption or indeed
by descent, Britain actually *is* Israel:

> After this [some victories in the wars with the invaders,
> notably by Ambrosius Aurelianus and his progeny],
> sometimes our countrymen, sometimes the enemy, won
> the field, to the end that our Lord might this land try
> after his accustomed manner these his Israelites,
> whether they loved him or not, until the year of the
> siege of Mons Badonis, when took place also the last
> almost, though not the least slaughter of our cruel foes,
> which was (as I am sure) forty-four years and one
> month after the landing of the Saxons, and also the
> time of my own nativity.[10]

The idea that the British were descended from the

Israelites was not forgotten in the centuries that separated Gildas from the Tudors. It is clear from certain letters and other documents that at least some people were aware of the Israelite legends and believed in them. Over a period of time the idea that the British were really Israelites in disguise gradually displaced the earlier legends, recorded by Geoffrey of Monmouth and others, that they came from Troy. We have already seen how, during the Wars of the Roses from 1455 to 1485, the dynastic claims of the major participants were of primary importance, and that the Yorkist King Edward IV had his genealogy mapped out on a scroll 18 feet long, tracing his ancestry right back to Jehoshaphat and the kings of Judah.

King Henry VIII too seems to have regarded himself as not just a Protestant king but an Israelite. In 1545 he had a medal struck to celebrate his new-found status as head of the Church of England. On the obverse side was a bust of the king with a Latin inscription; on the reverse was an inscription in Hebrew which translates as: 'Henry VIII, triple King [i.e. of England, France and Ireland], defender of the faith, and of the church of England and Ireland, under Christ, supreme head.' A similar medal was struck in 1547 to commemorate the coronation of Henry's son, the boy-king Edward VI. Examples of both of these medals can be seen in the British Museum. At that time there were no Jews in England and Latin was the official language of communication; so undoubtedly Hebrew scripts were put on these important medals to emphasize a believed connection between England and ancient Israel.

The notion that the British were Israelites continued as a theme in the writings of many authors right up to and long after the time of Queen Elizabeth. In 1588, following the destruction of the Spanish Armada, James Melville wrote an essay concerning the castaways of the Spanish fleet who landed in Fife. After describing the fear of invasion he explains how God himself had destroyed the menace to protect his 'awin' (own) Israel: 'And in very deed, as we knew certainly soon after, the keeper of his awin Israel, was in the meantime convoying that monstrous navy about our coasts, and directing their hulks and galiates to the islands, rocks and sands, whereupon he had destined their wreck and destruction.'[11] At the time of writing there was no state of Israel in Palestine, it being over 1,500 years since the Romans had expelled the Jews from Judea and some 2,200 years since the expulsion of the Israelites from Samaria by the Assyrians. The reference is clearly to Britain as God's 'awin Israel'.

During the Elizabethan period there were many who believed in Britain's perceived destiny as Israel reborn: that Britain would succeed where the earlier nation had failed and would ensure that God's plans for the redemption of the world came to fruition. Whether or not Elizabeth herself went along with the idea that the British were direct descendants of the ancient Israelites, she certainly believed in England's divine calling. Her Protestant faith was not just a rejection of Roman Catholicism but rather an affirmation of Britain's special destiny. In pursuit of the fulfilment of this destiny she was even willing to forgo marriage, lest her husband, not sharing her vision, should usurp her throne and for seemingly pragmatic reasons reverse her policies.

Another great influence on Elizabeth's thinking was the upsurge in interest around that time in what is called hermeticism. This tradition embraced all sorts of arcane pursuits from the relatively orthodox, such as alchemy and astrology, to the decidedly fringe activity of invoking angels by means of magical formulae. The dominant figure of the times in all such matters was the court astrologer, Dr John Dee, whose importance as a philosopher – one might say prophet – of the Elizabethan age is only now becoming apparent. Among his many activities Dee engaged in what we would today call spiritualism. Using various magical formulae, he would summon spirits and 'channel' what was said by and to them. He would have long discussions with archangels such as Uriel and Michael, and the results of these seances, which generally seem to have concerned the practice of magic, were recorded. Some of these records were later published, in five books known as *De Heptarchia Mystica*, 'The Seven Mysteries'. Accompanying this edition was a preface by its publisher, Elias Ashmole, a figure who will appear more prominently in a later chapter.

Dr Dee had considerable influence at the Elizabethan court. He was regarded as probably the greatest sage of his time; using his knowledge of astrology, he had even chosen the date for Elizabeth's coronation. He had an extraordinary mind that ranged over every subject under the sun and, besides his 'channelled' material (most of it, it has to be said, unintelligible nonsense), produced some outstanding work of his own. A graduate of St John's College, Cambridge, and a Fellow of Trinity, he was an accomplished mathematician. Though he is now better known for his *Monas Hieroglyphica*, a corpus of esoteric thought firmly in the hermetic tradition of Pico della Mirandola and Cornelius Agrippa, he also wrote a famous preface to an English translation of Euclid's geometry. In this he was again before his time, for prior to the seventeenth century mathematics was looked upon with deep suspicion in Christian Europe. It was thought by many pious people to be a species of magic and therefore an invention of the devil.

Dee clearly enjoyed playing the role of Renaissance magus, even though on several occasions – notably during the reign of Elizabeth's elder, and very Catholic, sister Mary – he was in danger of being charged with witchcraft. He drew around himself an ardent band of followers which included in their number the earl of Leicester, the earl's nephew Sir Philip Sidney, the Gilbert brothers Sir Humphrey and Adrian, and their half-brother, Sir Walter Raleigh. All of these gentlemen would come to Dee's house in Mortlake, a magnet for free-thinkers, to peruse his extensive library on the occult and discuss matters of religious, philosophical and national importance. Thus Dee's house became a species of neoplatonic academy, much in the tradition of the Florentine Accademia of the Medicis.

Not all of Dee's studies were so esoteric; he was passionately interested in British history and the advancement of a 'British empire' – a term that he seems to have been the first to use. Like Elizabeth he was proud of his ancestry and could trace his own lineage back to Welsh princes. For this reason, if for no other, he took an active interest in the Arthurian legend. He believed it to be England's destiny, now that it was united with Wales and restored to the rule of the line of monarchs descended from Brutus, to act as leader and guide to the world. He was far-sighted enough to see that if this were ever to become a reality, then England would have not only to challenge Spain in Europe but to colonize America. A curious justification for

Fig. 10. Frontispiece from Dr John Dee's *Monas Hieroglyphica*.

England's annexation of the vast territories of North America that currently lay beyond the reach of Spain was that according to legend it had been visited many centuries earlier by a Welsh prince named Madoc, a relative of King Arthur. As Madoc had claimed America for Britain long before Columbus made his famous voyage of 1492, it followed that Britain had prior title over Spain. Of course, it was not enough just to say this; to assert such a claim entailed exercising real power across the seas. For Britain to establish an overseas empire it would need to develop a navy. This project Dee now promoted vigorously, both to the queen herself and among his friends at court. All this is very well put by Dame Frances Yates:

> Dee's views on the British-imperial destiny of Queen Elizabeth I are set out in his *General and rare memorials pertayning to the Perfect art of Navigation* (1577). Expansion of the navy and Elizabethan expansion at sea were connected in his mind with the vast ideas concerning the lands to which (in his view) Elizabeth might lay claim through her mythical descent from King Arthur. Dee's 'British imperialism' is bound up with the 'British History' recounted by Geoffrey of Monmouth, based on the hypothetical descent of British monarchs from Brut, supposedly of Trojan origin, and therefore connecting with Virgil and the Roman imperial myth. Arthur was the supposed descendant of Brut, and was the chief religious and mystical exemplar of British imperial Christianity.
>
> In the *General and rare memorials* there is a complicated print based on a drawing in Dee's own hand, of Elizabeth sailing in a ship labelled 'Europa', with the moral that Britain is to grow strong at sea, so that

through her 'Imperial Monarchy' she may perhaps become the pilot of all Christendom.[12]

Dee's *Art of Navigation* actually has very little to do with the skills of sailing, though as a close friend of Gerardus Mercator, whom he met while studying at Louvain, he must have been familiar with modern techniques of map-making. He must also have realized that as the earth is a globe, the shortest distance between two places is governed by spherical geometry. This meant that the shortest, and therefore seemingly quickest, route to China on the other side of the Pacific Ocean would be via northern Canada. To prove this, in 1576 he set sail with Martin Frobisher to search for a north-west passage that would enable British merchant ships to go beyond the Spanish New World directly to the other side of Asia. They got no further than the Hudson Bay; but the journey did at least provide the inspiration for his book on navigation.

In the years that followed, English and Spanish rivalry over the New World intensified. In the decades after the Spanish conquest of Mexico in the 1520s, the Aztec silver and gold that flowed into the coffers of King Philip II made Spain the strongest power in Europe. Dee's own maritime exploits may have been behind him by now, but he retained his interest in the development of a British empire. Among the charmed circle of his friends was Sir Francis Drake, a privateer – a polite description for a government-sponsored pirate. Drake had been carrying out daring raids on Spanish shipping and coastal towns in the West Indies and Central America since 1570. In 1577 he undertook his greatest challenge yet: a round-the-world voyage. Almost certainly Dee was one of the sponsors of this expedition, which set out from England on 13 December 1577 and was to last nearly three years. In the course of this voyage Drake sailed around Cape Horn, up the west coast of South America and up most of North America, as far as latitude 48° north. This huge stretch of territory he annexed in the name of the queen, naming it 'New Albion'.

Drake was not only an ardent royalist but seems also to have believed in Britain's identity with Israel. In 1587 he wrote a letter to a famous preacher called James Foxe. Towards the end of this letter, Drake asked that prayers be said so that 'God may be glorified, his church, our queen [Elizabeth I] and country preserved, that we may have continual peace in Israel.' It goes without saying that by 'Israel' he meant England. But in 1588 this peace was shattered as, with the blessing of the pope, Philip of Spain launched his Armada with the intent of bringing England back into the Catholic fold by force and conquest. The tactic employed by Drake of putting fire-ships among the lumbering hulks of the Spanish galleons certainly contributed to the destruction of this formidable fleet; however, even at the time it was recognized that the defeat of the Spanish owed as much to the weather as to British seamanship. This was taken as proof positive that God had been listening to Britain's prayers and was still protecting his 'awin Israel'. What Drake may not have known is that a hex had been put on the Armada by England's grand magician, John Dee, who was then living in Prague.

The navigators of Dee's circle were not just adventurers content to sail along the coasts of America; they attempted to settle the land. Prime movers here were Sir Humphrey Gilbert and his brother Adrian Gilbert of Compton in Devon. In 1578 Queen

Elizabeth granted them a charter entitling them, in her name, to discover and colonize remote heathen lands. Later that year the Gilbert brothers made another attempt at finding that Holy Grail of British shipping: the north-west passage. As was inevitable, the expedition was a failure and they returned to England the following year. In 1583 they set sail again, this time with the firm intention of planting a permanent English colony in America. They made their first landfall at St John's in Newfoundland, but evidently deemed it unsuitable for settlement and sailed southwards. The unfortunate loss of one of their three ships at Cape Breton caused them to abandon their plans altogether and to set sail for home; but when a second ship, the *Squirrel*, went down off the Azores it took the Gilbert brothers with it, thereby putting paid to any further colonizing attempts by them.

In 1584 a new patent was issued by the queen, this time to the Gilberts' half-brother Sir Walter Raleigh. Thus it was that in 1586 a truly heroic attempt was made at establishing a colony on Roanoke Island off the coast of what is now North Carolina but was then part of a new land called Virginia in honour of England's virgin queen. This colony might have succeeded had it not been for the outbreak of war between England and Spain. This meant that for several crucial years the colonists were left to fend for themselves; and, as no ships could be spared to bring them supplies from England and they were not yet self-sufficient, they perished. The exact reasons why this pioneering colony failed are a matter of great debate, but nevertheless lessons were learnt which would be crucial to future pioneers' success. As it was, the most tangible fruits of Sir Walter Raleigh's American efforts were the introduction to England of a blessing and a curse: respectively, the potato and tobacco.

When Queen Elizabeth died in 1603 most of the Dee circle had already passed on: Leicester, Sidney, Drake and the Gilbert brothers, to name but a few. Dee himself, at one time the Merlin of Elizabeth's court, was to die five years later in 1608, in great poverty, at his house in Mortlake. At that time Sir Walter Raleigh, for most of his adult life a great favourite of Queen Elizabeth, was in the Tower of London under sentence of death for treason. He was executed in 1618, charged with breaking his word to the king that he would harm no Spaniards during a quest for what turned out to be fool's gold in the Orinoco.

With Raleigh's death, the era which gave birth to the notion of a British empire came to its end. It would be a long time before Britain again felt itself strong enough to challenge other European powers for control of the seven seas. However, the seeds of imperial endeavour sown at the time of Elizabeth would eventually produce a harvest larger than either she or any of her contemporaries could have imagined. In the meantime, many other forces were to come to bear, shaping the destiny of the island nation that would be Israel.

CHAPTER THREE

THE KING FROM THE NORTH

The accession of James VI of Scotland to the throne of England as James I in 1603 had very important political and cultural results, not just for Britain but for the whole of Europe. James's claim to the English throne came primarily through his mother, Mary, Queen of Scots, who was the granddaughter of Henry VIII's sister Margaret. He therefore had the same Tudor lineage as Elizabeth, his first cousin twice removed. On his father's side the Stuart or Stewart lineage went back to one Alan son of Flaad, brother to Alan the seneschal of Dol in Brittany. Given the location of the family in Brittany and the repeated family name of Alan, it seems likely that they were descended from the kings of Brittany, who ruled over the province at the time of King Arthur and indeed were closely interlinked with his dynasty in Wales.[1] A son of this Alan was Walter, who was made seneschal or steward of Scotland by King David I. The Stewarts were prominent in the medieval period of Scottish history, fighting against the English in the wars of both William Wallace and Robert the Bruce. A later Walter Stewart subsequently married Marjorie, the daughter of Robert the Bruce, their son ascending the throne of Scotland as King

Robert II. Mary, Queen of Scots, mother to James I of England, was a direct descendant of theirs.

James's character was contradictory in the extreme. Though a Protestant, he was by no means sympathetic to the Puritans. Similarly, though he was not unsympathetic to Catholics, he remained a Protestant all his life and had an 'authorized' Protestant edition of the Bible translated into English. Physically James was not prepossessing, having been a sickly child. He is said to have had one leg shorter than the other and, because his tongue was too long for his mouth, to have dribbled a lot. Unlike his immediate predecessors on the English throne, Henry VIII, Elizabeth I and, to some extent, Mary, he could not dominate his court simply by his sheer presence. Yet he had an absolute conviction that he ruled his kingdom by divine right and as a result was liable to follow policies – notably in foreign affairs – of his own choosing without consulting Parliament. This attitude of absolutism, characteristic of most European states at the time, took little account of the special role in English politics of Parliament, whose privileges had been won over many centuries. Also, as many people came to discover, James was not a man whose word was reliable. A weak man himself, his idea of kingcraft was to play his enemies off one against the other. His contemporaries, many of whom had fond memories of Elizabethan etiquette, found him uncouth, slovenly and lacking in dignity. His foreign policy was contradictory, seeking to appease the strong, Catholic powers of Spain and France while at the same time promoting himself as the de facto leader of the Protestant states of northern Europe. For a time this dualistic policy worked well, but ultimately the mixed signals that he sent to the Continental powers were to lead to disaster – not so much for England as for Europe.

James I was well educated, wrote a number of books and took a particular interest in foreign languages and theology. However, he was also superstitious, with not a little fear of the occult. In 1587, while still king only of Scotland, he had written and published a book called *Daemonologie*, in which as well as condemning witchcraft he denounced the conjuration of spirits. This was seen as an attack on the crystal-gazing of Dee and his associate Edward Kelley, during whose seances, or so it was reputed, demons would appear and communicate all sorts of nonsense. Consequently, when in 1603 James ascended the throne vacated by Elizabeth, Dee had more to fear than most over charges of witchcraft. As his defence, in 1604 he addressed a pamphlet to the new king in which he begged him to understand that all that he had heard about him as a magician was incorrect. These tales, he said, were all malicious rumours, put about by the enemies of England against a good Christian. But his appeals did not convince James. Thus it was that Dr John Dee, who in Elizabeth's time wielded considerable influence on account of his esoteric knowledge, was frozen out of James's court and left to die in extreme poverty. He was lucky to escape imprisonment or worse. Far from receiving royal favour on account of his sterling work in promoting the cause of empire, he was now an anachronistic embarrassment. His passing in 1608 marked the end of one era, the early Renaissance, and the start of another. This 'new age' would be one of enlightenment, and its crowning achievement would be not magic but rather the establishment of a natural philosophy whose working methodology we now call science.

Just as Queen Elizabeth and the other Tudor monarchs took pride in their Welsh ancestry and a lineage that went back to King Arthur, so the Stuarts looked with fondness on traditions associating them with the ancient kings of Scotland and Ireland. By tradition the kings of Scotland were crowned at Scone, just to the north of Perth.[2] Originally the ceremony was performed with the king sitting on the 'Stone of Scone', a flat block of sandstone said to have been brought to Scotland from the island of Iona by the Dal Riata tribesmen and to have been moved to Scone from Dunstaffnage Castle on Loch Etive by King Kenneth MacAlpin (d. *c*.860). In 1296 King Edward I of England, known as the 'Hammer of the Scots', asserted his authority as overlord of all Britain by taking this stone back to London. It was then placed inside the coronation seat he had specially made and kept in the national shrine of Westminster Abbey. This coronation seat was designed by the king's goldsmith, Master Adam of Shoreditch, and decorated by the king's painter, Master Walter of Durham. On the back of it was originally a portrait of the king. This was later removed and the seat was given four lion supporters as legs, to symbolize that it was truly the throne of David – the lion-king of Judah. Thereafter, with the notable exception of Queen Mary I,[3] all subsequent English kings and queens were to be crowned sitting on this seat.[4]

This stone (also known as the 'Stone of Destiny') has many other traditions associated with it. At Iona it had served as the throne of the early Scots, who migrated to Britain from Ireland in the sixth century AD. Prior to this migration it had been an Irish coronation stone, apparently kept at the hill fort of Tara, in County

Meath, for the purpose. According to Irish legends, it was called the Lia-Fail or 'Stone of Wonder', which would cry out if any true heir to the throne of Ireland should sit upon it.

The Danann were most notable magicians, and would work wonderful things thereby; and when they pleased, they would trouble both sea and land, darken both sonn and moone at their pleasures. They did frame a great broad stone which they called *Lya Fail*, or the stone of Ireland, by their art, and placed the same at Taragh, which by enchantment had this property; when anyone was born to whom to be a King of Ireland was predestinated, as soone as the party soe born stood upon This Stone, forthwith the Stone would give such a shouting noyse that it was heard from sea to sea, throughout the whole kingdom, which presently would satisfy the party standing on the Stone and all the rest of his future fortune to the Right of the Crown. This Stone remained a long time in the King of Ireland's palace at Taragh, whereon many Kings and Queens were crowned, until it was sent over to Scotland by the King of Ireland with his son Fergus, who was created the first King of Scotland on that Stone, and for a long time after all the Kings of Scotland received their crownes thereon untill the time of King Edward I, King of England, whoe took the same as a monument from thence into England in the warres between him and Scotchmen, and placed it in Westminster Abbey.[5]

There is a further legend concerning the Stone of Scone which, if true, would give it a vastly greater antiquity. According to these legends (contained in the *Chronicles of Eri*, written in 1788/9 and based on a Phoenician

Fig. 11. The coronation seat of Britain.

manuscript), the Lia-Fail was brought to Ireland from the east by an ancient called Olam Fola.

Correctly or incorrectly, later commentators have identified this Olam Fola with the biblical prophet Jeremiah and associated the stone he is said to have brought with him to Ireland, after the destruction of Jerusalem by the Babylonians in *c.*586 BC, with one formerly used as a throne by King David – the first king of Israel from the House of Judah, and the king who made Jerusalem the capital city of the Israelites. In the Bible David makes a covenant with God and is promised in turn that his throne will endure for ever. This prophecy is passed on to David by Nathan the prophet in the Second Book of Samuel:

> When your [David's] days are fulfilled and you lie down with your fathers, I [God] will raise up your offspring [Solomon] after you, who shall come forth from your body, and I will establish his kingdom. He shall build a house for my name, and I will establish the throne of his kingdom for ever. I will be his father, and he shall be my son. When he commits iniquity, I will chasten him with the rods of men, with the stripes of the sons of men; but I will not take my steadfast love from him, as I took it from Saul, whom I put away from before you. And your house and your kingdom shall be made sure for ever before me; your throne shall be established for ever. (2 Sam. 7: 12–16)

When on the point of death, David calls his son Solomon to him and repeats God's promise: 'If your [David's] sons take heed to their way, to walk before me in faithfulness with all their heart and with all their soul, there shall not fail you a man on the throne of Israel' (1 Kings 2: 4).

In addition to these references to the throne of Israel, there are numerous places in the Old Testament where David refers to his God in connection with a *tsur* (translated into English as 'rock'). Thus in the Second Book of Samuel, for example, we read: 'The Lord is my rock, and my fortress, and my deliverer, my God, my rock, in whom I take refuge, my saviour; thou savest me from violence' (2 Sam. 22: 2–3). That David is perhaps referring to an actual rock rather than simply using the word in a metaphorical sense seems to be implied in the record of his last words. These are contained in the following chapter of the same book of the Bible:

> The oracle of David, the son of Jesse, the oracle of the man who was raised on high, the anointed of the God of Jacob, the sweet psalmist of Israel: 'The Spirit of the Lord speaks by me, his word is upon my tongue.
>
> 'The God of Israel has spoken, the Rock [*tsur*] of Israel has said to me: When one rules justly over men, ruling in the fear of God, he dawns on them like the morning light, like the sun shining forth upon a cloudless morning, like rain that makes grass to sprout from the earth.' (2 Sam. 23: 1–4)

From this extract it would appear that the 'Rock of Israel' had some sort of oracular function; the king was able to receive God's instructions when in its presence. This is rather like the Lia-Fail crying out when a trueborn future king should sit upon it.

Yet according to traditions associated with the Stone of Scone, though David was the first king of the line of Judah to sit on the throne of Israel, his witness stone had an even greater antiquity. This is implied by yet another of the Stone of Scone's alternative names: Jacob's Pillow Stone. According to these legends, its importance as a witness to the coronation of rightful kings came from the fact that it was none other than the stone raised by Jacob at Bethel following his dream of a ladder with angels ascending and descending it:

And Jacob went out from Beer-sheba, and went toward Haran.

And he lighted upon a certain place, and tarried there all night, because the sun was set; and he took of the stones of that place, and put them for his pillows, and lay down in that place to sleep.

And he dreamed, and behold a ladder set upon the earth, and the top of it reached to heaven: and behold the angels of God ascending and descending on it.

And, behold, the Lord stood above it, and said, I am the Lord God of Abraham thy father, and the God of Isaac: the land whereon thou liest, to thee will I give it and to thy seed;

And thy seed shall be as the dust of the earth, and thou shalt spread abroad to the west, and to the east, and to the north, and to the south: and in thee and in thy seed shall all the families of the earth be blessed.

And, behold, I am with thee, and will keep thee in all places whither thou goest, and will bring thee again into this land; for I will not leave thee, until I have done that which I have spoken to thee.

And Jacob awoked out of his sleep, and he said, Surely the Lord is in this place and I knew it not.

And he was afraid, and said, How dreadful is this place! this is none other but the house of God [*Beth-el* in Hebrew], and this is the gate of heaven.

And Jacob rose early in the morning, and took the stone that he had for his pillow, and set it up for a pillar [*matstsebah*], and poured oil on top of it.

And he called the name of that place Beth-el: but the name of that city was called Luz at the first.

And Jacob vowed a vow, saying, If God will be with me, and will keep me in this way that I go, and will give me bread to eat and raiment to put on,

So that I shall come again to my father's house in peace; then shall the Lord be my God:

And this stone, which I have set for a pillar, shall be God's house [*beth-el*]: and of all that thou shalt give me I will surely give the tenth unto thee. (Gen. 28: 10–22)

In the Bible, Jacob's Pillow (or Pillar) Stone is said to have been a witness to this contract or covenant he had made with God. This made it a very important cult object for the ancient Israelites. Jacob's Pillow Stone or *matstsebah* functioned as a *beth-el*, the Hebrew equivalent of what in Greek would have been called a baitulos or *baitulos*. Such *baitula*, or 'witness stones', were very common in the ancient world. Often they were meteorites, which, naturally enough, were regarded as having been sent down from heaven by God himself. One of these was the so-called 'Sybil Stone' that resided at the oracular centre of Delphi in Greece. Another meteorite was venerated in what is now Anatolian Turkey, and was there regarded as the personification of Cybele, the mother of the gods. Until 205 BC this important cult object was kept at the centre of Cybele's cult, the city of Pessinus in Galatia, until it was taken back to Rome by the Romans. They had inferred from their own Sibylline books, oracular records which were kept in the Temple of Jupiter, that they needed to bring this meteorite to Rome if they were to win the war they were then fighting against Carthage. The Cybele meteorite was brought back to Rome, and the Romans won their war.

Cybele was identified by the Greeks with their own mother-goddess, Rhea. According to Greek mythology Rhea and her husband Cronos, the Greek equivalent of the Roman god Saturn, were Titans, whose children were destined to become the gods of the Olympian age. To avoid being displaced by his offspring, Cronos swallowed each one whole as it was born. Thus Rhea's first five children were disposed of. However, in place of the sixth, Zeus, Rhea gave Cronos a stone wrapped in swaddling clothes to look like a baby, preserving the child unharmed. When Zeus grew to adulthood he duly displaced his father as ruler of the heavens. Cronos was given an emetic and vomited up the stone along with the other gods. The Cybele stone therefore represented, or was a double for, Zeus himself. (The symbol of Cronos

Fig. 12. Saturn vomiting the stone of Zeus. From Michael Maier's *Atalanta Fugiens*.

vomiting up the stone of Zeus was used by the alchemist Michael Maier in his famous book of 1617, *Atalanta Fugiens*, as a symbol of the work of freeing the 'philosopher's stone' from base matter. We shall see more of Maier in later chapters.)

In Egypt there were several equivalent meteorites recorded as having been regarded as sacred objects, including some believed to have oracular powers. During the earlier period of Egyptian history known as the Old Kingdom (*c*.2800–2200 BC), a stone called the Benben was kept as a cult object in the Temple of the Phoenix at Heliopolis. This stone, almost certainly an oriented meteorite,[6] disappeared at around the time the Pyramids were built. During New Kingdom times (*c*.1550–1050 BC) another meteorite was kept at Thebes (Luxor) as a cult object sacred to the priapic god Min, and a third, sacred to the sun-god, Amun-Re, resided at the oracular oasis of Siwa. This one may still have been there when Alexander the Great made his famous pilgrimage to the oasis in *c*.331 BC.

We have no reason to believe that, if David did actually have a sacred stone for his throne, it was such a meteorite. However, it is clear that Jacob's Pillow Stone, the Lia-Fail of Ireland and the Stone of Scone, even if not one and the same, all functioned as witness stones and that, like the Sibylline stone, they were somehow emblematic of numinous divine power. As to whether James I was aware of the mythic connection between the Stone of Scone and these ancient meteorite cults, it seems unlikely; and given his animosity towards magic and the occult, if he had known about it he would probably have disapproved. However, the idea that the throne of Britain was one and the same as that of King David of Israel was very much in his mind.

Coming into London, James would have seen how Elizabeth's Ludgate featured statues of herself and her supposed illustrious ancestors, King Lud and his sons Avarwy and Teneufan. Not to be outdone, in 1617 he rebuilt Aldersgate, another of the ancient gateways to the City of London – significantly, the one that faced north towards Scotland. A plaque was put on the gate when it was repaired in 1670 with the following explanation:

ALDERS-GATE so named because of its antiquity as ALD-GATE was so called from its Age, so this from being the alder-Gate of the two [the other, presumably, being Ald-Gate]. It has several times been increased in its Buildings, but at length being ruinous it was taken down and rebuilt in a more beautiful manner anno 1618. The north side is adorned with the figure of King James the first on horseback, between 2 niches wherein are the figures of the prophets Samuel and Jeremiah, with these texts vizt. I Samuel Chap. 12 verse 1 & Jeremiah Chap. 17 verse 25. On the south side is King James I in his robes sitting in his chair of state. This gate received great damage in the Fire of London but was again repaired and this inscription placed on the south side. This gate was repaired and beautified at the sole charge of this city in ye year of Mayoralty of Sr. Samuel Sterling Knt. Anno Dom. 1670.

The placing of James's statues and also his choice of figures to accompany his own image on the north side of the gate is very interesting. Samuel was the prophet who appointed Saül as the first king of Israel. The text referred to (1 Sam. 12: 1) is as follows: 'And Samuel said unto all Israel, Behold, I have hearkened unto your

Fig. 13. Aldersgate in around 1700.

voice in all that ye said unto me, and have made a king over you.' In the context of Aldersgate this is clearly intended as a reference not to Saul but rather to King James himself.

The choice of Jeremiah as the second prophet may have been connected with the belief that he was to be identified with Olam Fola, the ancient who is said to have brought the Lia-Fail to Ireland. However, the principal reason why a statue of Jeremiah of all people was placed on a gateway to London is indicated by the text of the inscription that was put up below his statue (Jer. 17: 25). This read: 'Then shall enter into the gates

105

of this city, kings and princes, sitting upon the throne of David, riding in chariots and horse. And this city shall stand for ever.'

Aldersgate was immediately to the north of St Paul's Cathedral, on the old Roman road of Watling Street, which ran from the Kent coast, via Canterbury, London and St Albans, all the way to north Wales. Jeremiah was, therefore, presiding over the principal gate on the principal highway of the kingdom. On the north side of the gate King James is shown riding his horse and it is likely, though this is difficult to confirm, that it was through this very gateway that James arrived in London after being proclaimed king in succession to Elizabeth; this might be an explanation for the reference to kings and princes on horseback arriving by this gate. Similarly, on the inner, southern side of the gate he is shown sitting on his throne. This is clearly intended to symbolize him sitting on the 'throne of David', which could obviously be an allusion to the way that he, as James VI of Scotland, sat on the throne once occupied by David I of Scotland. However, as so often, there does seem to have been a further, deeper meaning to these symbolic representations. The passage from which the inscription is taken offers further illumination. It begins and ends as follows:

Then said the Lord to me: 'Go and stand in the Benjamin Gate, by which the kings of Judah enter and by which they go out, and in all the gates of Jerusalem, and say: "Hear the word of the Lord, you kings of Judah, and all the inhabitants of Jerusalem, who enter by these gates. Thus says the Lord: Take heed for the sake of your lives, and do not bear a burden on the Sabbath day or bring it in by the gates of Jerusalem . . .

' "... But if you do not listen to me, to keep the Sabbath day holy, and not to bear a burden and enter by the gates of Jerusalem on the Sabbath day, then I will kindle a fire in its gates, and it shall devour the palaces of Jerusalem and shall not be quenched." ' (Jer. 17: 19–27)

In ancient Israel the tribe of Benjamin had its territories immediately to the north of Jerusalem. Actually, technically speaking, Jerusalem was within the tribal estates of Benjamin, though it was on the border with Judah, only five miles from Bethlehem. Thus, like Aldersgate in London, the Benjamin Gate of Jerusalem would have been on the north side of the city. By placing Jeremiah's statue and the quote from this chapter at Aldersgate, James seems to have been hinting at secret knowledge concerning both himself as David's heir and London's identity as the capital of Israel; a 'New Jerusalem', so to speak.

It was undoubtedly the conviction that he was God's anointed sitting on the throne of the biblical David that lay at the root of James's belief in his divine right to govern. Just as the Tudors had made use of Welsh legends concerning King Arthur and his Round Table in the development of their programme for building a British empire, so James Stuart brought with him from Scotland ideas and people that were to have a profound effect on the development of English thinking in the seventeenth century. The most important of these was Scottish Rite Freemasonry, whose origins are shrouded in mystery.

For all his dislike of occultism, James I is the first British monarch definitely recorded as having been a Freemason. According to Christopher Knight and

Robert Lomas, Freemasons themselves, he was initiated in the Lodge of Scone and Perth in 1601 at the age of thirty-five.[7] It is perhaps noteworthy that James's mother lodge should have embraced Scone, the ancient seat of the Scottish kings. Freemasonry in Scotland has a very different pedigree from that prevalent in England. Scottish Rite Freemasonry claims to derive, at least in part, from an inheritance brought to Britain around 1307 by Christendom's most famous military order: the Knights Templar.

In 1118, about twenty years after the knights of the First Crusade set out from Europe to retake the Holy Land for Christendom, the Order of the Knights Templar was established. Its patron was the then king of Jerusalem, Baldwin II, who was of the French House of Lorraine and who had, like his cousin Baldwin I before him, previously been count of Edessa.[8] Initially there were just nine of these knights, led by one Hugues de Payen, who was the first Grand Master of the order. For nine years there were no further recruits to the order other than Hugues Count of Champagne who, abandoning his family, joined the order in 1125. The order was initially called 'The Poor Knights of Christ' but because Baldwin gave them the use of the Temple Mount with its huge Al-Aqsa Mosque, as their head-quarters, they came to be called 'Templars'.

Without a doubt the Knights Templar looked upon themselves, and were to some extent regarded by others, as a medieval version of King Arthur's Order of the Round Table. However, there were differences. Whereas King Arthur's order had been secular, with knights free to marry if they wished and under no obligation to stay permanently at court or in monasteries, the Templars were a species of warrior monks. As such they observed a monastic rule which was based on that of the Cistercians. At the head of the order was a Grand Master, who resided at Jerusalem, although his authority was not absolute.[9] As it developed the order became multinational, with preceptories throughout Europe. In each country where they were present there was a provincial commander and subordinate officers below him. It is said that at their height the Templars had no fewer than 16,000 lordships and 40,000 commanderies, which made them far and away the richest and most powerful organization in Christendom.

The origins of the Templars' wealth, which seems extraordinary given that their rule committed them to poverty, are not hard to find. Substantial gifts were made by pious Christians to further their work as crusaders; in addition, knights joining the order would bequeath lands and other property to the order in perpetuity, thereby providing it with a capital base. These donations, however, important as they were, were not the Templars' only source of wealth: they also operated what we would now call a multinational corporation.

The stated remit of the Templars was the protection of pilgrims to the Holy Land, making them a sort of police force. However, they also acted as bankers across Europe. Pilgrims could deposit money in one Templar house and take with them promissory notes that could be used in hostels all along the way to Jerusalem. This obviated the need for carrying large amounts of cash, a serious consideration when travelling through often hostile territory. As the amount of credit given was less than the value of the deposit made, the difference represented a profit for the order. This 'high street' banking was not the only type of transaction the Templars carried out; they also provided very large amounts of money on loan to kings. It was their effectiveness in this regard which was ultimately to prove their undoing.

King Philip IV of France (r. 1285–1314), known as 'the Fair', was a spendthrift who not only envied the Templars' wealth but owed them a lot of money. In 1307 he issued warrants for the arrest of all the Templars in his kingdom on trumped-up charges of blasphemous conduct.

In a most appalling episode of religious persecution they were interrogated by the Inquisition, threats of torture usually being enough to gain confessions of heresy. After some prevarication the order was dissolved by the pope, who at Philip's instigation ordered the kings of other European states similarly to arrest all Templars under their jurisdiction and to hand over their property to the rival order of Knights Hospitallers. The final indignity came in March 1314 when Jacques de Molay, the last Grand Master, was taken out on a scaffold in Paris to make a public confession of guilt before the gathered crowds. He refused and instead declared both himself and his order innocent of all charges. As a result he, along with Geoffrey de Charnay, the preceptor of Normandy, were immediately taken away and burnt at the stake for heresy.

On the face of it this was the final, ignoble end of what had been the greatest military order in Christendom. Yet as things turned out it was just the start of something new. For although the pope's orders were carried out with brutal efficiency in France, not everyone in the other countries over which he claimed authority obeyed him. In Spain large numbers of Templar knights were allowed to join the Order of Calatrava. In Portugal a new 'Order of Christ' was created especially for them. In other places, notably in England, they were simply merged with the Knights Hospitallers. However, not all of the Templars were willing to change their colours. For some, escape into exile was a better option and, as it happens, Scotland provided a perfect retreat.

In 1305, just two years before King Philip's arrest of the Templars of France, the Scottish nationalist Sir William Wallace was hanged, drawn and quartered in London at the bloody end of what had for a time been a successful rebellion, under his leadership, against English rule in Scotland. After his death his mantle was picked up by Robert the Bruce, who now claimed the crown of Scotland for himself by virtue of his descent from the Scottish king David I. Knowing full well that this would not be tolerated by Edward I of England, who favoured a rival candidate that he could more easily control, he had himself crowned at Scone on 27 March 1306.[10] Almost immediately the English invaded Scotland once more and Robert the Bruce was defeated in battle at Methven and Dalry. Edward declared Bruce an outlaw and he had to flee to the Island of Rathlin for shelter.

This was the low point of Robert's career. He had also been excommunicated by the pope for the crime of the cold-blooded murder of a rival claimant to the throne, and his position looked hopeless. Indeed, he would probably have suffered the same fate as William Wallace had not Edward I died in 1307 and been succeeded by his son Edward II. This king, though handsome and athletic in physique, was weak in character and in particular lacked his father's resolve in dealing with Scotland. Thus it was that between 1307 and 1313 Robert the Bruce was able gradually to win back most of his country. The climax came on 24 June 1314 when at Bannockburn he was once more faced by a large English army. This time Bruce was victorious; his triumph confirmed him as king and established Scotland's independence from England.

The Battle of Bannockburn is rightly celebrated as a great Scottish victory in the struggle for independence. How a Scottish force of only some 6,000 defeated an English army of over 21,000 is a matter of some surprise, even allowing for the undisciplined condition of the English army and the inferior generalship of Edward II compared with his illustrious father. The principal reason why Robert was able to defeat this much larger army would seem to be that he had a corps of well-armed, professional soldiers fighting under his banner; and all indications are that this contingent was the remnant of the Knights Templar. Their intervention turned the tide of battle, which up until then had been going against Robert. Though no doubt brave, the poorly equipped English levies – mostly farm labourers and the like – were no match for properly trained, professional soldiers.

That the Templars should have rallied to the Scottish banner is not really surprising given that Robert the Bruce, like themselves, had been excommunicated by the pope. For his part, Robert was in desperate need of any help he could get in facing the might of a larger English army. The timely arrival of even a relatively small force consisting of probably the best and most disciplined knights in Christendom was a godsend as far as he was concerned.

Robert's right to the Scottish throne, and that of his successors, was confirmed by an Act of the Scottish Parliament held at Ayr on 26 April 1315. Between 1315 and 1320 he continued to consolidate his position in Scotland and even found time to wage war against the English in Ireland. Infuriated by his successful insurrection and, no doubt, his flouting the papal edict in respect of the Templars, the pope sent legates to Scotland: Cardinal Gaucelin and Cardinal Luke. Robert refused even to see them; instead, he responded in a letter to the pope, explaining in no uncertain terms just what the Scots' position was, and that they were not about to be told by anyone how to govern their own country. This letter, known as the Declaration of Arbroath, was signed and sealed by some 120 Scottish nobles and can still be seen today in the Register House at Edinburgh.

Tellingly, this letter (written, of course, in Latin) includes the following passage:

We know, Most Holy Father and Lord, and from the chronicles and books of the ancients, that among other illustrious nations, ours, to wit the nation of the Scots, has been distinguished by many honours; which passing from the greater Scythia [i.e. southern Russia] through the Mediterranean Sea and the Pillars of Hercules, and sojourning in Spain among the most savage tribes through a long course of time, could nowhere be subjugated by any people however barbarous; and coming thence one thousand two hundred years after the outgoing of the people of Israel, they, by many victories and infinite toil, acquired for themselves the possessions of the West which they now hold . . . In their kingdom one hundred and thirteen kings of their own royal stock, no stranger intervening, have reigned.

The allusion to the migration of a Scythian or Scottish horde from Egypt to the Mediterranean and thence to Britain by way of Spain and Ireland was well known at this time, as it is related in the *History of Britain* by the eighth-century Welsh writer Nennius.[11] In Nennius' account the Scythian ancestors of the Scots were present in Egypt at the time Moses led the Israelites over the Red Sea. Although their leader was married to the pharaoh's daughter, Scotta or Scotia, the Egyptians regarded them as a threat and they also were expelled from the country, whence they eventually made their way to Ireland. The unstated implication of the Declaration of Arbroath is that the Egyptian 'Scythians', from whom the Irish and Scots believed themselves to be descended, were in some way related to the Israelites who crossed the Red Sea with Moses. Nennius' account does seem to refer to a real historical event. This was the expulsion of the Hyksos or 'shepherd kings' who are believed by Egyptologists to have been foreigners and to have been thrown out from Egypt by the pharaohs of the New Kingdom in *c.*1567 BC. Whether or not the Scots (or indeed the Israelites) were really descended from the Hyksos is a matter of contention. However, Egyptian bas-reliefs of Hyksos captives, which can be seen on temple walls and in museums today, depict bearded foreigners who do not look Egyptian.

Whatever the truth of the matter, by 1328 Bruce's position was unassailable and the pope, bowing to the inevitable, finally recognized his jurisdiction over Scotland. Thereafter Scottish kings ruled independently of England until the merging of the two thrones under James I in 1603.

A leading figure on the Scottish side at the Battle of

Bannockburn was Sir William Sinclair (or St Clair), the Grand Master of the Templars in Scotland and possessor of the Barony of Rosslyn. After the Scottish victory he was well rewarded for his help by Robert the Bruce with additional lands and they remained lifelong friends. Sir William advanced his position further by marrying the daughter of the earl of Strathearn, Caithness and Orkney. They had a son, Sir Henry Sinclair, who was made earl of Orkney by King Haakon VI of Norway – the islands at that time being a Norwegian possession. In 1454 Henry's son, another Sir William Sinclair, lord of Rosslyn and earl of Orkney, was made chancellor of Scotland. This Sir William set about building a most remarkable chapel at Rosslyn Castle, the design of which is believed by many to have been based upon the plans of the Temple of Solomon as drawn up by the Knights Templar. These plans, so it is said, were derived from the Templars' own archae-ological investigations, which they conducted on the Temple Mount of Jerusalem during the time of their occupation of that holy site. According to Christopher Knight and Robert Lomas, who are both Freemasons, other senior members of the Scottish establishment besides Sir William Sinclair were also either Templars or Templar affiliates. They now sought to conceal the identity of the Templar order in a new guise:

As soon as Scotland was once again officially part of Christendom it was imperative that the Templars should disappear from sight by becoming a secret society, as the power of the Vatican was now able once again to prosecute its enemies across the whole of Europe. Fortunately during the transition period [immediately after the pope recognized Bruce as king in

October 1328 and his subsequent death the following June] a member of the Templar Moray family was Regent, ruling on behalf of the infant King David II, and this gave them the level of control they needed to plan the future of the organisation that had already replaced their doomed Order, so that they could retain the great secrets with which they had become entrusted.[12]

The organization to which they allude is, of course, Freemasonry, the claim being that a masonic secret society was created in Scotland some four centuries prior to Freemasonry's official beginning in Britain with the founding of London's Grand Lodge in 1717. That this might indeed be so is borne out by some very interesting evidence that has only recently come to light. On Saturday, 10 July 2000 the *Daily Telegraph* printed an article concerning a secret scroll which had been hanging in a masonic lodge at Kirkwall in the Orkneys and which is believed to have Templar connections (see plate 16). The article's author, Thomas Harding, explained how the 18-foot-long sailcoth had been carbon-dated to the fifteenth century. This early date is contested by other writers, who maintain that its origin is no earlier than the late eighteenth century. However, if true, it would put the origin of the scroll back to a time maybe as much as two centuries before the accession of James VI and I to the throne of England. What is beyond doubt is that it resides in a masonic lodge at Kirkwall in the Orkneys, a territory historically associated with the Sinclairs; and, as we have seen, the same Scottish family was closely associated with the Templars at the time of Robert the Bruce. If the Kirkwall Scroll truly dates from the fifteenth century, then it was painted around the time when Sir William Sinclair, third earl of Orkney and earl of Caithness, was chancellor of Scotland.

The nature of the Templars' masonic knowledge and how it affected the development of London in the seventeenth century will be the subject of a later chapter. However, it is worth remarking here that the design on that part of the Kirkwall Scroll pictured in the *Daily Telegraph* article is strikingly similar to the coat of arms of London's Grand Lodge (see plate 17). As the scroll has now been dated to the fifteenth century and the Grand Lodge was created in the eighteenth, we can be confident that this design was brought to London from Scotland and not vice versa. The secrets contained in this design and their significance may well have been known to James I, who as noted previously is the first monarch known to have been a Freemason, the Templar legacy being part of what he brought with him to England.

The influence of Freemasonry on Britain's destiny and the development of the British empire is considerable. However, before considering this subject further, it is necessary first to consider other influences that came to Britain from Europe in the early seventeenth century. These had as their point of origin the capital of what is now the Czech Republic but was then called Bohemia: the city of Prague.

CHAPTER FOUR

THE BOHEMIAN CONNECTION

Around Elizabeth I there grew a cult of sorts with far-reaching implications, not just for England but for Europe as a whole. This cult had to do with the identification of the queen with figures representing justice. In Edmund Spenser's poem *The Faerie Queene* she is identified with Astraea, the Roman goddess of justice and just virgin of the Golden Age. In the Roman world, Astraea was symbolically linked as an archetype with the constellation of Virgo, which precedes Libra, the sign of the zodiac symbolized by the balances of just measure. All this was an inheritance from ancient Egypt where the constellation of Virgo was considered to be a personification of Maat, the wife of Thoth and goddess of the rule of law. Outwardly Spenser's poem implies that, as an earthly incarnation of Astraea, Elizabeth was thought to personify the concept of law as the balancing of opposing forces. However, its secret message was that Elizabeth, as the goddess returned to earth, was in fact inaugurating a new, golden, 'Augustan' Age.[1] Under her just rule, law and order would be upheld and a new age of enlightenment would prevail not just in England but throughout the world.

Even before the defeat of the Spanish Armada in 1588, England was regarded as the leading Protestant state of Europe. Consequently, the small Protestant principalities of Germany looked upon it as their best guarantor against suppression by the Catholic powers. Throughout Elizabeth's long reign the central fact of political life was the power of Catholic Spain. As far as the Spanish king Philip II was concerned, Elizabeth, as the daughter of Anne Boleyn, Henry VIII's second wife, was illegitimate; thus, as far as he and the rest of Catholic Europe were concerned, her occupation of the throne of England was illegal. The fact that Elizabeth was a Protestant served to complicate matters further.

Given that the English queen showed no inclination to be drawn back into the orbit of Rome, from the Catholic point of view there were two possible solutions to this problem. The first and perhaps most attractive option was to foment a Catholic revolution inside England in favour of her cousin, Mary, Queen of Scots. Mary, a flamboyant and passionate woman who had once been queen of France, was no stranger to intrigue, having married the murderer of her second husband, Lord Darnley. She would not, it was thought, be squeamish about deposing Elizabeth or even having the 'usurper' executed. With Mary on the throne, or so it was hoped, English Protestantism could be stamped out once and for all. Unfortunately, from the conspirators' point of view, plans to replace Elizabeth with her cousin were never really likely to come to fruition. Elizabeth was held in high esteem by most of her compatriots and a rebellion in favour of Mary, made difficult by her imprisonment in 1569, became impossible after she was beheaded in 1587. Mary's death made all the more urgent the second alternative: an invasion of England and Elizabeth's forcible removal from the throne. This plan too was thwarted, at least for a time, by the defeat of the Spanish Armada in 1588.

Given these threats not just to her life but to everything she believed in, Elizabeth knew that if England were to survive as an independent, Protestant state she needed friends – and, just as importantly, her powerful Catholic enemies needed to be kept divided. Accordingly, she formulated a European foreign policy for England that was to last for four hundred years – a policy entirely in sympathy with her identity as the goddess Astraea: the maintenance of the balance of power.

During the sixteenth century central and eastern Europe were dominated by the Austrian Habsburg empire, which included modern Austria, Germany, large parts of Italy and parts of Poland, Hungary and Croatia. The Habsburgs who ruled over this sprawling imperium were cousins of King Philip of Spain. Even so, Elizabeth knew there were tensions within the family that could be exploited. Moreover, unlike Spain, where to be a Protestant was to risk death or worse, the Austrian empire was quite a loose affair. It had many Protestant citizens and was generally more tolerant of them.

The kingdom of Bohemia, today largely Catholic and part of the Czech Republic, at this time had a large Protestant population. It was in this important component of the empire, and in particular its capital, Prague, that the flames of European Protestantism had first been ignited at the time of Jan Huss (1369–1415). He had publicly proclaimed what were then deemed heretical teachings and for this he had been burned at the stake. The story of Jan Huss had a special poignancy for English Protestants, for many of his ideas had been taken from the works of their own prophet of reform, John Wycliffe.

Wycliffe, a highly distinguished theologian and master of Balliol College, Oxford, had come to prominence during the reign of Edward III (1327–77). He preached against corruption in the church, which he saw as being rife, and was particularly scathing on the unlawfulness of taxes being paid to the pope. He also denied the doctrine of transubstantiation – that the bread and wine of communion were actually turned into the body and blood of Jesus Christ – saying that to believe such a thing was 'blasphemous folly'; instead, he urged a return to the simple teachings of the gospels without the trappings of sacraments. To aid in this return to fundamentalist practices, he directed the first translation of the Bible into English. This made it possible for ordinary people – at least, those who were sufficiently educated in their own language – to read the scriptures for themselves without relying on a priest to interpret them from the Latin. Though the England of his time was not yet ready for a full-blown religious reformation, he had sown seeds that were destined to germinate and burst into flower in a most unexpected way.

Wycliffe lived to see Edward III succeeded by King Richard II, who as a boy of sixteen married Anne of Bohemia. She was the daughter of the Holy Roman Emperor Charles VI, and much political advantage to both countries was expected to come from this union. Although John Wycliffe was an old man at the time of the marriage in 1383 and close to death, his ideas concerning the need for reform of the church were still very much current; and a number of scholars from Bohemia who were in the marriage party of Anne took Wycliffe's writings back home with them when they departed. Around 1400 these came into the hands of Jan Huss, who as rector of the University of Prague and of the newly built Bethlehem Chapel had access to the libraries in which Wycliffe's writings were kept. He, though of humble birth, was an educated man, able to read Latin and with a passionate interest in Christian philosophy. Up until then he had not questioned the authority of the Catholic Church on matters temporal or spiritual. However, Wycliffe's books fired his own sense of indignation that the theories and practices of the church of which he was an ordained minister should be so widely divergent. Thus it was that Wycliffe's seeds found fertile ground in which to germinate – not in England but in far-off Bohemia.

In 1403 Huss had Wycliffe's *Triologus* (one of his last works) translated into the Czech language. As a free-thinking intellectual he was much influenced by the power of Wycliffe's arguments and in 1405 he published a paper of his own, *De Omni Sanguine Christi Glorificato*, which urged people to study Christ's words and not to worry so much about supposedly miraculous sacraments. Huss's ideas were well received by the ordinary people of Bohemia, who were in any case somewhat inclined towards the Eastern Orthodoxy branch of Christianity – a less hierarchical and more democratic church than that of Rome. He also received some support – at least at first – from the Bohemian ruler King Wenceslaus. However, his writings put him on a collision course with the church establishment, whose authority lay primarily in its control not just of the word of God but of the administration of the very sacraments that he was denigrating.

In 1409 Pope Alexander V issued a bull condemning the work of Wycliffe and ordered the destruction of his works. As a result the archbishop of Prague publicly burnt some 200 books and excommunicated Huss. This led to a popular uprising. Ignoring an injunction by the archbishop forbidding preaching on non-authorized premises, Huss responded to the mood of the people by continuing to give sermons in the Bethlehem Chapel. This conflict between the church authorities and the lay people of Prague escalated further in 1411 when a fresh ban was placed on Huss and the whole city was placed in interdiction. This was a terrible thing to happen as far as believers were concerned, for it meant not only that they themselves could not receive the sacraments but that anyone who died had to be buried in unconsecrated ground without the benefit of the church's benedictions. This spread fear and despondency throughout the city.

The final straw, as far as Huss was concerned, came the following year when legates of the pope arrived in Prague to sell indulgences. According to church doctrine, after a person died, his or her soul would be judged. Even if, on balance, the person had been found to be good, the soul would have to spend a certain time undergoing the torments of purgatory – a sort of watered-down hell – before, cleansed of sin, it could enter into heaven. It had always been believed (and still is by Catholics) that the remission of sins and consequently a lessening of the time to be spent in purgatory could be earnt through prayer, the religious life and making pilgrimages to holy shrines. A papal indulgence, however, was something else. It was a sort of 'get out of gaol free' card, a 'certificate' that could be bought for money. It was believed that the possession of such an indulgence meant not just forgiveness of sins but partial or even total cancellation of the need to spend time in purgatory. Better still, the person buying the indulgence did not have to go through the bothersome requirements of wearing sackcloth and ashes, going on pilgrimages or whatever. All they had to do was find enough cash to buy one.

Few people, not even Huss, objected to the comforting thought that the pains of purgatory could be avoided, at least in part, if one made reparation for the consequences of one's sins in this life. What upset him (and later Martin Luther) was the idea that indulgences could be bought and sold like futures on a spiritual stock exchange. It was this obscene abuse of presumed church authority that provoked him to proclaim publicly his belief that the selling of church indulgences was not lawful and that forgiveness of sins could be achieved only by contrition and penance on the part of the sinner.

The response of the church was extreme, if predictable. When three of Huss's followers protested in church against the indulgence vendors, they were arrested by the city authorities and executed. Like nearly everybody else, Huss was shocked by these events; reluctantly he was persuaded, for his own safety, to leave Prague and to carry on his work in the countryside of Bohemia. Here, delivering sermons to the ordinary peasants and lower nobility, he drew even larger audiences than he had in the capital. As a result, what had started as a small academic protest in Prague university now became a countrywide movement for reform.

In 1413 Huss was summoned to attend the Council

of Constance, a gathering of bishops whose main task was to bring an end to the scandal of there being more than one pope at the same time. To induce him to leave the relative safety of Bohemia he was granted a guarantee of safe passage by King Sigismund, the Holy Roman Emperor. According to the terms of this accord it was agreed that, whatever the outcome of his trial at Constance might be, he should be allowed to return unhindered to Bohemia. It would then be down to his own king, Wenceslaus of Bohemia (Sigismund's brother), to enforce the judgment of the council. This guarantee, which was accepted by Huss, turned out to be worthless. A few months after he arrived he was arrested and placed in confinement under the juris-diction of the bishop of Constance. Tried for heresy, he was unanimously condemned and a sentence of death was passed, to be carried out immediately. Huss was burnt at the stake on 6 July 1414. To forestall the possibility that his place of execution might become a shrine, his ashes, along with the earth on which the fire had stood, were scattered on the Rhine. Furthermore, in a bizarre act of retrospective retribution, the council declared that John Wycliffe was also a heretic and should receive the same fate. These orders were carried out in 1427 by the bishop of Lincoln, who had Wycliffe's bones disinterred and burnt. The ashes from this fire were similarly thrown into the River Swift.

The bishops at Constance may have hoped that this would be the end of the matter; but, not surprisingly, the treacherous way in which Huss had been lured to his death caused an outcry back in Bohemia. The Hussite movement, which till then had been a purely religious affair, now took on a political dimension. Letters were sent to the Council of Constance protesting in the strongest terms about Huss's execution – and about the acquiescence in this act of Sigismund, the Holy Roman Emperor whose promise of free passage had been broken. King Wenceslaus attempted to control the Hussite movement, but it was by now too late and a full-scale rebellion broke out.

From very early on the Hussites were split into two rival groups or factions. The more moderate of the two, the 'Ultraquists', were in the main based in Prague itself; the more extreme party, later called the 'Taborites', had left Prague to escape repression and begun preaching around the country, denouncing Sigismund everywhere they went. Right from the start the Taborites had a conception of themselves as a holy people, set apart, who would bring about the renewal of corrupted Christendom. Like the early Christian communities of Galilee, they would share property in common; a new 'Israel', they would ignore the teachings of man and be subject only to the will of God. Accordingly, they established a community of their own on a site some 50 miles south of Prague. Here they built the new town of Tabor, which was organized along principles we would describe as communist. The choice of name for the new community is highly significant: Mount Tabor is the peak near Nazareth where, according to tradition, the transfiguration of Jesus had taken place (Matt. 17: 1–9). The name Tabor therefore symbolized a place of religious transformation and numinous spiritual power.

Meanwhile, in Prague in July 1419 a Hussite procession going down a street was stoned by opponents from the town hall. The people were outraged and what had been a religious procession turned into an ugly mob. A group of Hussites led by Jan Zizka, a nobleman who would later play a prominent role in the history of Bohemia, burst into the town hall and threw the burgomaster and several other councillors from the windows to be set upon and killed by the angry crowd below. When news of this appalling event, known to history as the 'first defenestration of Prague', was brought to the attention of King Wenceslaus, it brought on a stroke; he died a few days later, leaving his brother Sigismund, the villain of the piece as far as the Hussites were concerned, as titular king of Bohemia. To prevent his coronation, which they rightly saw as being very bad for their cause, the people of Prague took up arms.

Sigismund, enraged at the impudence of the Bohemians in daring to oppose his coronation, came with an army to force his way into Prague. His plan was simple: to invest the city and starve his opponents into submission. This tactic might have worked had not Jan Zizka, probably the best general of his day, already joined the Hussites at Tabor and begun to organize their militia into one of the most formidable armies of its time. He now brought this army to the aid of Prague, decisively defeating Sigismund and his 'Romanists' at the Battle of Sudomer. However, any thought that this might be the end of the matter were quickly dashed. As far as both church and emperor were concerned, it only served to raise the stakes yet further.

As noted above, the Council of Constance had not been called primarily to address the matter of the Hussite 'heresy', though this was certainly seen as important business; of more pressing concern was that there were at this time three 'popes', each of them claiming that the other two were impostors. The emperor's man was John XXIII, vying for his tiara with the rival claims of Gregory XII and Benedict XIII. At the Council of Constance all three were persuaded to abdicate and on St Martin's Day 1417 a fresh election was held. As a result of the ballot an outsider, Cardinal Otto Colona, was made undisputed father of the church, taking the titular name Pope Martin V.

In March 1420 this new pope, aghast at the failure of Sigismund to capture Prague and bring to an end the Hussite uprising, proclaimed a crusade against Bohemia. By 20 June a huge army of crusaders had arrived at Prague, intent on the utter destruction of the Hussites and all other adherents of the heretical teachings of Jan Huss and John Wycliffe. The Hussites knew what they could expect if they were defeated. They had only to think of the fate of the thirteenth-century Albigenses (also known as the Cathars) of France, who had faced a similar crusade and ended up being massacred en masse by the soldiers of the church. Accordingly, a period of urgent negotiations was entered into in an attempt to defuse the situation, with the Hussites formulating their position in the form of a document known as the Declaration of Prague. Their demands were quite simple: that the word of the Lord should be preached freely in Bohemia; that there should be equality in the administration of the sacrament of communion so that the laity, like the priests, should receive it in both kinds, wine as well as bread; that as worldly wealth is contrary to the teachings of Christ and a detriment to its proper role, the church should give up its property and the clergy live in poverty, as had Christ and his apostles; that living a life of sin (i.e. the taking of mistresses by the nobility and clergy) should be prohibited, no matter how high-ranking the person. Needless to say this declaration was rejected by Sigismund, who was in the business of re-establishing papal and imperial authority, not having it reduced or bound by puritanical regulations.

Fortunately for the Bohemians, they had Jan Zizka, the 'one-eyed' general on their side.[2] A military genius, he realized that if his peasant army were to have any chance against the professional soldiers sent against them, they would have to use novel tactics. At that time the cavalry charge, followed up by infantry attack, was still the standard way of fighting battles. As the Hussites had little in the way of cavalry themselves, they needed to develop tactics that would suit them rather than their opponents. Zizka therefore worked out a system of warfare based on heavy wagons. Using these wagons, the Hussites were able to take the war to their enemies while fighting actual battles defensively. Having decided on a suitable location, the Hussites would place their wagons, of which there were many, in a circle. Gaps between and beneath the wagons were blocked up with large wooden beams and earth-fortifications. On board the wagons were placed men operating crossbows and hand-cannons, along with pike-men to defend them in combat at close quarters. Within the protected centre of the circle were placed artillery pieces, sighted to shoot over the tops of the wagons at the approaching enemy. Jan Zizka had, in effect, invented tank warfare nearly five hundred years before the invention of the tank. His tactics proved to be extremely effective. Everywhere they went the Bohemians were victorious, defeating the armies of not just one but five separate crusades. The Hussites even sent armies on the offensive into what is now Germany, Austria, Slovakia and Poland, winning victories wherever they went.

By 1433 Sigismund and the then pope, Eugenius IV, were ready to talk peace. What they had been unable to impose by force of arms, they were now to gain by stealth. As part of the peace treaty they promised the Bohemians that adults could continue to choose between a Catholic or Bohemian confession. These terms were agreed to by the Hussites of Prague, who were by now tired of fighting. Being mainly drawn from the upper and middle classes, they were not as puritanical as the Hussites of Tabor and lacked their zeal. A further brief war between the different factions of Hussites led to the defeat of the Taborites, and in 1436 Sigismund was eventually crowned king of Bohemia. His enjoyment of this position, which in any case carried little real power, was short-lived: he died the following year.

In all, the Hussite Wars had lasted for seventeen years. Though the movement was suppressed after 1621 and the Catholic Church re-established in Bohemia, the teachings of Jan Huss profoundly affected the development of Protestantism throughout northern Europe. Out of the ashes of the Hussite movement was born the Bohemian Fratrum Unitum or 'Unity Brethren'. They made up the largest Christian denomination throughout Bohemia and Moravia and, as we shall see, during the early seventeenth century their successors were to have a profound influence on developments in Europe.

During the late sixteenth and early seventeenth centuries Prague became a true city of enlightenment. Under the rule of a relatively benevolent king, Maximilian II (1527–76), who was also the elected Holy Roman Emperor, the people of Bohemia enjoyed a freedom of thought almost without parallel throughout the rest of mainland Europe. Though himself a Catholic and a Habsburg, Maximilian was a pragmatist who was able to keep the peace between his Protestant and Catholic subjects. He was succeeded by his eldest surviving son, Rudolf II, who was crowned king of Hungary in 1572, king of Bohemia in 1575 and Holy Roman Emperor in 1576. It was unfortunate for not just Bohemia but the whole of Europe that he lacked the political abilities of his father. His portraits and sculptures show the face of a depressive with sagging eyelids and pursed lips, grimly attempting to deal with life's complexities.

Rudolf would probably have been happier if he had not been burdened by the responsibilities of running an empire. Though not highly intelligent himself, he nevertheless enjoyed the company of some of the wisest men of his day and was also a great sponsor of the arts. His *Kunstkammer*, or art gallery, grew to become the largest collection in Europe, while his library of rare books was second to none. As a sponsor of science he acted as patron to some of the greatest innovators of his age, including the famous astronomers Tycho Brahe and Johannes Kepler. This in itself would be enough to earn him a place in history; but there was more.

Though less tolerant of Protestantism than his father, Rudolf II was deeply interested in esotericism. Indeed, his esoteric interests were wide and eclectic, for he was an avid student of alchemy and astrology as well as chemistry and astronomy. Perhaps as a gesture of rebellion against his extensive family of Habsburgs, he made Prague his home in preference to Vienna. There he lived a fairly isolated life in his castle of Hradcany, becoming more and more of a recluse as he got older.

Thus it was that under his at times eccentric rule Prague became a magnet for alchemists and other fringe intellectuals.

The friendly relations between England and Bohemia, established at the time of Richard II's marriage to Anne, continued into the sixteenth century and intensified after the Reformation. In 1575, soon after his coronation, Emperor Rudolf II was visited by Sir Philip Sidney. Famous throughout Europe as a statesman as well as a soldier and poet, Sidney was a favourite of Queen Elizabeth and acted as her roving ambassador for the Protestant cause. She was well aware of Bohemia's Hussite past and, even though the country was now once more Catholic, was anxious to maintain friendly relations with its rulers. She also knew that many Bohemians were still Protestants. In the past their ancestors, the Hussites, had shown themselves to be doughty fighters; it followed that, should the need arise, they might turn out to be important allies in her struggles with Spain. It was no doubt with these considerations in mind that she sent Sidney to Prague. Outwardly, Sidney's mission was to offer Queen Elizabeth's congratulations on Rudolf's elevation to the throne of Bohemia, but the real purpose of his embassy was to ascertain where the new king stood politically, especially as he was sure soon to succeed his father as emperor.

Sir Philip Sidney was a member of the Dee circle and a frequent visitor to the good doctor's house in Mortlake. Given a shared interest in alchemy and astrology, it would be surprising if, in addition to politics, Sidney did not discuss esoteric ideas with the new king. Doubtless he cleared the way for his friend and former teacher who, as a professor of mathematics,

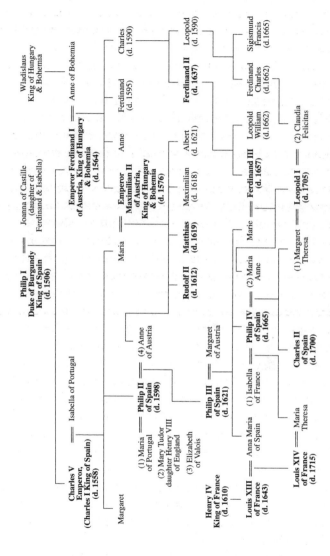

Fig. 14. The family tree of the Imperial Habsburgs.

133

alchemist, and court astrologer to Queen Elizabeth, was considered one of the most learned men in Europe. In 1583–9 John Dee and an associate called Edward Kelley paid an extended visit to Bohemia and Poland. Along with his wife, family and a considerable baggage train, Dee brought with him to Prague at least one copy of his magnum opus, *Monas Hieroglyphica*, which had been published in Antwerp in 1564. This monumental work remains one of the most obscure yet revealing works of sixteenth-century hermeticism. It takes as its emblem the 'hieroglyphic monad', which is at once a variant of the symbol for the planet Mercury and also a composite sign made out of the symbols for all the seven planets. The book itself was an attempt to draw together into one system hermetic philosophy, the Kabbalah, alchemy, astrology and cosmology. Dee used the book as his calling-card, politely presenting a copy of it to Rudolf, now emperor. As the book contained a dedication to his father, Maximilian, Rudolf was delighted to accept the gift. However, he admitted that its contents went way over his head.

Cordial relations having been established with the emperor, Dee had every expectation that a suitable position might be found for him, either as imperial mathematician (a post later filled by Tycho Brahe) or perhaps as court astrologer. Dee's ideas, however, especially his magical conjurations of angels, ruffled feathers in the church, and on 10 April 1586, at the instigation of the archbishop of Prague, three of Dee's books were publicly burnt as heretical. Worse still, on 29 May of the same year Pope Sixtus V issued a papal edict banishing Dee and Kelley from Prague and ordering them to leave the city within six days. Behind this attack was an Italian priest named Francisco Pucci, who had pretended to befriend the English visitors and had attended at least one seance with them. He now tried to persuade them to go to Rome, where they could present their case before the pope. Unlike Jan Huss, Dee was not taken in.

In a letter to Francis Walsingham, chancellor of the Order of the Garter and secretary of state to Queen Elizabeth, Dee complained about the duplicity of his hosts. This duplicity, however, may not have been entirely one-sided. Dee's letters to Walsingham, who was also Elizabeth's spymaster-general, have inclined many to believe that his real mission to Bohemia was on her account: namely, to investigate the possibility of an Anglo-imperial alliance against the burgeoning power of Spain. Dee may have been a good mathematician, astrologer and even alchemist (though he seems to have failed in all his attempts actually to make gold from base metal), but did he have the temperament to make a good spy? On the face of it he was too garrulous by far, and too open and trusting in talking to acquaintances about his spiritualistic activities. For even in sixteenth-century Prague, a city where many intellectuals were receptive to new ideas, these interests must have struck most people as at best eccentric and at worst plainly heretical. However, Dee did make important contacts at Prague and there is no doubt that his influence – or rather, that of his ideas – was profound, even if less than obvious. Also, his writings, particularly the journal he wrote concerning his travels and talks with angels, may not be so innocent as they seem at first glance.

That there is a hidden message contained in Dee's writings was certainly the opinion of the seventeenth-century scientist Robert Hooke, who some sixty years after Dee's death, in a commentary on his *Book of Spirits*, was to write:

> To come to the book itself [Dr Dee's *Book of Spirits*]. Upon turning it over, and comparing several Particulars in it one with another, and with other Writings of the said Dr Dee, and considering also the History of the Life, Actions and Estate of that said author, so far as I can be informed, I do conceive that the greatest part of the said Book, especially all that which relates to the Spirits and Apparitions, together with their Names, Speeches, Shews, Noises, Clothing, Actions, and the Prayers and Doxologies etc., are all Cryptography; and that some Parts also of that which seems to be a Journal of his Voyage and Travels into several parts of Germany, are also Cryptographical, that is that under these feigned stories, which he seems to relate as Matter of Fact, he hath concealed Relations of quite another thing; and that he made use of this way of absconding it, that he might thus more securely escape discovery, if he should fall under suspicion as to the true Designs of his Travels, or that the same should fall into the hands of any spies, or such as might be employed to betray him or his intentions, conceiving the Inquisition that should be made, or Prosecution if discovered, would be more gentle for a Pretended Enthusiast, than for a real spy.[3]

In Hooke's opinion the key to Dee's writings was the *Book of Enoch*, a collection of prophetic writings believed to be by the biblical patriarch Enoch, a copy of which he carried with him on his journey. If so, the cryptographic system he was presumably employing was that of word substitution. This form of cipher could be understood only by someone who knew which book to consult. As the master of this sort of cryptography was Walsingham, to whom Dee addressed a number of letters during the period of his travels, it is not impossible that a cipher of this type was employed. However, this remains conjecture as nobody has yet proved that Dee's strange 'messages from the spirit world' were indeed coded messages of any kind.

After a short period of exile in Germany, Dee and Kelley returned to Bohemia. They did not stay in Prague, however, but now went to live with a new patron: William Ursinus, Count Rosenberg, who, on their behalf, had obtained a revocation of the papal decree of expulsion. Count Rosenberg was a powerful and wealthy man, being viceroy of Bohemia and a Knight of the Golden Fleece; the Order of the Golden Fleece being the Catholic counterpart to the Order of the Garter. Dee and his party stayed with Ursinus at his castle of Trebona for some eighteen months, and during this time Kelley carried out alchemical experiments, some of them by all accounts successful. Trebona lay in southern Bohemia, not very far from Tabor which a century earlier had been the Hussites' communal centre. Importantly, it was on the main road linking Prague with Vienna and about equidistant between the two. Here, in the safe surroundings of Trebona Castle and under the protection of Count Rosenberg, Dee was able to entertain guests and to pass on at least some of his wisdom gained over long years of esoteric research. This influence, though largely unnoticed at the time, was to have profound repercussions a generation later.

Dee left Bohemia on 11 March 1588, arriving in England in December after an extended stay in Germany. Edward Kelley stayed on in Prague, his apparent success as an alchemist earning him rich praise and even a knighthood. However, the adulation was short-lived. Eventually it was realized that he was a confidence trickster who had never actually made gold at all but on the contrary had run up considerable debts. Kelley was thrown into prison in 1591; later freed for a time, he was reincarcerated in 1595 and died shortly afterwards, under suspicious circumstances, while trying to escape.

Another visitor to Prague and to the court of Rudolf II, arriving in 1589, was Giordano Bruno. Though he would have missed Dee he may have met up with Kelley, who had not yet fallen into disgrace. In any case he was moving in the same circles as they had, for like them he was a friend of Count Laski. A polymath like Dr Dee, Bruno was in many ways an even more controversial figure. Born in 1548 in Nola, a small town near Naples, he joined the Dominican Order in 1563. However, Bruno was not cut out to be an obedient monk and in 1576, having been accused of heresy, he left the order and fled Italy. From then until his death in 1600 he was a wanderer among the nations of Europe, preaching a philosophy of enlightenment.

We have no evidence to suggest that Bruno ever met Dee, but it would have been fascinating to have overheard a conversation between the two esoteric masters. Dee would no doubt have appreciated Bruno's extravagant discourses, but they would have disagreed on the subject of mathematics and its importance as a tool for the unlocking of the secrets of nature. For though Dee was deeply immersed in occult studies, there was also a practical side to his work – as already noted, he was a professor of mathematics who had written a much-acclaimed preface to Henry Billingsley's translation of Euclid, and for all his enthusiasm for spiritualism and invocations of angels he had also produced the *Art of Navigation*. Bruno, by contrast, worked on the basis of intuition rather than scientific principles; indeed, during the six months he spent in Prague he published a book with the title *Articuli adversus mathematicos* (Articles against mathematicians). This book includes some extraordinary diagrams which among other things show the esoteric nature of patterns derived from such geometric devices as the *vesica piscis*. However, though the diagrams show a certain skill in regard to geometry, Bruno was no mathematician. His great interest was cosmology, and he energetically promoted, wherever he went, the new astronomical work of Copernicus, including the revolutionary idea that the earth turns around the sun.

Bruno's lectures, which challenged the philosophical system of Aristotle as well as the orthodox Ptolemaic conception of the universe, got him into trouble almost everywhere he went. At Oxford those he called 'pedants' turned out to be quite unwilling to accept that the Aristotelian world view with which they had grown up – and which they now taught to their students – was in any way in error. Bruno was heckled when he spoke and forced into ignominious retreat. Undaunted, he left England and went to France – but, unfortunately, in Paris his attacks on Aristotelian philosophy earned him not just verbal abuse but even physical attack. From there he was lucky to get away with only his reputation in tatters. As a consequence he moved onwards to Germany, where from 1586 to 1592 he was able to live in relative peace. It was during this time that he visited Prague.

Bruno, who liked to refer to himself as 'the Nolan' after his birthplace, wrote a number of books,

Fig. 15. Illustration from Bruno's *Articuli Adversus Mathematicos*.

developing an innovative philosophy that was quite at odds with current Christian dogma. Whereas Wycliffe's and Huss's arguments with the church authorities of their day had centred on abuse of privilege, the administration of sacraments and the role of the clergy within the greater Christian community, Bruno's disputes were altogether more philosophical; but in many ways his ideas were more radical than those of Copernicus, who had simply said that the earth goes round the sun, and more heretical than the teachings of Wycliffe and Huss. Bruno taught that not only was the earth not at the centre of the universe, nor was the sun. According to him the universe, being of infinite expanse, had no centre. The stars, he said, were simply other suns and they looked small only because they were a long way away. This meant that there was a probability that, like our own sun, each of the stars had a solar system of its own. Thus there must be other planets like our earth and in all probability there were men and women, just like ourselves, living on them. This raised an important ethical question: were these people living on other planets affected by the sin of Adam? Or, to put it another way, was the unique sacrifice of God's only begotten son, Jesus Christ, necessary only for the redemption of the earth or did it apply to the whole universe of stars and planets as well? Needless to say these were questions the church would rather not have had asked, still less be forced to answer.

The role of the sacraments in the church versus the authority of scripture does not seem to have bothered Bruno overmuch. This is because his world-view came not from the gospels but rather from the *Hermetica*, a strange collection of pagan essays that emanated from Egypt as opposed to Palestine. Brought back to Florence from the east shortly after the fall of Constantinople in 1453, the *Hermetica* had had a profound effect on the development of Renaissance thought. It was generally believed that they were the work of Hermes Trismegistus, the Greek name for Thoth, the Egyptian god of wisdom. Christians, Muslims and Jews alike equated Hermes with Enoch, an antediluvian biblical patriarch. In the Bible little is said about Enoch except that he 'walked with God: and he was not: for God took him'. This implied that, like Elijah, he was a wise and holy prophet who did not need to experience death but was instead taken straight into heaven. As Enoch pre-dated Noah and lived long before Moses, the author of the earliest books in the Bible, it was concluded that the *Hermetica* was the oldest wisdom literature in the world. Following this line of logic, the books of Hermes/Enoch had precedence over those of Moses and could therefore be safely studied in the secure knowledge that what they taught was not really pagan at all but rather prophetic insight most profound.

Bruno found that the teaching of Hermes Trismegistus was pertinent to the development of his own philosophy, which appealed to reason as a function of enlightened thinking as opposed to the exactitude of mathematically based science. Nevertheless, the revolutionary ideas that Bruno promulgated of a universe of infinite extent, containing myriads of worlds not unlike our own, helped to shape the development of enlightenment thought. His world-view weakened the hold of religious orthodoxy and encouraged a more scientific approach to the study of nature.

His months in Prague having failed to bring the offer of a suitable position, Bruno set off for Venice. Though he was still indicted as a heretic in Italy, it seemed safe enough; he had, after all, been invited to come as the guest of a nobleman, Zuane Mocenigo, who wanted to be taught his 'Art of Memory' – a visualization technique – and Venice was a proud republic, not directly under the control of Rome. Believing he had nothing to fear, Bruno arrived in Italy in 1592, staying for a few weeks in Padua before moving to Venice itself. Unfortunately for Bruno, trusting Mocenigo turned out to be a gross miscalculation. He had been living there for only a few months when he was arrested by the Venetian Inquisition and thrown into gaol. Here he was held for eight long years. At the end of this time he was taken to Rome, where, on 17 February 1600, still unrepentant of his 'heresies', he was burnt at the stake.

By this time the intellectual atmosphere at Prague was moving away from the occult towards the truly scientific. With Edward Kelley the alchemist dead and all but forgotten, Rudolf II had other, less controversial foreigners on his payroll. In June 1599 he had installed the Danish astronomer Tycho Brahe in the castle of Benatky with the title 'imperial mathematician' and a salary of 3,000 florins. Tycho was then the most famous astronomer in Europe, it being nearly thirty years since he had published his first paper concerning a new star which he had identified in the constellation of Cassiopeia. Since then, under the patronage of King Frederick II of Denmark, he had built up a fabulous astronomical observatory called Uraniburg on a small island off Copenhagen. Here he had perfected a variety of instruments for the exact observation of the heavens. Using these, he had been able to catalogue the positions of some 777 stars. An unfortunate falling out with Frederick's successor, Christian IV, led to the closure of his observatory and his having to leave his native Denmark; so he had been glad to accept a position at the court of Rudolf – especially one so remunerative.

From his new base in Bohemia, in 1600 Tycho invited Johannes Kepler, a young professor of mathematics from Graz University in Austria, to join him as his assistant. The Protestant Kepler was a gifted mathematician, but this distinction had not saved his position when, under the Counter-Reformation, all Protestants in the province of Styria (in Austria) had been ordered to convert to Catholicism or leave. A research post at Prague, where he could continue in his religion unmolested, was as much of a godsend to him as it was to Tycho Brahe. When the latter died in 1601 it was only natural for Rudolf to promote Kepler to the prestigious post of imperial mathematician. Thus it was that, at the age of thirty, one of the greatest mathematicians of his generation inherited the records of Europe's greatest observational astronomer and found himself occupying a position that would enable him to make full use of them.

Prague was now the undisputed capital of the world where astronomy was concerned, and this did much to shape the self-image of the Bohemians. Like his superior, Kepler had been schooled in the new astronomy of Copernicus, which taught that the planets rotated around the sun and not the earth. However, whereas Tycho Brahe, perhaps for religious reasons, could not quite accept that the earth was not at the centre of the universe, Kepler was prepared to go the whole hog, and over the course of the next few years he was to make some startling discoveries of his own that pushed back the frontiers of astronomical thinking. In 1609 he published a book entitled *Astronomia Nova*, giving details of his first two laws of planetary motion. Making full use of Tycho's recorded movements of stars and planets – observational records that went back over decades – he had developed mathematical formulae to describe planetary motions. The planets, he announced, move not in circular orbits as had previously been thought, but rather in ellipses; and the sun was at one of the foci for each of these ellipses. This explained the sometimes erratic and irregular movements of the planets, which speed up as they approach the sun and slow down as they retreat from it. In this way he showed that celestial bodies, far from being pushed along by angelic entities, as had been supposed, were subject to physical laws. A few decades later Sir Isaac Newton would show that the planets were governed by the same laws of gravity and motion that ruled over the falling of an apple. In other words, God's *fiat*, by means of which he created the universe, was not analogous to a papal edict but resembled

1. Old London in flames, September 1666.

2. Angel reveals plans for a New Jerusalem to St John of Patmos in the Book of Revelation. (Armenian Cathedral of St James, Jerusalem.)

3. Fragment of the tomb monument of Gaius Julius Classicianus, Roman Procurator for Britain after the Boudicca rebellion of AD 60.

4. Ancient church of St Martin's-within-Ludgate where in c. 660 Cadwallon, last but one of the pre-Saxon kings of Britain, was buried in a golden, equestrian statue.

5. Tombstone of Vivius Marcianus, from the Brittano-Roman cemetery at old Ludgate.

6. Jack Cade at the London Stone in 1450, which he used as witness to his claim to be a Mortimer and therefore rightful heir to the throne of England.

7. Victorian monumental dragon supporting the arms of London at the site of Temple Bar, Fleet Street.

8. Gog and Magog strike the hours at St Dunstan-in-the-West, Fleet Street.

9. Winchester Round Table, probably made in c. 1290 for Arthurian celebrations, repainted with the Tudor rose by order of Henry VIII.

10. Statue of Queen Elizabeth I, which once graced old Ludgate. Now at the church of St Dunstan-in-the-West, Fleet Street.

11. Statues of King Lud (who is said to have first built the walls of London) and his sons Teneuvan and Avarwy. From old Ludgate, now at the church of St Dunstan-in-the-West.

12. Portrait of the famous Elizabethan alchemist and magus, Dr John Dee.

13. Wax disc with magical markings used by Dr Dee for casting spells.

14. Dr Dee's crystal ball, used for invoking angels and spirits.

15. The Stone of Destiny, coronation seat of the monarchs of Great Britain.

16. Part of the Kirkwall Scroll, showing the Ark of the Covenant and Seraphim.

17. Coat of arms of the United Grand Lodge of England with similar design to the Kirkwall Scroll.

18. Painting of Israel (Jacob) blessing Ephraim and Manasseh, titular 'patriarchs' of Britain and America.

19. Emperor Rudolf II, patron of artists, alchemists and astronomers.

20. The Rosicrucian Queen Elizabeth of Bohemia, daughter of James I, wife of Elector Frederick V of the Palatine and grandmother of King George I.

21. Gresham College, home to the Invisible College and probable centre of a secret Rosicrucian movement.

22. Rosslyn Chapel, built by the Sinclair family as a shrine for the performance of Templar and masonic rituals and incorporating many secrets in its design.

23. James I, first king of Great Britain, wearing the robes of the neo-Arthurian Order of the Garter.

rather the creation of the *logoi* or laws which governed the entire universe. This realization, to a large extent made possible by the receptive atmosphere of Prague which allowed for the discovery of Kepler's laws, was possibly the defining moment in the birth of enlightenment philosophy.

Rudolf II was by no means a successful king or even popular with his subjects. Even when Dee met him for the first time in 1585 he was on the verge of insanity. In succeeding years, while he was busy fussing around alchemical stoves, his imperial powers were leaching away. The brief golden age of enlightenment that had for a short time made Prague the scientific capital of the world was coming to an end. The stage was being set for another revolution: one which would affect not just Bohemia but the whole of Europe.

CHAPTER FIVE

THE ROSICRUCIAN FURORE

The start of the seventeenth century saw Europe in the grip of what might be called 'new age' fever. There was a feeling abroad that the new century would be a time of great change. True, it began inauspiciously enough with the execution in Rome of Giordano Bruno, self-styled prophet of hermeticism. However, his martyrdom at the Campo de' Fiori on 17 February 1600 was more symptomatic of the insecurity of his persecutors than of the way that modern philosophy was moving. It was a medieval response to a challenge which was not merely heresy, in the old sense of the word, but rather the beginnings of a seismic change in the way people think about the world and their place in it. As the century wore on, so the conflict between old and new age views of the world would sharpen, leading rapidly to the catastrophe of the Thirty Years War.

Bruno died nearly eighty years before Isaac Newton published his *Philosophiae Naturalis Principia Mathematica*, explaining scientifically how the motion of the planets is governed by gravitational attraction and not by angelic forces propelling them around crystal spheres. By that time, owing to the revolution of ideas we know today as the enlightenment, the world was a different place. How this new world was born is not as obvious as may at first appear; to a large extent, it owed its origins to an undercurrent of thought known as Rosicrucianism.

In England the change of centuries was marked by the death of Queen Elizabeth in 1603 and the accession of James I. If the seventeenth century began badly with the execution of Bruno for heresy, the death of Elizabeth symbolized the passing of a magical age that had seen a renaissance in such mystical pursuits as astrology, alchemy and spiritualism. A further portent of change, if any were needed, was the sudden appearance in 1603 and 1604 of two new and very bright stars: supernovae in the constellations of Cygnus and Serpentarius. Traditionally, stars were thought to embody principles of nature, each star governing some aspect of life on earth. The appearance of a bright, new star could therefore be thought to herald the birth of some new influence. Serpentarius, 'the Serpent', is a fairly dim collection of stars that winds its way around the middle of Ophiuchus. This constellation, the 'Serpent Bearer', was anciently linked with Asclepius, the Greek god of healing, who among other things was revered for his ability at curing snake bites. As the serpent is, on one level, a symbol of the devil, so the appearance of a nova in this constellation could symbolize the appearance of an antidote to sin. On the other hand Cygnus, the Swan, has the alternative, Christian name of the 'Northern Cross' and seen from Europe its brightest star, Deneb, culminates close to the zenith. To Christian astrologers the appearance of a nova or 'new star' in this constellation could perhaps seem to herald the imminent return of Jesus Christ himself.

Living in Prague at the time of these thrilling stellar events was Johannes Kepler, who in his privileged position at the court of Rudolf II would have been more aware than most of the winds of change blowing through the Holy Roman Empire. An astrologer as well as the greatest astronomer of his time, he was to write in his book *De Stella Nova* (1606) that these new stars portended religious and political changes. However, he did not need to be an astrologer to see that changes, quite possibly for the worse as far as he himself was concerned, were inevitable. As Rudolf grew older, so he forgot the need to treat his Protestant subjects with tact. In 1600 he had allowed Catholic radicals to dictate his policy towards the Unitas Fratrum, the 'Unity Brethren' who were the spiritual heirs, as it were, of the Hussites, and in 1602 he issued a decree against the Brethren which was enforced in a large part of Bohemia. They appealed to his brother Matthias for support and a rebellion against Rudolf's rule and in favour of Matthias spread across the empire. In 1604, with the new stars shining brightly, the Hungarians rose up against the rule of the emperor. Increasingly divorced from political reality, Rudolf had foolishly sought to deprive the country of its constitution as well as the Protestants of their rights. As a response Stephan Boksay, a nobleman from Transylvania, advanced from the south and drove the imperial forces out of Hungary.

For Rudolf the price of failure was extreme. It was now clear to all that his eccentricity was degenerating into madness – with dangerous consequences for the Habsburg empire. Consequently the Habsburg family in Vienna rallied around his younger brother, Matthias, and recognized him as their head. To prevent Hungary from seceding altogether from the Hapsburg empire,

Matthias entered into negotiations with Boksay, culminating in a peace treaty signed at Vienna on 23 June 1606. Under the terms of this treaty the Hungarians had their rights restored to them and Boksay was recognized as prince of Transylvania. Rudolf, still nominally Holy Roman Emperor as well as king of Bohemia, was sidelined. He was forced to give up rulership of Austria, Hungary and Moravia to Matthias, who now became king of Hungary.

Further breakdown was yet to come. In 1608 the rebels entered Bohemia, and the following year, in an attempt to curry favour with the country's nobility, many of whom were still Hussite Protestants, Rudolf issued his famous 'letter of majesty'. Though he himself was a Catholic, this charter guaranteed Protestants their religious freedom. This should have led to an amicable arrangement between crown and estates, but unfortunately, however good his intentions, he was still not in control of the situation on the ground. Soon after the charter was signed his own troops, led by a cousin, the Archduke Leopold, mutinied and began to ravage Bohemia. Knowing that, however sympathetic he might be, Rudolf would be of little help to them, the Bohemian nobles now also turned to Matthias, who raised an army and in 1611 put down Leopold's rebellion. The Emperor Rudolf, whose dominion now stretched little further than the walls of his castle in Prague, was subsequently forced to cede to his brother the crown of Bohemia to add to those of Austria, Moravia and Hungary.

Rudolf died on 20 January 1612 and Matthias, already fifty-five years of age, succeeded him as Holy Roman Emperor. It was the end of an era that, for all its contradictions, had seen at Prague the birth of something special. Rudolf may have been a manic depressive and a rotten politician, but he had proved to be a great patron of both arts and sciences. His library and museum were the envy of Europe, while his court mathematician, Johannes Kepler, was laying down the basis of modern astronomy. Under his mostly benign rule Prague had risen from obscurity to become the most fashionably avant-garde city in Europe. It was a golden age that would be remembered fondly by the Bohemians for generations to come.

The death of Rudolf, who epitomized the philosopher king, left many in Germany feeling uneasy about the future. Protestants in particular had to wonder if such religious freedoms as they now enjoyed would endure for long once Matthias too departed this world. For while they believed that he could be relied upon to act pragmatically, he was himself getting on in years and his reign could only be regarded as an interim. At the same time the forces of the Catholic Counter-Reformation were daily growing in strength and they knew that it remained the policy of the papacy, as it had been at the time of the Hussites, to extirpate Protestantism altogether.

It was in this climate that around 1614 the first of a series of anonymous pamphlets appeared in Germany. Entitled the *Fama Fraternitatis or a Discovery of the Fraternity of the most noble order of the Rosy Cross*, it was followed the next year by a second: the *Confessio Fraternitatis or the confession of the laudable fraternity of the most honourable order of the Rosy Cross, written to all the learned of Europe*. These manifestos announced to a startled world that there was in existence a secret 'Rosicrucian' Brotherhood whose identity was entirely unknown to all but a few initiates.

The pamphlets promised not just a reformation in the old sense of the word but a wholesale revelation of the divine intention. Once this new knowledge was made known, the differences between Catholics and Protestants would seem immaterial and the world would move into a new age of enlightenment.

The pamphlets spoke of a wondrous teacher called Christian Rozencreutz or 'Brother C.R.C.', who had set up a mystical order. This order was in possession of his secret teachings, gleaned during a long journey through Islamic countries, that would be of great benefit to the world. According to the *Fama*, Brother C.R.C. was born in 1378 and died in 1488 at the age of 110. Evidently he was buried in a special tomb whose location was kept secret even from later members of the order – those appointed to take the place of the founders at their deaths. This tomb had apparently been rediscovered by accident in 1604, in accordance with Rosencreutz's prophecies.[1] In that year some remedial work was carried out at the house of 'N.N.', a brother of the third generation in succession to brothers 'D' and 'A'. In the course of this work a secret door had been found, concealed behind some plaster-work, with an inscription that read: *Post CXX Annos Patebo*, 'After 120 years I will be opened.' The *Fama* describes what N.N. and his companions found when they went inside:

> In the morning following we opened the door, and there appeared to our sight a vault of seven sides and seven corners, every side five foot broad, and the height of eight foot. Although the sun never shines in this vault, nevertheless, it was enlightened with another sun, which had learned this from the sun, and was

situated in the upper part in the centre of the sieling [*sic*]. In the midst, instead of a tomb-stone, was a round altar, covered with a plate of brass, and thereon this engraven:

A. C. R. C. *Hoc universi compendium unius mihi sepulchrum feci*. [I have made for my tomb this summary of the one universe].[2]

Brother N.N. lifted the brass plate and under it found the still uncorrupted body of the order's founder: Brother C.R.C. Clutched in his hand was a parchment detailing the history of the order as outlined in the *Fama* as well as certain secret teachings not previously divulged. Continuing in this vein, the *Fama* describes how the two brothers resealed the tomb before going public with their discovery. It then moves on to its primary purpose: that of inviting interested parties to join them in the general reformation of the world. It ends with the curious saying, which is evidently a species of prayer: *Sub umbra alarum tuarum, Jehova* – 'Under the shadow of your wing, O Jehovah'.

The Rosicrucian documents made their first appearance in Germany, the country from which the founder of the order was said to come. As well as describing his tomb, the *Fama* told the story of how Christian Rosencreutz came by his strange knowledge. According to the pamphlet this holy brother, whose name was not to be found in the records of any known society or religious order, had travelled to the east as a youth of sixteen with the intention of visiting Jerusalem. However, this pilgrimage had not gone according to plan. While in Damascus, en route to the Holy City, he had met up with members of a secret Arabic sect. He was impressed with their obvious wisdom and they, equally impressed with his precocious abilities as a physician, agreed to take him to an Arabian city named 'Damcar'.[3] There he learned Arabic and was taught advanced mathematics and 'Physick' (which in this context does not mean physics in the modern sense of the word but rather medicine). Leaving Damcar after several years, he travelled onwards to Egypt and from there went to Fez. Here he remained for a further two years and had many secret teachings revealed to him concerning magic and the Kabbalah.

His education now complete, C.R.C. left the Muslim world and went to Spain, where he set about teaching what he had learnt. However, he quickly discovered that those who were already considered wise were not at all inclined to be shown the error of their ways:

After two years Brother R. C. departed the city of Fez, and sailed with many costly things into Spain, hoping well, as he himself had so well and profitably spent his time in his travel, that the learned in Europe would highly rejoice with him, and begin to rule and order all their studies according to those sure and sound foundations. He therefore conferred with the learned in Spain, shewing unto them the errors of our arts, and how they might be corrected, and from whence they should gather the true *Inditia* of the times to come, and wherein they ought to agree with those things that are past; also how the faults of the Church and the whole *Philosophia Moralis* were to be amended. He shewed them new growths, new fruits and beasts, which did concord with old philosophy, and prescribed them new Axiomata, wherein all things might fully be restored. But it was to them a laughing matter, and being a new thing unto them, they feared that their great name would be lessened if they should now again begin to learn, and acknowledge their many years' errors, to which they were accustomed, and wherewith they had gained enough.[4]

Leaving Spain, Brother C.R.C. returned to his native Germany and built for himself an abode 'in which he ruminated his voyage and philosophy, and reduced them together in a true memorial'. This work accomplished, he set about founding an order of his own through which, at a more propitious time, his knowledge might be passed into the world. Into this order were recruited eight brethren, most of whom were close family members. Having instructed them in the use of a magical language and other esoterica, he sent them off into different countries where they could both interact with the learned and observe if anything new were to be discovered. These devotees, and their subsequent successors, swore to live by the following rules of the order:

First, That none of them should profess any other thing than to cure the sick, and that gratis.

Second, None of the posterity should be constrained to wear one certain kind of habit, but therein to follow the custom of the country.

Third, That every year, upon the day C., they should meet together at the house *Sancti Spiritus*, or write the cause of his absence.

Fourth, Every Brother should look about for a worthy person who, after his decease, might succeed him.

Fifth, The word R.C. should be their seal, mark, and character.

Sixth, The Fraternity should remain secret one hundred years.[5]

The *Fama Fraternitatis* was followed into print by the *Confessio*, a more prolix work addressed to 'the learned of Europe'. That the brotherhood as it then existed (1611) was a Protestant organization is made clear in the first chapter, where the writer condemns the pope (along with Mahomet) for blasphemies against Jesus Christ. In this work the still unknown Rosicrucian brothers proclaim that though the world is approaching its end, prior to this there will be a new age of enlightenment:

> One thing should here, O mortals, be established by us, that God hath decreed to the world before her end, which presently thereupon shall ensue, an influx of truth, light, and grandeur, such as he commanded should accompany Adam from Paradise and sweeten the misery of man: Wherefore there shall cease all falsehood, darkness, and bondage, which little by little, with the great globe's revolution, hath crept into the arts, works, and governments of men, darkening the greater part of them . . .
>
> And we now confess that many high intelligences by their writings will be a great furtherance unto this Reformation which is to come, so do we by no means arrogate to ourselves this glory, as if such a work were only imposed on us, but we testify with our Saviour Christ, that sooner shall the stones rise up and offer their service, than there shall be any want of executors of God's counsel.[6]

The authors then lay out in general terms their proposition for a reformation based on close scrutiny of the 'Book of Nature' and through this a better understanding of God's laws. The appearance of the new stars in Serpentarius and Cygnus is, they say, to be viewed as heralding this reformation of ideas:

> God, indeed, hath already sent messengers which should testify His will, to wit, some new stars which have appeared in *Serpentarius* and *Cygnus*, the which powerful signs of a great Council shew forth how for all things which human ingenuity discovers, God calls upon His hidden knowledge, as likewise the Book of Nature, though it stands open truly for all eyes, can be read or understood by only a very few.[7]

'Following the footsteps of nature' became a metaphor for pursuing scientific research through observation of the phenomenal world as opposed to Aristotelian scholasticism. It is the secret teaching behind Emblem 42 of *Atalanta Fugiens*, a unique work that appeared in 1617; combining fugues (verses set to music) with pictures or 'emblems', it purports to be an interpretation of the alchemical process of transmutation using the Greek myth of the flight of Atalanta. Its author, Michael Maier, who had been physician to the emperor Rudolf II and was a highly esteemed alchemist, lived for a time in both Prague and Heidelberg, and became an apologist for Rosicrucianism; several of his works contain Rosicrucian allusions.

According to the legend, Atalanta was a young huntress who was extremely fleet of foot. Reluctantly she agreed to her father's wishes that she should marry whoever could beat her in a running race. Many suitors tried and failed to win her hand before the right man, Hippomenes, came along. He had been instructed by the goddess Aphrodite, who had told him that if he wanted to win the race he should throw three golden apples in Atalanta's path. This he did, and while Atalanta stopped to pick up the apples, either out of desire for gold or in order to let him win, he was able to reach the finishing line first. Without waiting to be properly wed, the young couple consummated their passion within the hallowed precincts of a temple to Cybele. As a consequence of this insult, she turned them into lions.

Within the alchemical lexicon of images, Atalanta clearly stands for *pneuma*, the spirit of nature or 'first matter' which has to be fixed in order for the transmutation to occur. The golden apples symbolize the 'seed pattern' or 'form' of gold which, according to alchemical theory, has to be 'projected' on to the 'first matter' in order to make 'philosophical gold'. The coupling of Atalanta and Hippomenes in the temple of Cybele, i.e. the natural world, signifies the process of multiplication. The reference to their being turned into lions probably came about in the first place because Cybele is traditionally shown as riding in a chariot drawn by paired lions, symbolic of the sun.

Drawing on this rich symbolic tradition, the emblems of *Atalanta Fugiens* are full of significance. Yet it is clear that Maier himself was not just a romantic philosopher of the old, alchemical tradition but was keenly aware of the new winds of reason that were blowing away superstition. He knew that the way forward lay with science, not archaic mysticism, and that this entailed studying closely the laws of nature. Emblem 42 carries the legend: 'For him versed in Chemistry, let Nature, Reason, Experience, and Reading be his Guide, staff, spectacles and lamp.' The accompanying verse is:

Let Nature be your guide, and with your art
  Follow her closely. Without her you'll err.
Let reason be your staff; experience lend
  Power to your sight, that you may see afar.
Let reading be your lamp, dispelling dark,
    That you may guard 'gainst throngs of things and
      words.[8]

The writers of the Rosicrucian *Confessio* hint again
at a secret language which their fraternity has adopted
the better to understand the workings of nature:

Fig. 16. Emblem 42 from Michael Maier's *Atalanta Fugiens*.

These characters and letters, as God hath here and there incorporated them in the Sacred Scriptures, so hath he imprinted them most manifestly on the wonderful work of creation, on the heavens, the earth, and on all beasts, so that as the mathematician predicts eclipses, so we prognosticate the obscurations of the church, and how long they shall last. From these letters we have borrowed our magick writing, and thence have made for ourselves a new language, in which the nature of things is expressed, so that it is no wonder that we are not so eloquent in other tongues, least of all this Latin, which we know to be by no means in agreement with that of Adam and of Enoch, but to have been contaminated by the confusion of Babel.[9]

This reference to a secret language is itself prophetic of the way in which science – or natural philosophy, as it was then called – was indeed to develop a language and terminology of its own. The shorthand notations and recondite symbols of the scientist, by means of which the workings of nature are described in the form of equations, do indeed make up different language from Latin or any other known to man. Yet there is a more esoteric meaning here that seems to connect the author with a possible 'school' set up by or at least based on the work of Dr John Dee. For he and his associate Edward Kelley claimed to have been given, in the course of their channelled conversations with angels, a secret 'Enochian' alphabet, supposedly that used by the angels themselves. This is not the only reference to Dee's influence to be seen in the Rosicrucian documents, and we shall be returning to this connection later on.

The sudden appearance of the Rosicrucian

documents caused a furore throughout Europe. Their impact on seventeenth-century thought can be compared with that of the communist manifestos of Karl Marx three centuries later. Suddenly everybody who mattered wanted to join the mysterious society and to be initiated into their mysteries. The authorship of these two manifestos has never been truly proven, though it is generally assumed that they, as well as a later work called *The Chemical Wedding of Christian Rosencreutz*, were penned by one Johann Valentin Andreae, a Lutheran pastor and mystic from Württemberg in Germany. However, although he later admitted to being the author of the *Chemical Wedding* and may have secretly been a member of some sort of brotherhood with Rosicrucian pretensions, Andreae flatly denied writing either the *Fama* or the *Confessio*. Internal evidence from the manifestos also suggests a different authorship. What seems more likely, and certainly seems to have been the opinion of the historian Dame Frances Yates, is that the real writer of the pamphlets had royal connections.

The concept of the 'chemical wedding' is to be found throughout alchemical literature of the seventeenth century and even before. Though the laws of chemistry as we would understand them today had not yet been worked out, it was well understood that nature was polarized into male and female. It followed that the 'marriage', namely a controlled and regulated union between the male and female aspects of nature, was one of the most important steps on the path to creating the alchemical stone of the philosophers. For obvious reasons, such a union of opposite principles was generally symbolized by the metaphor of human marriage. As a practising alchemist Andreae would

160

have understood this arcane symbolism. However, in his book he seems to be saying more: his concerns are as much political as alchemical, and concern the situation in Germany at the time of the Rosicrucian furore.

Andreae's home province of Württemburg, one of the patchwork of small states that made up seventeenth-century Germany, was sandwiched between Baden and Bavaria, just to the north of Switzerland. That Württemburg should have a connection with the Rosicrucian movement is entirely plausible, for unlike Bavaria it was Protestant, adhering to the Lutheran confession. In 1600 the reigning duke was the anglophilic Frederick I, who a year before had paid a large sum of money to have Württemburg, while still remaining part of the Holy Roman Empire, freed from Austrian hegemony. Like the emperor Rudolf II, to whom the money was paid, this Frederick was intensely interested in alchemy. He had also visited England on a number of occasions and was well known to Queen Elizabeth. One of his great ambitions had been enrolment into the Order of the Garter, Europe's premier order of nobility, founded in 1348 by King Edward III of England in emulation of the legendary Knights of the Round Table under King Arthur. With the Queen's permission, he had been elected to this honour in 1597; but he was not actually received into the order until after her death in 1603. The event of his investiture at Stuttgart, the major city of Württemburg, in 1605 was one of the great occasions of the early seventeenth century. A special embassy, including a company of actors, was sent over from England and there were processions and much feasting to celebrate the occasion.

When Frederick of Württemburg was enrolled as a Knight of the Garter he would have been well aware of

161

the connection between the order and that of King Arthur's Round Table; indeed, this could explain his strong desire to join. However, Elizabeth, like her father, was a canny politician where symbols were concerned. She understood that, through its connections with King Arthur and Joseph of Arimathea, the Order of the Garter represented something both more ancient than and alternative to the primacy of the papacy. Membership of the order implied connection with the mysteries of the Holy Grail without the necessity of kowtowing to Rome to receive benediction. While most of the Garter knights of her time were drawn from her own court, she actively pursued a policy of recruiting foreign kings and princes into the order. This was not a simple matter of piety or even of adding some foreign glamour to an old and perhaps somewhat fusty institution: it was connected with her policy of maintaining the balance of power in Europe. During the early years of her reign Duke Adolphus of Holstein, King Charles IX of France and the Emperor Maximilian of Germany, all heads of state, were enrolled into the order. Elizabeth further endeavoured to keep these great houses of Europe allied to England by having membership of the order pass from generation to generation. Thus following the death of Charles IX, first Henry III and then Henry IV of France were enrolled to the order; the Emperor Maximilian was followed by Dr John Dee's one-time patron, Rudolf II. To these august heads were added King Frederick II of Denmark, Count John Casimir of the Palatinate and now his neighbour Duke Frederick of Württemburg. What all these heads of state had in common, Catholic and Protestant alike, was a fear of domination by Spain. For all of them, membership of the Garter 'Round Table' represented security in the form of a loose alliance of mostly Protestant states in opposition to the papacy and its principal supporter, Spain.

James I inherited Elizabeth's foreign policy and, at least in the earlier years of his reign, carried on with it. He hastened to have Frederick of Württemburg fully installed as a Garter knight in 1605. John Casimir, the Elector Palatine, was succeeded in this office by his nephew, Frederick IV. This count died before he could be enrolled in the order but his son, Count Frederick V, who took over as ruler of the Palatinate in 1610, was duly installed. This, however, was to be no ordinary election to the august ranks of the Order of the Garter, for Frederick was also engaged to James I's daughter, Elizabeth Stuart. The marriage of these two in London in February 1613 was an even more glittering occasion than the investiture of Frederick of Württemburg as a Garter knight. It involved pageants and masques, elaborate dress, fireworks, parties, plays and, of course, the ceremony of the installation of Frederick V into the Order of the Garter. This was an 'alchemical' marriage on a grand scale: the union of Protestant Germany (in the form of Frederick) with Great Britain (represented by Elizabeth Stuart). The offspring of this alliance would in time occupy the thrones of Europe and rule over the greatest empire the world has yet seen.

At the time of the wedding, that happy outcome was a long way in the future; and behind all the festivity, storm clouds were brewing. For European Protestants the start of the second decade of the seventeenth century was full of foreboding. In May 1610 King Henry IV (Navarre), still Protestant at heart though he had outwardly converted to Catholicism in order to obtain the throne of France, had been assassinated. A shrewd monarch who had led the European opposition to Habsburg power, his loss was a disaster not only for Protestants within France but also for the small kingdoms and principalities that made up the loose confederation of Protestant powers. When he died his son, King Louis XIII, was still a boy of only nine, and it was Marie de' Medici, Henry's wife and Louis' mother, who as regent now held the strings of power in France. Unfortunately for the Protestants, she was a Catholic, and quickly reversed her late husband's foreign policy by forging new alliances between France, Spain and Austria. As we have seen, matters were further complicated by the death of Rudolf II in 1612. For though his brother Matthias was careful not to antagonize his Protestant subjects, the fact that he also was of advanced years created uncertainty for the future. It seemed likely that the next Holy Roman Emperor would be more in sympathy with the Jesuits and aid the forces of Counter-Reformation in the reassertion of Catholic hegemony over not just Bohemia but Germany too. For Protestants, therefore, the marriage of Frederick V, Count Palatine, to Elizabeth Stuart represented something more important than simply the union of two royal houses: it was the cornerstone on which they hoped an anti-Habsburg alliance could be rebuilt.

At the centre of these Protestant intrigues was Christian of the German state of Anhalt. Prior to 1610 he had been actively supporting King Henry IV of France in his efforts to curb the power of the Habsburgs. Now that Henry's assassination had brought these plans to naught, he transferred his allegiance to the young Count Frederick V of the

Palatinate. Christian was of an older generation of diplomats and had been a close friend of that great Elizabethan ambassador Sir Philip Sidney. He had also enjoyed most friendly relations with not only Frederick's father, Frederick IV, but his great-uncle, Count John Casimir. It seems likely that it was Anhalt who had hatched the idea of drawing England more closely into a European alliance of Protestant states by means of the marriage of Frederick and Elizabeth, a union which might just fill the political vacuum left by the death of Henry IV. With the wedding achieved, it was generally believed in Europe that the Palatinate – and with it the other Protestant states of Germany – would now be under England's protective wing. This alliance in itself would go a long way towards re-establishing the balance of power upset by Henry IV's untimely death. However, it was only the first stage of Anhalt's great plan; for he had other ambitions for the young Frederick that in the fullness of time were to lead to disaster.

This, then, was the political atmosphere which prevailed in Europe at the time the Rosicrucian pamphlets were published. In Germany especially it was a time of both uncertainty and hope. There was fear among the Protestants that the time of tolerance was running out, that the forces of the Counter-Reformation were gathering in preparation for a fresh attempt at wiping out their brand of Christianity. At the same time there was a millennial expectation, heralded by the appearance of the new stars, that a new age was dawning. There was a widespread belief that, however dark and forebidding the gathering clouds might seem, behind them the sun was shining with a greater radiance than before.

This feeling of millennial expectation coupled with angst about the current situation is shown very clearly in the frontispiece to a book entitled *Speculum Sophicum Rhodo-Stauricum* (Mirror of Rosicrucian wisdom), written by Theophilus Schweighardt but published anonymously in 1618. It shows the invisible or secret Rosicrucian college as a movable fortress on wheels. Banners proclaim 'Collegium Fraternitatis' (College of the Brotherhood) and 'S.S.' (Speculum Sophicum). Above its bell tower is the word 'Fama', the name of the first Rosicrucian pamphlet. The college itself is suspended, like a puppet, from a string that goes to heaven – to the very hand of God. The words which end the *Fama*, *Sub umbra alarum tuarum, Jehova* (Under the shadow of your wing, O Jehovah), are indicated by the wings that shade the college.

The new stars in the constellations of Serpentarius and Cygnus are shown as portents of what is happening below on earth. The good news of 'C.R.F.' (Christian Rozencreutz Fraternitas) is being trumpeted from the side of the college. Noah's Ark, symbolic of God's first covenant with humankind, when he promised he would never again destroy the world with a flood, is shown stranded on the top of Mount Ararat. As at the time of Noah, messenger birds are being sent out from and returning to the college. A hand brandishes a sword bearing the word *Cavete!*, 'Beware!' A man is winched out of a well, symbolic of being raised from the ignorance of 'opinion'. Another man clasps and kisses an anchor, recognizing at last that he is ignorant and needs salvation through the name of God. He has a hat, staff and satchel by his side, indicating that he is a pilgrim in search of the truth. Over the windows in the upper storey of the building is

Fig. 17. The 'College of the Fraternity' from *Speculum Sophicum Rhodo-Stauricum* by Theophilus Schweighardt, 1618.

written *Jesus nobis omnia*: 'Jesus to us everything'. To either side of the door are a rose and a cross: the symbols of the Rosicrucian Brotherhood. However, people walk or ride by in complete ignorance of the mysterious school that stands next to them. One even falls off a cliff-side to his certain death.

The stated reason for the publication of the Rosicrucian pamphlets was that the hitherto secret fraternity of the Rosy Cross was intending to go public. Like all societies, it needed recruits if it was to grow from a mere handful of initiates into an organization with the power and influence to make a real impact on the world. Thus written above the door are the words *Venite Digni*: 'Those who are worthy, let them come'. This echoes the invitation to join that is issued in the *Fama*:

So, according to the will and meaning of *Fra.* C. R. C., we his brethren request again all the learned in Europe who shall read (sent forth in five languages) this our *Fama* and *Confessio*, that it would please them with good deliberation to ponder this our offer, and to examine most nearly and sharply their arts, and behold the present time with all diligence, and to declare their minde, either *communicato consilio*, or *singulatim* by print. And although at this time we make no mention either of our names or meetings, yet nevertheless every one's opinion shall assuredly come to our hands, in what languages so ever it be, nor any body shall fail, whoso gives but his name, to speak with some of us, either by word of mouth, or else, if there be some lett, in writing. And this we say for a truth, that whosoever shall earnestly, and from his heart, bear affection unto us, it shall be beneficial to him in goods, body, and soul; but he that is false-hearted, or onely greedy of riches, the same first of all shall not be able in any manner of wise to hurt us, but bring himself to utter ruine and destruction. Also our building, although one hundred thousand people had very near seen and beheld the same, shall forever remain untouched, un-destroyed, and hidden to the wicked world. *Sub umbra alarum tuarum, Jehova.*[10]

Clearly it was felt that such an organization was needed at this potentially dangerous time in European history. The secret knowledge, which had up until then been restricted to the few, was now to be disseminated, if not to the many, at least to those of the 'learned' of Europe deemed worthy of such an honour. In this way rationalism might triumph and disaster might be averted.

Needless to say, would-be candidates were not slow in coming forward. The description as given in the *Fama* of the mysterious tomb of Brother C.R.C. excited curiosity, and the opportunity of joining such a select club was enough to attract applicants from among the intellectual elite of Europe. Unfortunately, the Rosicrucian Brotherhood, if it really existed, ignored these entreaties. In fact, it proved to be nearly as elusive as the Holy Grail. All attempts to track down flesh and blood members of this invisible order failed. Gradually, it became clear to many that the Rosicrucian pamphlets were an elaborate hoax. Yet, as Dr Yates has shown, this is not the full story. For there is evidence that during the early part of the seventeenth century, though the secretive society mentioned in the pamphlets was 'invisible' and may indeed have been entirely fictitious, there were indeed what might more loosely be called

'Rosicrucians' secretly active throughout Europe. Their main centre of operations was Germany and the core of the movement, if such we may call it, would appear to have been in Heidelberg, capital of the Palatinate.

The court of Frederick and Elizabeth was by all accounts a glittering affair. Their beautiful palace at Heidelberg Castle, with its gardens and mechanical wonders, enjoyed a majestic setting overlooking the valley of the River Neckar, a tributary of the Rhine. As, following the death of its eccentric ruler Rudolf, Prague's light dimmed and the Bohemian capital became an ever less attractive destination for free-thinkers, so Heidelberg shone more brightly. Around the young couple grew a court of admirers, and the Palatinate in general enjoyed a cultural renaissance. Even Oppenheim, a small, unimportant town some 25 miles north of Heidelberg, benefited, becoming a major centre for publishing. Around the time of Frederick and Elizabeth's wedding, Johann Theodore de Bry had moved his father's celebrated printing works to this cultural backwater from Frankfurt. Here, enjoying the freedom of ideas allowed by the young ruler, he published works on alchemy and other esoteric subjects, including books by Michael Maier, author of *Atalanta Fugiens*. He also brought into print the *History of the Macrocosm and Microcosm* by an English alchemist and polymath, Robert Fludd. These were large, profusely illustrated books that must have been very expensive to print and even more to purchase. Yet, as Joscelyn Godwin records in his brief biography of Robert Fludd, not only did de Bry not demand payment from Fludd for producing the books, he paid out an advance against future royalties:

To Fludd, the De Bry firm's efficiency and experience must have come as a godsend, for he says in his answer to Foster that 'our home-borne Printers demanded of me five hundred pounds to print the first volume, and to find the cuts in copper; but beyond the seas, it was printed at no cost to mine, and that as I would wish. And I had 16 copies sent me over, with 40 pounds in gold, as an unexpected gratuitie for it.'[11]

Fludd and Maier were important thinkers whose ideas and writings were enthusiastically received on the Continent. Though not themselves members of the secretive Rosicrucian Brotherhood spoken of in the *Fama* and *Confessio* – an organization which, as we have seen, in any case probably did not exist in the way described – they became its principal cheerleaders. In 1616 a book by Fludd with the long title *Apologia compendiaria fraternitatem de Rosea Cruce suspicionis et infamiae maculis aspersam, veritatis quasi Fluctibus abluens et asbstergens* was published by Gottfried Basson in Leiden. This was followed by another defence of the Rosicrucians in 1617, also published by Basson, with the title *Tractatus Apologeticus Integratem Societatis De Rosae Cruce defendens*. It may have been Fludd's fulsome praise of the mysterious Rosicrucian Brothers that brought him to the attention of the Palatinate publisher Johann de Bry, and it is not at all unlikely that de Bry was being subsidized to do this work by other – perhaps royal – benefactors of whom Fludd himself was unaware.

Also in 1617, as noted earlier, *Atalanta Fugiens* was published. Close study of the images it contains indicates that it is not only about alchemy but also includes secret messages to do with the politics of the

171

time. It is thought by many that the engravings for which it is rightly famous are the work of either Johann Theodore de Bry himself or his son-in-law, Matthieu Merien. Examination of the Emblems and the often irrelevant verses that accompany them suggest that the engraved plates were already in existence before Maier wrote his texts and were connected with some secret enterprise. The impression one gets is that this set of engravings were lying around in the de Bry workshop (possibly left over from some other project(s) that had been abandoned) and that Michael Maier had been asked to compose some suitably esoteric verses to accompany them.

This is very interesting because, as we have seen, at the time *Atalanta Fugiens* first went to press in 1617 the De Bry printing works were based in Oppenheim in the Palatinate. Several of the prints contained in the book have been identified as using Heidelberg itself as their background, most especially Emblem 7: 'There is a chick, flying up from its nest, that falls back into the nest again.' It is clear that this picture, which shows two young eagles in an eyrie, about to embark on a flight, should have come after Emblem 12 (reproduced as figure 12), which shows Cronos vomiting the stone of Zeus on to the same mountain peak. Epigram 7 seems to make oblique reference to this with the words:

In hollow crag Jove's BIRD built its nest,
    In which it hid itself and fed its young.
One of these chicks wanted to fly with wings:
    Its wingless brother pulled it back again,
So that flying it fell back to its nest.
    Connect them, head to tail, and you'll not fail.

Fig. 18. Emblem 7 from Michael Maier's *Atalanta Fugiens*.

Taking these two prints together, it is clear that in the original work for which de Bry engraved the plates the stone of Zeus is in reality to be thought of as an egg: the egg of the imperial eagle. It has been laid on a mountain peak in Heidelberg, which implies the residence of the royal family of that city. This in turn would suggest that the two eagles of Emblem 7 were not originally drawn as symbols for some alchemical process but were secretly intended to symbolize the royal couple, Frederick and Elizabeth, who the Rosicrucians hoped would one day become emperor and empress of Germany.

Unfortunately, the golden age of the Palatinate was to prove short-lived, for events were now moving at a quickening pace. Bohemia was once more in turmoil following the abdication of Matthias as king and the taking up of the crown by his cousin, Ferdinand of Styria. Suddenly the Bohemian Protestants found their worst fears realized: they were now to be ruled over by a Habsburg king who was not only Catholic but deeply hostile to Protestantism. In a replay of history, Ferdinand was to take Bohemia back to the bad old days of strife that followed the martyrdom of Jan Huss.

One of the new king's first acts was to revoke the 'letter of majesty' by virtue of which Bohemian Protestants had been guaranteed a degree of religious freedom under the previous two emperors. He and his Jesuit advisers then began a policy of outright repression. Although Bohemia's more liberal Catholics disapproved of these moves, they were powerless to stop this new policy of extremism which was threatening to open old wounds. In May 1618 things came to a head. There was a furious meeting between members of the Protestant estates and two Catholic governors, William Stavata and Jaroslav Martinic, who had been sent to implement the emperor's new policy. These two, along with a secretary to the royal council, were arrested and, after a mock trial for violating the terms of the 'letter of majesty', were thrown from a window of Hracadny Castle into the moat below. This event, known as the second defenestration of Prague, had worrying echoes of the first, when almost exactly two hundred years earlier the Hussites had thrown anti-reform officials from the windows of the town hall. Though this time the governors were not seriously hurt, the Protestant Unity Brethren knew that this act of rebellion was going to have serious consequences and very likely lead to another imperial crusade against their land. Unfortunately for them, much had changed in the intervening centuries, and whereas the Hussites had been able to field a formidable army under their one-eyed general, Jan Ziska, modern Bohemia was a soft target. The country was divided along class lines; the Bohemian army was not the fighting force it had been at the time of the Hussite crusades and its generals were in no way the equal of Zizka. Unable to stand up to the power of the Habsburg empire alone, the rebels knew they needed powerful allies and a figurehead around which they could rally.

Replacing the royal board of governors with directors of their own, the estates began the process of mobilization. All-out war might still have been avoided had the situation not been further complicated by the death of Matthias in March 1619. At a general assembly the Bohemian estates declared that Ferdinand was deposed as king of Bohemia and that henceforth the crown of Bohemia should be elective, as it had been centuries earlier. Then, in a not wholly unpredictable move, they offered this poisoned chalice to Count Frederick V of the Palatinate. Thus the scene was set for that historic confrontation between Catholic and Protestant known as the Thirty Years War.

The young Frederick, though he must have had some misgivings about such a risky enterprise, was keen to respond to the Bohemians' plea. Both his mother and many friends cautioned him against acceptance of the proffered crown, but he could not be dissuaded. He was, after all, the son-in-law of the king of England and could therefore surely expect material support from the country which thirty years earlier had defeated the Spanish Armada. Not only that, he had in his pocket a letter from the archbishop of Canterbury advising him to accept the crown as a religious duty. In these circumstances it would be not only cowardly but an abdication of his religious obligations to ignore the plight of the Bohemians. Accordingly, on 28 September 1619 he wrote back to the rebels and accepted their offer. Then, believing in his destiny, this leader of the Protestant princes of Germany packed his bags and, with his wife and children, set off for Prague.

There was, of course, a wider agenda to all of this which seriously worried Ferdinand and the other Habsburgs back in Vienna. The loss of the crown of Bohemia to Frederick, though insulting, was not the real issue at stake. What was potentially of greater importance was Ferdinand's claim to the title of Holy Roman Emperor. This crown, though it had been held by the Habsburgs for generations, was also elective. In theory, at least, it might be possible for someone other than a Habsburg to be elected as king of the Germans and consequently, as these posts went together, as emperor. There were seven electors in all. Three, being drawn from the Catholic Church (the archbishops of Mainz, Cologne and Trier), could always be relied upon as long as the prospective emperor were a Catholic. The other four were from the laity. They were the count palatine of the Rhine, the duke of Saxony, the margrave of Brandenburg and the king of Bohemia. As count palatine Frederick already had one vote in his pocket; by becoming king of Bohemia he would gain a second. The margrave of Brandenburg was, like Frederick, a Calvinist and a member of the Evangelical Union; moreover, his son and heir was married to Frederick's sister. Thus, in theory at least, his vote could be added to Frederick's own two to cancel out those of the archbishops. This left just the duke of Saxony, who though Lutheran as opposed to Calvinist was still a Protestant and might well be tempted to vote against a Habsburg candidate.

Habsburg power was still a reality. In any conflict with the Protestant princes of Germany, Ferdinand could expect support from Spain and Bavaria, and in any show of force the Catholic powers would be more than a match for the Protestants. However, Ferdinand wasn't taking any chances with the vote, so, once he had dealt with a few other matters, he hurried to Frankfurt before Frederick could be crowned king of Bohemia and gain the crucial extra vote. There Ferdinand was indeed elected as emperor and crowned on 28 August. The vote being lost, Frederick set out for Bohemia on 27 September. A little over a month later, on 4 November, he was crowned king of Bohemia at Prague cathedral by the Hussite clergy. At last, or so they thought, the Bohemians had a Protestant king whose nobility, courage and, above all, powerful alliances with the English as well as other Protestant princes would guarantee them their religious freedom. They did not have to wait long to discover how wrong these assumptions were.

As soon as he heard of Frederick's coronation, Ferdinand began to prepare his counter-strike. He was already in close contact with the duke of Bavaria and with his cousins in Spain. Together they hatched a plan that would, they hoped, see the destruction of Protestantism once and for all. Frederick, meanwhile, found himself isolated. His friends, the Protestant princes, were unwilling to give their support to the risky venture on which he had embarked; and, worse still, his father-in-law completely disowned him. What he had failed to realize, or perhaps didn't want to believe, was that England under James had moved away from the confrontational politics of Elizabeth and was now decidedly neutral in its relationships with the great powers of Europe. True, James's beloved daughter Elizabeth was already married to the new king of Bohemia; but he also wanted his son, later to be Charles I, to marry the Catholic daughter of the king of Spain. While the English as a whole, people and Parliament alike, were wholly behind Frederick and would have liked to come to his assistance, their king was in no mood for such an adventure that might jeopardize his relationship with Spain.

For Frederick, and northern Europe as a whole, the crunch came a year after his coronation. Bohemia was invaded by a force commanded by the duke of Bavaria. On 8 November 1620 Frederick's army, commanded by Anhalt, the probable instigator of the plan to put him on the throne, was utterly defeated just outside Prague at the Battle of the White Mountain. In the meantime Frederick's home state of the Palatinate was being devastated by a Spanish army under the command of the great general Ambrose Spinola. Heidelberg itself was virtually razed to the ground; Frederick's castle with its impressive gardens was despoiled and the precious 'Rosicrucian' books from his library consigned to the flames. Frederick and his family were forced to flee, leaving Prague so quickly that they lost most of their valuables in the process. He and his wife Elizabeth were to spend the rest of their lives living in genteel poverty in exile in The Hague.

With their departure went Protestant dreams of a new age of enlightenment. The rest of Germany – to say nothing of England – looked on in appalled fascination at this bonfire of vanities. Yet, as it turned out, this was to be but the start of a long war that would devastate not just Bohemia and the Palatinate but most of the rest of Germany as well, and ultimately see both Spain and Austria eclipsed by the growing power of France. Though England managed to stay militarily aloof from this terrible European conflagration, probably the worst experienced by the Continent between the fall of Rome and the world wars of the twentieth century, it was nevertheless affected in other ways. The country became a magnet for many of those lost souls who had seen their dreams of a better world shattered. These men, some of the greatest scholars in Europe, would now help Britain on its way to becoming the first modern, industrialized state in the world.

CHAPTER SIX

SCIENCE AND SOCIETY

During the sixteenth century England began to develop its tradition of investigative science. This had its roots in the works of the medieval alchemists. At the time of the Renaissance most 'natural philosophers', as scientists were then called, were also alchemists. The current understanding of the science of chemistry did not then, as it does now, preclude the possibility that lead could be transmuted into gold by chemical means. That they were unsuccessful in their endeavours did not deter them, for they believed that it had been done in the past; accordingly, they pored over old texts, looking for clues in the writings of previous masters of the art. Even so illustrious a scientist as Sir Isaac Newton (1642–1727) at one time conducted alchemical experiments; in the seventeenth century it was considered no more strange that an enterprising philosopher should have an alchemical still brewing away in his garden shed than that he should have a telescope with which to study the planets. Provided he didn't confuse it with magic, alchemy was considered to be a worthy pursuit for a gentleman. Not only that, but it had the added attraction that one might just succeed in producing a 'philosopher's stone' and thereby become fabulously wealthy.

Alchemy has a long pedigree. Although it was also practised in the east in China and India, in its western form it owes its origins to ancient Egypt. Indeed, the term 'alchemy', from the Latin *al-chemia*, is ultimately derived from Khem or Chem, the old name given to the delta area of Egypt. In the ancient world the Egyptians were renowned for their knowledge of 'chemistry', the art of the transmutation of matter. They were highly skilled pharmacists and knew how to manufacture herbal extracts and how to prepare medicines from these. They also knew a great deal about metals: how to smelt them from ore-bearing minerals and how to blend them together, for example, to make bronze. Producing amalgams, such as brass, that had the appearance of gold even though they were composed of base metals, was well within their capabilities. So, too, was the mixing of gold with silver to produce electrum. The techniques for doing all these things they wrote down on papyri, the most famous surviving example of which we now know as the Leyden Papyrus. Following the conquest of Egypt by Alexander the Great in 330 BC, some of these 'alchemical' papyri were translated into Greek. Many of these Greek works found their way to Mesopotamia and were preserved by the Sabians of Harran, who in turn brought them to Baghdad. It was Arabic translations of these mostly Greek works which subsequently passed back to Europe via North Africa.

A number of alchemical texts were in circulation in the sixteenth and seventeenth centuries, and many of these were lavishly illustrated, for the advent of printing meant that woodcut engavings could be used to great effect. Whole series of these engravings were produced, and frequently re-used to illustrate

Fig. 19. Three alchemists in discussion: Thomas Norton,
Abbot Cremer and Basil Valentine. From Michael Maier's
Tripus Aureus, 1618.

alchemical books other than the ones for which they
had originally been prepared. As these images were
highly symbolic and in their imagery very far removed
from the mundane processes of calcination, solution,
distillation and the rest, alchemy became more and
more arcane.

The imagery employed by the alchemists frequently
drew on esoteric sources and traditions far removed
from alchemy itself. Playing with ideas in symbolic
form was as much part of the game as slaving over an
alchemical retort. The problem for the reader was not
just one of trying to understand recondite texts, it was
a matter of recognizing the symbols presented. Often
these were based on scenes from mythology, but at
other times they drew on the Bible for inspiration. Thus

the first illustration in a famous book called the *Mutus Liber* (Silent Book), which was published in 1677 at La Rochelle by Pierre Savouret, brings together Rosicrucian symbolism (crossed rose-branches) with the story of Jacob's dream at Bethel. Jacob/Israel sleeps with his head resting against his Pillow Stone (in Britain, as we have seen, identified with the Stone of Scone). As he sleeps, so the angels he dreams of blow

Fig. 20. *Mutus Liber*, Sleep of Jacob/Israel.
From *Bibliotheca Chemica Curiosa*, 1702.

183

trumpets in an attempt to rouse him. The ladder is to be understood Kabbalistically as representing the Tree of Life. The sleep of Israel represents humankind in a trance state, unable to see the reality of the ladder of creation that would take him back to the heaven from whence he came.

But the 'silent book' referred to is not the Bible; it is nature, the intense study of which is the real work of the alchemist. The true alchemist studies the laws of nature so that he can reproduce its work in his laboratory. He recognizes that transformations of matter cannot be achieved by wishful thinking but only by working within the laws set out by God. All this is a very far cry from the simple business of turning base metals into gold, and the Latin caption to the illustration tells us as much. It translates as: 'The Silent Book, in which nevertheless the whole of Hermetic Philosophy is portrayed in hieroglyphic figures, dedicated to God the merciful, thrice good in the highest degree, and dedicated to the sons of the art only, the name of the author being Altus.'

The philosophy that underpinned alchemy also owed its origins to Egypt. Alchemists such as Basil Valentine took their inspiration from the corpus of writings attributed to Hermes Trismegistus, most especially his *Tabula Smaragdina* or 'Emerald Table'. The belief of the alchemists was that metals had their particular characteristics because of the pattern or 'form' that was stamped upon them. This was considered to be something different from the actual 'matter' from which a piece of metal was composed. Thus the matter or material aspect of gold was no different from that of lead; it differed only in its appearance and character, differences which came about because gold had projected upon it the seed-form or pattern of gold whereas lead, for example, had a coarser pattern appropriate to its own, duller nature. It was believed that if the matter of a base material, such as lead, could be freed from its coarse form, then it could be reconstituted as gold. In principle, at least, this was very easy to do. All that was required was for the base metal to be reduced to a black 'first matter' and then to be mixed with a seeding substance that would give to this amorphous mass a higher form: that of gold. The stages of this process were normally considered to be twelve in number: the 'Gates' of Sir George Ripley, or the 'Keys' of Basil Valentine. In practice, of course, things were not so easy, and alchemists spent months or even years slaving away in their laboratories with nothing to show for all their labours.

During the sixteenth and seventeenth centuries many books on alchemy were written in England, some of which gained a high reputation abroad as well as at home. The antiquarian Elias Ashmole (1617–92), who brought together a number of these writings in his *Theatrum Chemicum Britannicum* of 1652, records that Michael Maier, possibly the most famous German alchemist of his day, came to Britain 'purposely that he might so understand our English tongue and to translate Norton's *Ordinall* into Latin verse, which most judiciously and learnedly he did'.[1]

Along with alchemists, England, with its liberal regime, also produced good mathematicians. John Dee's preface to Henry Billingsley's translation of Euclid, published in 1570, was regarded with admiration throughout Europe, and he was not alone; there were other English scientists who studied mathematics as well. Probably the most notable of these was

Dee's contemporary William Gilbert (1540–1603).

Member and then president of the Royal College of Physicians, physician-in-ordinary to Queen Elizabeth and to her successor King James I, Gilbert was by the standards of the day undoubtedly a good doctor; but this is not chiefly why he is remembered. For, when not ministering to his patients, he was busy conducting scientific experiments. His chief field of interest was magnetism, then a matter of unexplained mystery. A true scientist, Gilbert collected together everything that anybody had written on the subject of magnetism and then took the study further into entirely new fields. He was the first to name the two ends of a magnet the 'north and south poles' and to recognize that opposite poles were attracted to one another. His book *De Magnete*, first published in 1600, was read with admiration throughout Europe as well as in England. It earned the approval even of Galileo, who described Gilbert as 'great to a degree that is enviable'.[2]

Gilbert's study of magnetism represented a new style of scientific research. At the time he was writing (which corresponded with the period of Giordano Bruno's peregrinations), Aristotelian philosophy still reigned supreme. The thought that Aristotle's works might yet be superseded and that it was down to the scientists of the day to push back the boundaries of knowledge by making observations of their own was only just beginning to take root. The solarcentric astronomy of Copernicus, which was enthusiastically received by mathematicians such as Gilbert, was banned by the Roman Church; so subversive were these modern ideas considered in Catholic Europe that Bruno would be burnt at the stake and Galileo imprisoned for daring to say the earth went around the sun and not vice versa.

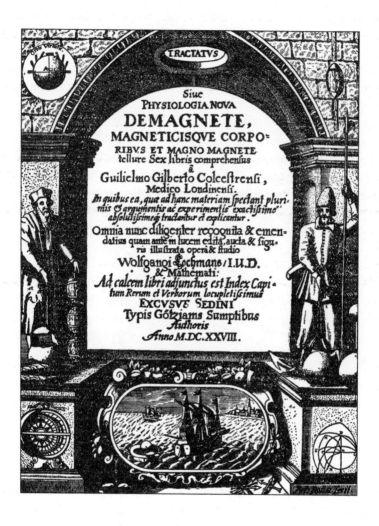

Fig. 21. Title page from *De Magnete*. (Second edition, 1628.)

187

Yet in England, where the pope's edicts held no sway, such ideas could be discussed openly. This made it an island of toleration where science was concerned – with important practical consequences. Gilbert's study of magnetism, for example, aided commerce, for magnetic compasses were needed for navigation. This is why a ship in full sail is shown at the bottom of the frontispiece to *De Magnete*.

There is another of Dr Gilbert's activities that deserves comment: for almost thirty years, after an extended trip to Europe in his early thirties, he ran a

Fig. 22. The coat of arms of William Gilbert.

private 'college' at his home on St Peter's Hill in Colchester. What were the concerns of this college and what was discussed during its meetings it is impossible to say, but we may suspect that its aims were in line with those proclaimed in the Rosicrucian pamphlets. While we cannot be certain that Gilbert's college was some sort of Rosicrucian fellowship, his coat of arms, printed on the verso of the title page of his book on magnetism, is certainly strikingly Rosicrucian in its conception. This may be purely accidental, but it is still interesting.

William Gilbert's shield is divided into quarters. In the upper left and lower right quarters are his father Jerome's arms. The visitation of Essex of 1634 reveals these as 'Argent, on a chevron between three leopards' faces azure as many roses of the field'. These arms were confirmed to William Gilbert in letters patent by the Royal College of Arms on 27 November 1577. The fact that they were confirmed rather than granted indicates that they were already in existence and were presumably used, if not by his own father, by some traceable patriarch of the family. Now, these arms are similar to (though not identical with) those used by the Devon Gilberts. Their arms were 'Or, on a chevron Sable, three roses of the field, leaved ppr. a bordure Gules'. This similarity suggests that William Gilbert either was or believed himself to be related to Sir Walter Raleigh's half-brothers, Sir Humphrey and Adrian Gilbert.

In the illustration to the volume on magnetism, the Gilbert arms are quartered. In the opposite quarters are charged St George's crosses, each with a crescent moon at its centre. Surrounding these crosses are, one in each quarter, four scallop shells. Scallops are symbolic of pilgrimage, and the crescent moon – particularly in the

189

form it is shown here – would seem to indicate pilgrimage to an Islamic country. Could it be that this coat of arms is an oblique reference to C.R.C. with whose pilgrimage to Damascus and instruction by a secret brotherhood in an Islamic country the *Fama* begins? As the *Fama* itself was not even written in Gilbert's day, this becomes even more intriguing, for it would imply that he knew about the legend of C.R.C. before the pamphlets made these ideas available to the wider world. We may never know the truth about this connection. However, whether accidentally or not, it is undeniable that this intriguing coat of arms includes the elements of roses and crosses: symbols of the Rosicrucian order.

While there is no absolute proof that Gilbert was a member of a secret Rosicrucian order, the indications are that, had such an order existed in the Germany of his day, he had the opportunity of joining it. We know that he became a fellow of St John's College, Cambridge, in 1560–1, a mathematical examiner in 1565–6 and an MD in 1569. In that year he would have been twenty-nine years of age and considered to have reached full maturity. Being in the same year elected a senior fellow of St John's, he could therefore be said to have settled on a life within academia. However, having attained his fellowship, he almost immediately left England and went to Europe (probably Germany) for several years. It appears to have been during this time abroad that he was awarded his PhD – though at what institution is unknown – and began practising as a physician. He returned to England in 1573 and was immediately elected a member of the Royal College of Physicians. He was clearly highly regarded in his new profession as a doctor, for he held many important offices for the society, eventually becoming its president in 1600, and in 1601 he was appointed physician to the queen herself.

During nearly all of this time (1573–1601), Gilbert held regular meetings of his private college or society at his house in Colchester. What was discussed at these meetings is unknown. However, given Gilbert's own interests as a mathematician, physician and experimental scientist, one would assume that its general purpose was the study of natural philosophy. Gilbert himself was certainly interested in chemistry, which in those days was not distinct from alchemy. Indeed, this was a necessary prerequisite for a physician, for at that time there were no high-street chemists and prescription remedies had to be prepared by hand – usually by the physician himself. However, what distinguished Gilbert from most of the alchemists of his day, who were sometimes referred to rather disparagingly as 'Geber's Cooks' after a celebrated Spanish alchemist of the fourteenth century, was his scientific attitude of mind. First and foremost he was an experimentalist, and he was one of the first scientists – if not the first – to make use of the inductive method of reasoning. Gilbert's *De Magnete* was the first modern textbook on the subjects of electricity and magnetism. It contained details of his numerous experiments into the properties of iron, lodestone and amber, and put forth the then novel theory that the earth is itself a gigantic magnet. In breaking new ground by using experimental observation and inductive reasoning rather than falling back on the old Aristotelian logic, he was in the vanguard of enlightenment thinking.

For men of Gilbert's interests, private groups had hitherto been the only way of meeting like-minded individuals for discussion and experimentation; but at the time he was writing, the idea of a more open London-based college for the study of science was in the air. During the Tudor period there emerged a new merchant class for whom trade was not a dirty word. One of the most active of these new merchants was Sir Thomas Gresham, who in 1551 had been appointed 'King's Merchant', that is to say royal agent, at Antwerp. At that time England was suffering from a decline in exports of textile goods to what had traditionally been one of its strongest markets. Gresham realized that the key to commercial success was stability in the value of money, and that this ultimately depended on confidence that obligations would be met. As manager of the royal debt he made sure that payments were made on time and in the amount expected. As a result, first Mary's and later Elizabeth's credit was held in such high regard that they could borrow in Antwerp at highly advantageous rates. With his own stock also riding high as a result, Gresham was able to undermine the privileged position then held by the Hanseatic League in British–European trade and to acquire a new monopoly for the Merchant Adventurers' Company, of which he was a member. This arrangement proved to be highly beneficial both to the exchequer and to Gresham himself. As a result he became an extremely wealthy man. However, even the wealthy cannot stay the hand of the grim reaper. His son Richard died in 1564 and his daughter, Anne, who was married to Nathaniel Bacon (half-brother of Sir Francis) also died young. Thus it was that when Sir Thomas came to write (or rewrite) his will in 1575, he had no direct heirs to consider and was able to put the bulk of his estate to philanthropic purpose.

Much to the annoyance of his more distant relatives, Gresham stipulated in his will that, following his widow's death, his house near Bishopsgate, in the heart of the City of London, was to be turned into a college.[3] This institution, unique for its time, was to be independent of the already existing universities of Oxford and Cambridge. With a foresight rare among businessmen of this period, Gresham realized that one of the things holding England back as a trading nation was the poor standard of education of the merchant classes. At that time the universities were largely geared to the study of the classics: Latin and Greek. Oxford and Cambridge might be among the best centres of scholarship in the world, but unfortunately what they taught was almost irrelevant to the world of commerce. Latin and Greek were all well and good for the training of lawyers and ministers of the church, but a classically based education made a poor foundation for business. Moreover, taking time out from life to spend as a student was a luxury that could be afforded by only a small section of the populace. Gresham realized that what was needed was an institution in London that would offer lectures that anyone could attend. In this way the general level of education of the ordinary people, on whom so much depended, could be raised. Then both they and business would benefit.

In ancient times the matter of study had been divided into seven 'liberal arts': grammar, logic, rhetoric, arithmetic, geometry, music and astronomy. With some variations, these arts were to be represented by the seven faculties at Gresham College; however, right from the start the emphasis was to be on practical knowledge as opposed to sophistry and purely theoretical argumentation. For example, knowledge of astronomy was linked with navigation by the stars and was therefore a subject that would prove very useful for sailors taking British goods overseas. Knowledge of rhetoric could be helpful in developing the skills of business negotiation. Geometry was – and indeed still is – the basis of architecture, and was therefore a requirement for progressing beyond the most basic levels of the building trade. For anyone embarking on a career in business, a sound knowledge of numbers, of rhetoric and of navigation would be of more use than Latin and Greek literature. It was on this basis that Gresham College was to be set up.

Sir Thomas Gresham died very suddenly in 1579, but the college was not brought into being for a further eighteen years. Sir Thomas had stated in his will that Gresham House should continue to be his wife's home for as long as she lived; only after her death would it provide premises for the new college. As it turned out his widow, Dame Anne Gresham, proved to be made of sterner stuff than her husband and remained in occupation of the house for a further seventeen years until her own passing in 1596. So Gresham College finally opened its doors to students for the first time at the end of 1597. The will had stipulated that a further portion of Gresham's estate, including revenue from the Royal Exchange, was to be put into a trust fund to pay for the upkeep of the college and to provide salaries for its resident professors. There were to be seven of these at any given time, and each was to receive an annual salary of £50, which in those days was a considerable amount of money. Furthermore, each professor was to be provided with chambers inside the college where he would live as well as give private instruction to students. In exchange for such beneficence, the professors had to remain unmarried (a stipulation common to the universities at the time, which caused little grief as most professors were also clerics) and to give three hours of lectures a week.

There was no shortage of willing candidates for the new professorships. Queen Elizabeth herself recommended that Sir John Bull, from her Chapel Royal, be offered the chair in music. He was duly appointed, along with six other professors: Edward Brerewood (astronomy), Matthew Gwinne (physic), Caleb Willis (rhetoric), Anthony Wotton (divinity), Henry Briggs (geometry) and Henry Mountlow (law). The inaugural lecture was delivered by Dr Bull on 6 October 1597 and the college was declared open.

Sir Thomas Gresham's intention was that his college should act as a catalyst in raising the standard of education among the ordinary people of London: the clerks, sailors, shopkeepers and the like who made up the bulk of the city's working population. For this reason the public lectures were to be free of charge, and he expected that, when not so engaged, his professors would take delight in giving private tuition to their part-time students. All this would be done under the watchful yet benevolent eyes of the Corporation of London and the Mercers' Company, his own trade guild, who were made joint trustees of the college. However, as things turned out, it very soon became clear that the ideal and the reality were two different beasts. The professors, far from delighting in sharing their knowledge with the hoi polloi of London, found even three hours a week of lecturing irksome. They therefore demanded – and received – a cut in hours to a more manageable two, to be given on only one day in the week. At the same time, willing students proved harder to find than had been imagined. The ordinary folk of London, tired from their work in the docks and sweatshops of the city, were more interested in the customary pleasures of life. Far from clamouring to hear lectures on the intricacies of geometry and rhetoric, in their free time they were to be found in the taverns, theatres and bear-gardens that made London a tolerable city in which to live. Thus all too often the Gresham professors would find themselves lecturing to just one or two students and sometimes even to an empty room.

It would be easy to brand Gresham College as a failure in that, contrary to its founder's wishes, it did little to raise the educational standard of the ordinary people of London. However, on another level it had a profound impact on London society that ultimately was to have ramifications well beyond Sir Thomas's wildest imaginings. For although the public lectures were poorly attended and the professors seem to have done little in the way of private instruction, the college nevertheless provided a forum and a focal point for learning in the city of London. The extraordinary freedom of study enjoyed by the Gresham professors – a freedom untrammelled by the traditions associated with the ancient universities – provided an opportunity for young men of talent, in the early days of their academic careers, to experiment with new ideas. Moreover, the practical curriculum and outlook of the new college favoured the study of science, then in its infancy. Because of these factors Gresham College very quickly became a major centre of advanced learning and a point of focus for enlightenment thinking.

Of the early Gresham professors, none better exemplifies this modern attitude to science than John

Greaves, who was appointed Gresham Professor of Geometry in 1630. Like many of his generation he was in favour of the new astronomy pioneered by Copernicus, Kepler and Galileo; and, like these masters, he realized that this new science depended on careful observation of the heavens. A lunar eclipse was expected in 1638 and it was calculated that the best place to view it would be in the Middle East. Accordingly, in 1637, with sponsorship from William Laud, the archbishop of Canterbury (who hoped Gresham would bring back some valuable Arabic manuscripts), he sailed for Egypt. While there he took the opportunity of making a survey of the pyramids of Giza – the first European to do so since the days of the pharaohs.

That Greaves's primary motive in making this survey was connected with his own field of interest as Gresham Professor of Geometry cannot be doubted; for what could be more geometrical than a pyramid? Yet there does seem to have been a religious interest too in this survey of the pyramids. After all, it was generally believed by Christians that the Israelites had, as the Bible teaches, sojourned for a time in the land of Egypt. If so, then it seemed likely that evidence for this period of captivity might be found among the abundant ruins of the pyramids, and that study of these would therefore lend support to the Bible. This religious dimension to the Greaves expedition and its connection with the 'new science' is described in detail by Charles Piazzi Smyth in his nineteenth-century classic, *Our Inheritance in the Great Pyramid*:

Living as he did before the full birth of European science, but on the edge of an horizon which is eventful in scientific history; with an unusual knowledge too of Oriental languages, and a taste for travelling in the then turbulent regions of the East, Professor Greaves belongs to the almost heroic time. Immediately behind him were, if not the dark ages, the scholastic periods of profitless verbal disquisitions; and in front, to be revealed after his death, were the germs of the mechanical and physical natural philosophy which have since then changed the face of the world. There is no better a life-point that can be taken than Greaves's, whereby to judge what Europe has gained by the exercise of civil and religious liberty, coupled with the study of nature direct, through two and a half centuries of unrestricted opportunity. When as much more time has passed over the world as now separates us from Greaves's age, then, if not rather much sooner than then – say all the safest interpreters of the sacred prophecies – a further Divine, and hitherto un-exampled, step in the development of the Christian dispensation will have commenced.[4]

John Greaves's measurement of the outside of the Great Pyramid was inevitably not all that accurate, as at that time it was half-buried in sand. Nevertheless he did make a careful survey of the interior and brought back interesting data on the dimensions of the sarcophagus contained in the King's Chamber. He found that it measured ' "on the west side, six feet, and four hundred and eighty-eight parts of the English foot, divided into a thousand parts" (that is, 6 feet, and 488 of 1,000 parts of a foot); "in breadth at the north end, two feet, and two hundred and eighteen parts of the foot divided into a thousand parts" (that is, 2 feet, and 218 of 1,000 parts of the English foot). "The depth is

2 feet and 860 of 1,000 parts of the English foot." [5]

That he was able to make measurements with this sort of accuracy is less surprising than that he should have wanted to. For up until his visit to the pyramids in 1637, where geometry was concerned European commentators had been content merely to quote what had been written about them by Greek sages such as Strabo and Diodorus Siculus. These ancients had written that the length of the apotherm of the Great Pyramid (the distance from its apex to the centre of one of its sides) was exactly one stadium (600 feet). People either accepted or disputed this figure, but nobody had thought actually to go and measure the pyramid to see if this statement was true or false.

It was this new attitude to the material world – that it should be observed, and deductions made on the basis of these observations – which characterized the new age of science. John Greaves was an early exponent of this new attitude of enquiry, which was encouraged by the lenient atmosphere of Gresham College. In 1646, by which time he had moved on to become Savilian Professor of Astronomy at Oxford University, he published the results of his work at the pyramids in a book entitled *Pyramidographia*. By that time science was well rooted in England, the more so because it fitted with the prevailing philosophy. This philosophy, which underpinned this new thinking, was put into words by another remarkable Englishman (and probable Rosicrucian): Francis Bacon.

CHAPTER SEVEN

THE PROPHET OF SCIENCE

Following the invasions of Bohemia in 1620 and the onset of the Thirty Years War, the European mainland became a decidedly unsafe place for Protestant intellectuals. In Bohemia itself the leaders of the rebellion were executed and anyone else who had been involved with the cause had their lands confiscated. The former Emperor Rudolf's letter of majesty having been rescinded, Protestantism was outlawed and a wholesale programme of reconversion to Catholicism was put in train.

One of the people watching these events from the safety of England was Francis Bacon, Baron Verulam. A man of extraordinary talent, he is thought by some to have been the real author of Shakespeare's plays as well as of the first two Rosicrucian manifestos.[1] Whatever the truth behind these rumours – and, even assuming he could maintain his anonymity, it seems scarcely possible that he could have found the time to write the collected works of Shakespeare – his known achievements were monumental. The youngest son of Sir Nicholas Bacon, Queen Elizabeth's Lord Keeper of the Great Seal of England, by his second wife Anne, he was born in 1561 into elevated circles. However, his promising career as a courtier received a setback when his father died suddenly in 1579. For whatever reason, Francis was not included in his father's will and suddenly found himself without any inheritance. Thrown back on his own resources, he entered the legal profession while at the same time pursuing a parliamentary career. In both these ventures he was successful, being elected Member of Parliament in 1581 and graduating from Gray's Inn in 1582.

As a lawyer Bacon was outstanding, rising to the level of Reader in 1586 and Double Reader in 1600. His political career, though, was slower to take off, mainly owing to his opposition in Parliament to the Queen's demands for additional taxes. However, Elizabeth, who no doubt recognized that such a talented young man could be of use to her, seems eventually to have forgiven him his reluctance to fund her, and in 1596 he was given the honorific title of Queen's Counsel Extraordinary. In this post he found himself having to prosecute his erstwhile friend and patron, the earl of Essex, who was tried for treason following his abortive uprising of 1601. It is said that Essex might have got away with his head had not Bacon made such a brilliant speech summing up his guilt before the court. Later the queen, who suffered some unpopularity among the people for putting to death their hero, ordered Bacon to write an official account of the proceedings. He must have felt guilty about his role in all of this, for after Elizabeth's death he published a self-defence for his role in the trial and execution of Essex.

Bacon's career as a politician really took off after James I came to the throne in 1603. James, himself a legally minded and suspicious man, obviously liked

Bacon, and the feeling seems to have been mutual; by this time Bacon was himself middle-aged and understood much about the foibles of royalty. Almost immediately he was knighted, and other honours were to follow. In 1617 he was appointed Lord Keeper of the Seal (the post once occupied by his father) and the following year he was promoted to the position of Lord Chancellor. For this dignity he was shortly after raised to the peerage as Baron Verulam. Four years later, in 1621, his political star reached its apogee when he was created the first Viscount St Albans.

Bacon's portraits show him to have been quite a handsome man, with a poised and noble bearing. However, his face also betrays a steely determination and the saturnine quality of intensity. It is the face of an intelligent thinker, but one perhaps somewhat lacking in warmth; clearly a man of ambition as well as ability – so it would be surprising if he had not made enemies on his rise to fame and fortune. As a lawyer – indeed the greatest lawyer – of Elizabethan England he set the rule of law above friendship, as can be seen in his treatment of the earl of Essex. This high-mindedness was bound to irritate less fastidious colleagues enjoying neither the advantages of high office nor the ability to achieve it. That he had the king's trust was his great fortune and he certainly served his monarch well. However, within a few months his enemies saw their chance to bring down the new viscount.

Bacon's fall from grace was meteoric. Just a few months after being created viscount he was tried and convicted in the House of Lords on charges of taking bribes in one of the lower courts – a common enough and more or less accepted practice at the time. Bacon admitted the offences. It has been suggested that he did

Fig. 23. Portrait of Francis Bacon. (From *The Advancement
and Proficiency of Learning*, 1640.)

203

so to protect others from attack, most notably King James himself. There may be some truth in this, for he seems to have retained the king's favour throughout the period of his tribulation. There was never any suggestion that Bacon had given special favours to those who had proffered gifts, which raises the possibility that there may have been an element of, if not blackmail, certainly revenge in the charges being brought. For a few days Bacon was imprisoned in the Tower of London, where he may have been haunted by the ghosts not just of Essex but also of Walter Raleigh, at whose trial he had been on the prosecuting team. Eventually he was dismissed from his high office of Lord Chancellor and ordered to pay a fine of £40,000 – a huge sum in those days. Though the fine was later commuted by the king and he received a partial pardon, the damage to Bacon's reputation from this scandal was irreparable. He retired from public life and he might have merited little more than a footnote in history were it not that throughout his busy life he had been engaged in another less profitable but ultimately more notable career: that of philosopher.

By any standards Francis Bacon's literary output was unusually large; and it is all the more extraordinary in that he was regularly publishing books of the most learned nature throughout his time in public office when he had many other important matters on his mind. His writings reveal that he was a philosopher of the first rank, to be considered the equal of such luminaries as Plato, Aristotle and Descartes. He was also a scientist with an interest in alchemy, still an accepted area of research for any gentleman of means, and a theatrical impresario, capable of staging complex and expensive masques. He was, in short, a Renaissance Man in every sense of the term.

It must have come as a surprise to his contemporaries to discover that this legally minded minister was so academically gifted. His most important work, first published in 1605, was *The Advancement of Learning*. This opus in two books set out a new agenda which was in effect a prospectus for the development of what was then called natural philosophy and we would know today as science. The work is dedicated to King James I and in form it reads like a private essay addressed to the king. The first book is largely a defence of knowledge against charges that too much of it leads to heresy and loss of faith. In this first volume, which is an anticipatory defence against criticism of what he is going to lay out for the reader in the second, Bacon shows what a skilled politician he was. Throughout he displays his wide knowledge of the classics, of history and of religion, while tactfully reminding his sovereign of the essential role played by philosophers in the guidance of kings. The general drift of the book can be seen in the following passage:

> To conclude therefore, let no man, upon a weak conceit of sobriety or an ill-applied moderation, think or maintain that a man can search too far or be too well studied in the book of God's word [the Bible] or in the book of God's works [Nature]; divinity or philosophy; but rather let men endeavour an endless progress or proficience in both; only let men beware that they apply both to charity, and not to swelling; to use and not to ostentation; and again, that they do not unwisely mingle or confound these learnings together.[2]

Bacon knew that he needed the support of James if

his written works were to have any sort of practical impact; and to gain this support he needed to assure the king of his own devout intentions. The general proposition asserted here, that you can't have too much learning, may seem an obvious statement to today's reader, but it is one that needed defending in times of religious and philosophical persecution.

Having demonstrated to the king in his first book that he has a thorough grasp of the sort of classical education then in vogue, in his second Bacon makes the radical proposition that it is now time to go further and advance knowledge into new fields of learning. He criticizes the learned of his day for simply recycling the same old information, gained by reading classical authors such as Aristotle, rather than extending the depth of knowledge into uncharted waters: 'For why should a few received authors stand up like Hercules' Columns, beyond which there should be no sailing or discovering, since we have so bright and benign a star as your Majesty to conduct and prosper us?'[3] This seems to be the secret message contained in the title page of the 1640 edition of *The Advancement of Learning*. At a superficial level it salutes the twin obelisks of Oxonium (Oxford) and Cantabrigia (Cambridge), which stand on plinths made from Bacon's books and between which is slung a banner giving the title of this new book. However, at a deeper level these august institutions are being lampooned as the 'Pillars of Hercules' beyond which his ship sails to lands of knowledge as yet unchartered.

Bacon saw the need for practical, financial support for men of learning if colleges were to attract and retain the best men. This he perceived as a vital necessity not just to these institutions themselves but to the life of the

Fig. 24. Title page from *The Advancement and Proficiency of Learning*, 1640 edition.

nation as a whole. He therefore respectfully requests the king that he should set aside funds with which to endow laboratories of science, pointing out that there is a need not just for books but also for practical apparatuses in the pursuit of knowledge.

But certain it is that unto the deep, fruitful, and operative study of many sciences, specially natural philosophy and physic, books be not only the instrumentals; wherein also the beneficence of men hath not been altogether wanting; for we see spheres, globes, astrolabes, maps, and the like, have been provided as appurtenances to astronomy and cosmography, as well as books: we see likewise that some places instituted for physic have annexed the commodity of gardens for simples [herbal essences] of all sorts, and do likewise command the use of dead bodies for anatomies. But these do respect but a few things. In general, there will hardly be any main proficience in the disclosing of nature, except there be some allowance for expenses about experiments; whether they be experiments appertaining to Vulcanus [i.e. Alchemy] or Daedalus [i.e. Mechanics], furnace or engine, or any other kind; and therefore as secretaries and spials of princes and states bring in bills for intelligence, so you must allow the spials and intelligencers of nature to bring in their bills, or else you shall be ill advertised.[4]

What James made of this direct request for money to fund scientific laboratories can only be guessed. Certainly the king liked to think of himself as a very well-read and learned monarch; and, despite his fear of witchcraft, or anything else that smelled of magic, he was very interested in alchemy and possessed a considerable library on the subject. The idea of his funding a research institute for the furtherance of chemical studies might therefore not have been out of the question. In any case his high regard for Francis Bacon meant that he would have taken seriously from him ideas on the advancement of science that he would not have entertained from anyone else.

Throughout his life, Bacon was an opponent of orthodoxy with regard to science. Like Giordano Bruno, who in 1583 had visited Oxford and disputed natural philosophy with the professors there, he was not a supporter of Aristotelianism. He believed, quite rightly, that the prevalent attitude of treating the works of this long dead Greek as though they were holy writ was one of the factors holding back science. Aristotle's treatises on science came to be called the *Organon* or 'instrument' of scientific reasoning. This was the scientific Bible as far as medieval philosophers were concerned and, as Bruno had found to his cost, it was a kind of heresy to disagree with what was contained therein. In 1620 Bacon directly challenged the Aristotelian orthodoxy by publishing a work of his own entitled *Novum Organon*, planned as part of a larger work, never completed, entitled *The Great Instauration* (reformation). Once more Bacon's dedication to King James is revealing both of his intentions and of the great care he took to make sure he was not treading on any royal toes in attempting such a radical work:

MOST SERENE AND MIGHTY KING:
Your majesty will, perhaps, accuse me of theft, in that I have stolen from your employments time sufficient for this work. I have no reply, for there can be no

restitution of time, unless, perhaps, that which has been withdrawn from your affairs might be set down as devoted to the perpetuating of your name and to the honour of your age, were what I now offer of any value. It is at least new, even in its very nature; but copied from a very ancient pattern, no other than the world itself, and the nature of things, and of the mind. I myself (ingenuously to confess the truth) am wont to value this work rather as the offspring of time than of wit. For the only wonderful circumstance in it is, that the first conception of the matter, and so deep suspicions of prevalent notions should ever have entered into any person's mind; the consequences naturally follow. But, doubtless, there is a chance, (as we call it,) and something as it were accidental in man's thoughts, no less than in his actions and words. I would have this chance, however, (of which I am speaking,) to be so understood, that if there be any merit in what I offer, it should be attributed to the immeasurable mercy and bounty of God, and to the felicity of this your age; to which felicity I have devoted myself whilst living with the sincerest zeal, and I shall, perhaps, before my death have rendered the age a light unto posterity, by kindling this new torch amid the darkness of philosophy. This regeneration and instauration of the sciences is with justice due to the age of a prince surpassing all others in wisdom and learning. There remains for me but to make one request, worthy of your majesty, and very especially relating to my subject, namely, that, resembling Solomon as you do in most respects, in the gravity of your decisions, the peacefulness of your reign, the expansion of your heart, and, lastly, in the noble variety of books you have composed, you would further imitate the same monarch in procuring the compilation and completion of a Natural and Experimental History, that shall be genuine and rigorous, not that of mere philologues, and serviceable for raising the superstructure of philosophy, such, in short, as I will in its proper place describe: that, at length, after so many ages, philosophy and the sciences may no longer be unsettled and speculative, but fixed on the solid foundation of a varied and well considered experience. I for my part have supplied the instrument, the matter to be worked upon must be sought from things themselves. May the great and good God long preserve your majesty in safety.

Your majesty's

Most bounden and devoted,

FRANCIS VERULAM, Chancellor[5]

In his preface to the book he spells out his new approach to science, which is to involve a radical overhaul of the ancient Greek legacy:

It appears to me that men know not either their acquirements or their powers, and trust too much to the former, and too little to the latter. Hence it arises that, either estimating the arts they have become acquainted with at an absurd value, they require nothing more, or forming too low an opinion of themselves, they waste their powers on trivial objects, without attempting any thing to the purpose. The sciences have thus their own pillars, fixed as it were by fate, since men are not roused to penetrate beyond them either by zeal or hope: and inasmuch as an imaginary plenty mainly contributes to a dearth, and from a reliance upon present assistance, that which will really hereafter aid us is neglected, it becomes useful, nay, clearly necessary, in the very outset of our work, to remove, without any circumlocution or concealment, all excessive conceit and admiration of our actual state of knowledge, by this wholesome warning not to exaggerate or boast of its extent or utility. For, if any one look more attentively into that vast variety of books which the arts and sciences are so proud of, he will everywhere discover innumerable repetitions of the same thing, varied only by the method of treating it, but anticipated in invention; so that although at first sight they appear numerous, they are found, upon examination, to be but scanty. And with regard to their utility I must speak plainly. That philosophy of ours which we have chiefly derived from the Greeks, appears to me but the childhood of knowledge, and to possess the peculiarity of that age, being prone to idle loquacity, but weak and unripe for generation; for it is fruitful of controversy and barren of effects . . . Besides, if these sciences were not manifestly a dead letter, it would never happen, as for many ages has been the case in practice, that they should adhere almost immovably to their original footing, without acquiring a growth worthy of mankind: and this so completely, that frequently not only an assertion continues to be an assertion, but even a question to be a question, which, instead of being solved by discussion, becomes fixed and encouraged; and every system of instruction successively handed down to us brings upon the stage the characters of master and scholar, not those of an inventor and one capable of adding some excellence to his inventions. But we see the contrary happen in the mechanical arts. For they, as if inhaling some life-inspiring air, daily increase, and are brought to perfection; they generally in the hands of the inventor

212

appear rude, cumbrous, and shapeless, but afterwards acquire such additional powers and facility, that sooner may men's wishes and fancies decline and change, than the arts reach their full height and perfection. Philosophy and the intellectual sciences on the contrary, like statues, are adored and celebrated, but are not made to advance: nay, they are frequently most vigorous in the hands of their author, and thenceforward degenerate.[6]

In place of the endless repetition of old knowledge taken from the classics, Bacon proposed a new science based on observation and experiment. This he compares with the freeing of navigation once men had discovered the use of the magnetic compass.

To sum up, therefore, our observations, neither reliance upon others, nor their own industry, appear hitherto to have set forth learning to mankind in her best light, especially as there is little aid in such demonstrations and experiments as have yet reached us. For the fabric of this universe is like a labyrinth to the contemplative mind, where doubtful paths, deceitful imitations of things and their signs, winding and intricate folds and knots of nature everywhere present themselves, and a way must constantly be made through the forests of experience and particular natures, with the aid of the uncertain light of the senses, shining and disappearing by fits. But the guides who offer their services are (as has been said) themselves confused, and increase the number of wanderings and of wanderers. In so difficult a matter we must despair of man's unassisted judgement, or even of any casual good fortune: for neither the excellence of wit, however great, nor the die of experience, however frequently cast, can overcome such disadvantages. We must guide our steps by a clue, and the whole path, from the very first perceptions of our senses, must be secured by a determined method. Nor must I be thought to say, that nothing whatever has been done by so many and so much labour; for I regret not our discoveries, and the ancients have certainly shown themselves worthy of admiration in all that requires either wit or abstracted meditation. But, as in former ages, when men at sea used only to steer by their observations of the stars, they were indeed enabled to coast the shores of the Continent, or some small and inland seas; but before they could traverse the ocean and discover the regions of the new world, it was necessary that the use of the compass, a more trusty and certain guide on their voyage, should be first known; even so, the present discoveries in the arts and sciences are such as might be found out by meditation, observation, and discussion, as being more open to the senses and lying immediately beneath our common notions: but before we are allowed to enter the more remote and hidden parts of nature, it is necessary that a better and more perfect use and application of the human mind and understanding should be introduced.[7]

Although Bacon's 'instauration' of the sciences seems quite tame to us today, used as we are to a scientific method based on observation, hypothesis and the elucidation of natural laws, at the time he was writing these were radical ideas. It seems likely that at that time, such a book could have been published in no other country and perhaps by few other individuals without the author endangering both life and reputation – indeed, we have seen how previous attempts in Europe had met with calamity.

Nor does Bacon's significance end here; for his writings extended well beyond the philosophy of science. His last book, published posthumously in 1626 along with his alchemical work *Sylva Sylvarum*, concerns a utopian vision for the ideal society of the future. It is a work of fiction that in part is clearly intended to be a satire upon both Plato's *Timaeus* and Thomas More's *Utopia*. Entitled *The New Atlantis*, it tells the story of some sailors who, caught in a storm while sailing the South Pacific, stumble upon a hitherto unknown island called Bensalem. There is in this name a cryptic meaning. In the Bible *Salem* is the name of the city of the priest-king Melchizedek, who gave gifts and blessed Abraham (Gen. 15: 18–20). This city was later renamed Jerusalem. *Ben* is Hebrew for 'son'; thus Bensalem means 'son of Salem', i.e. the New Jerusalem.

The sailors who arrive at the island discover that the natives are not only friendly and hospitable but extremely knowledgeable, both about science and about the world around them. They explain that though their island home is unknown to contemporary Europeans, whose navigational skills have only recently become of such a standard that they are able to make such long journeys, it was visited frequently in the past by Phoenicians, Carthaginians, Chinese, ancient Egyptians, Persians and others. Also, in those former times they themselves regularly made long voyages, even as far as the Pillars of Hercules and the Mediterranean Sea. Indeed, before the great inundation (Noah's Flood), they also traded with the peoples of 'Atlantis'.

The story told in *The New Atlantis* seems quaint to

us today but it has to be remembered that when Bacon was writing it was still less than a hundred years since Cortes and Pizarro had made their famous conquests of Mexico and Peru. Like most Europeans of his day, Bacon equates the lost continent of Atlantis with these exotic civilizations of Central and South America. Tales of these strange lands, with their gold, their fabulous cities, their stepped pyramids, their colourfully dressed natives and their strange, hieroglyphic texts, captivated audiences throughout Europe. Though by the early seventeenth century America itself – at least, Mexico and Peru – was fairly well charted, the South Pacific was still a *terra incognita*. Another century and more would have to pass before Captain Cook would make his epic voyage, during which he visited many islands of the South Pacific as well as Australia. So there was every reason for Bacon to suppose that there might be islands in the Pacific every bit as civilized as Mexico and Peru. Since nobody knew any better, he could also fantasize that the islanders who lived in these semi-mythical realms were not only civilized but virtuous. In short he could, like Plato, invent a fantasy world where people actually lived according to the ideals he himself espoused.

The islanders of Bacon's fantasy are the very antithesis of the bloodthirsty Aztecs, whose large-scale human sacrifices so shocked the Spanish conquistadors. Nor are they imperialists like the power-hungry marauders of Plato's Atlantis. On the contrary, they shun contact with the rest of the world so that they may better live according to the laws of God. If not actually Christians in a recognized sense, they are at least people of the book, the Old and the New Testaments having been brought to them in a miraculous way in an ark.

The laws of their society, however, were framed for them by a 'King Salomona', who established among them a noble order or society named 'Salomon's House', a college analogous to the Rosicrucian society of the *Fama* pamphlet.

At this point Bacon moves on from his simple tale of an exotic paradise to enumerate the real message of his book: the need for an order of scientists, analogous to that of the Garter knights or Templars, to elucidate and unravel the mysteries of nature. The society of Salomon's House, he writes, is based upon the ideals of King Solomon's temple – Solomon being the archetype of the wise king:

Ye shall understand (my dear friends) that amongst the excellent acts of that king [Salomona], one above all hath the pre-eminence. It was the erection and institution of an Order or Society which we call 'Salomon's House'; the noblest foundation (as we think) that ever was upon the earth; and lanthorn of this kingdom. It is dedicated to the study of the Works and Creatures of God. Some think it beareth the founder's name a little corrupted, as if it should be Salamona's House. But the records write it as it is spoken. So as I take it to be denominate of the King of the Hebrews, which is famous with you, and no stranger to us. For we have some parts of his works which with you are lost; namely, that Natural History which he wrote, of all plants, from the 'cedar of Libanus' to the 'moss which groweth out of the wall', and of all 'things that have life and motion'. This maketh me think that our king, finding himself to symbolize in many things with that king of Hebrews (which lived many years before him), honoured him with the title of this foundation. And I am rather induced to be of this opinion, for that I find in ancient records this Order of Society is sometimes called Salomon's House and sometimes the College of the Six Days Works; whereby I am satisfied that our excellent king had learned from the Hebrews that God had created the world and all that therein is within six days; and therefore he instituting that House for the finding out of the true nature of all things (whereby God might have the more glory in the workmanship of them, and men the more fruit in the use of them) did give it also that second name.[8]

Bacon's linking of his ideal society of initiates with King Solomon has a purpose. In the Bible, Solomon is the personification of the wise king whose judgement is based on a deep understanding not just of the law but of human nature. This is no accident, for Solomon, when given an opportunity to ask God for any gift, chose wisdom.

In Gibeon the Lord appeared to Solomon in a dream by night: and God said, Ask what I shall give thee. And Solomon said, Thou hast showed unto thy servant David my father great mercy, according as he walked before thee in truth, and in righteousness, and in uprightness of heart with thee; and thou hast kept for him this great kindness, that thou hast given him a son to sit on his throne, as it is this day.

And now Oh Lord my God, thou hast made thy servant king instead of David my father: and I am but a little child: I know not how to go out or come in. And thy servant is in the midst of thy people which thou hast chosen, a great people, that cannot be numbered nor counted for multitude. Give therefore thy servant an understanding heart to judge thy people, that I may discern between good and bad: for who is able to judge this thy so great a people?

And the speech pleased the Lord, that Solomon had asked this thing. And God said to him, Because thou hast asked this thing, and hast not asked for thyself long life: neither hast asked riches for thyself, nor hast asked the life of thine enemies; but hast asked for thyself understanding to discern judgement; Behold I have done according to thy words: lo I have given thee a wise and an understanding heart; so that there was none like thee before thee, neither after thee shall any arise like unto thee. And I have also given thee that which thou hast not asked, both riches and honour: so that there shall not be any amongst the kings like unto thee all thy days. And if thou wilt walk in my ways, to keep my statutes and my commandments, as thy father David did walk, then I will lengthen thy days.

And Solomon awoke; and behold it was a dream. And he came to Jerusalem, and stood before the ark of the covenant of the Lord, and offered up burnt offerings, and offered peace offerings, and made a feast to all his servants. (1 Kgs 3: 5–15)

This story of Solomon, who put wisdom before riches that he might better judge the people, would obviously have had a strong appeal to a lawyer like Bacon who was himself Lord Chancellor of England. Yet it is clear that Bacon refers to the House of Solomon in *The New Atlantis* for another, more practical reason: for did not this king of Israel build the first Temple at Jerusalem? For the many Britons who believed they were descended from the lost tribes of

Israel – and perhaps we should count Bacon as well as James I in their number – this would have been a very important event. And, as we have seen, in his dedication to *The Great Instauration* Bacon makes flattering comparisons between James and Solomon.

Reading along these lines, we begin to understand that Bacon's allegorical island of Bensalem, 'Son of [Jeru]Salem', is not really to be understood as an unknown island in the Pacific; rather, it is Britain itself, the gathering place of the lost tribes of Israel and itself believed to be the son of Jerusalem. The wise king Salomona, who in *The New Atlantis* is said to have framed the laws of Bensalem, is intended to be symbolic of James I himself. This being so, the 'House of Salomon', where the wise gather to study the laws of nature, is perhaps symbolic of an existing but secret college with King James as its royal master.

Bacon's ideal of a scientific society linked to the 'House of Salomon' is strikingly similar to that of the Rosicrucian Order as presented in the *Fama* and *Confessio* – indeed so much so that many people believe him to have been if not the actual author, then certainly the instigator of these pamphlets. There is some substance in these charges. His utopian scientific society, which he calls Salomon's House, is very similar to, though not identical with, the invisible college of the Rosicrucians, whose ideals are the advancement of learning and healing of the sick. It is clear that Bacon, if not the author of the *Fama*, had at least studied it. That these allusions were understood by his near contemporaries is indicated by the work of a later Rosicrucian author, John Heydon, who in a plagiarized work of 1662 went so far as to rewrite parts of Bacon's *New Atlantis*. In this work, *The Holy Guide*, he makes it quite clear that Bacon's House of Salomon is to be understood as the secret college of the Rosicrucians. Yet at the time Bacon was writing there was already such an institution in existence of exactly the type he was describing: Gresham College. And this college was not on some remote island of the south Pacific but in the very heart of London itself.

For Bacon's patron, James I, the whole idea of a 'House of Solomon' would have had an even deeper and more esoteric interest. For James not only believed that he himself was linearly descended from the biblical kings David and Solomon, but knew that Scotland was home to later mysteries surrounding the latter's temple. As we have seen, there is a strong tradition that the Battle of Bannockburn, which secured Scotland's independence from England, was won with the help of the Knights Templar. It is also rumoured that the Knights Templar brought with them to Scotland a treasure beyond price. What this may have been is shrouded in mystery, but there are clues that this rumour is not entirely without basis. According to Christopher Knight and Robert Lomas, the chapel at Rosslyn in Scotland had a secret purpose that connects it with Solomon's Temple. As we saw in chapter 3, this chapel had been built by a Sir William Sinclair (or St Clair), a descendant of the Sir William Sinclair who, as Grand Master of the Scottish Templars, had fought at Bannockburn. The later Sir William had died in 1484 and there seems little doubt that he was himself also a Grand Master of the Templars or some successor organization. His chapel at Rosslyn, the building of which seems to have occupied him greatly, is one of the most mysterious buildings in Scotland and still has a haunting presence about it. It does not seem to have functioned as a church in the normally accepted sense of the word. For one thing, it contained no altar and had little in the way of Christian imagery. Today it is in a ruinous state, but even this is deceptive. For, according to Knight and Lomas, it always was a ruin. The 'chapel' was part of a 'building' that was never intended should be completed.

> Another point that has puzzled historians was the fact that the 'chapel' was never finished and was 'clearly intended as the first section of a much larger and grander building – a major cathedral'. There is no known reason why the St Clair family should have suddenly stopped building and forget the forty-five-year-old project if it had been their intention to build a collegiate church. Yet the west wall is huge, totally incompatible with the rest of the structure and very obviously incomplete . . . To all intents and purposes it looks like a ruin of a much larger structure, except that it is known that there never was one.[9]

Knight and Lomas are convinced that the Rosslyn chapel, which does not seem even to have been consecrated as a church before 1862, was intended to be a recreation of the ruined Temple of Jerusalem.

> Thinking about it, it would have been strange to complete a small chapel if the intention was to built a great medieval church; and a cathedral in the middle of nowhere at that. The west wall is incomplete and the obvious natural conclusion is that it was never finished – but there is another reason why single walls remain; they are the remains of a ruined cathedral, or more precisely in this case *a ruined temple* . . . The Rosslyn

shrine was completed exactly to plan; there never was any intention of building further because the huge west wall is a carefully executed reconstruction of Herod's Temple that the Knights Templar first entered in their exploration in Jerusalem in AD 1118.[10]

The idea that the Sinclairs were in possession of certain secrets connected with the Templars and that William Sinclair constructed Rosslyn Chapel as a replica of the ruined Temple of Jerusalem is perfectly plausible. As we also saw in chapter 3, the so-called Kirkwall Scroll, which resides in a masonic lodge in the Orkneys, has a connection with the Knights Templar; moreover, this scroll has now been carbon-dated to the fifteenth century, the period when the chapel at Rosslyn was built and when the Sinclairs were earls of Orkney. According to Knight and Lomas, a later still Sir William Sinclair – one living at the time of James I – was the first elected Grand Master of the Grand Lodge of Scotland.[11] If this is so, then the implication is clear for all to see. The Freemasons, via the Sinclairs, very likely do possess secrets dating back to the Templars; and these in the main probably concern discoveries made by the members of the order while they were living at the Al-Aqsa Mosque on top of the Temple Mount of Jerusalem.

Knight and Lomas believe that the first Sir William Sinclair concealed certain scrolls in the crypt at Rosslyn. These, they believe, were originally the possession of the Templars, having been found by them during their excavations on the Temple Mount. Unfortunately, more recent investigations of the crypt have found no evidence to support this hypothesis. However, though today the crypt would appear to be empty, this does not mean that it has always been so. It may be that whatever treasure was placed there at the time the chapel was built has since been moved to an even more secure location – perhaps even the Orkney Islands.

Rosslyn Chapel, with its Templar/masonic links, would have been well known to James I, who was, of course, king of Scotland prior to becoming king of England. Indeed, as we shall see later, there is strong evidence not only that James was knowledgeable about Freemasonry and its Scottish origins but that he was himself a Grand Master by royal prerogative. As such he would certainly have been regarded as a modern-day 'Solomon' to the brotherhood of his day. For though the United Grand Lodge of London was not inaugurated until 1717 – long after James's death – it is clear that a society of Freemasons already existed in Scotland during his lifetime. It would seem to have been James I, who took the English throne in 1603, who was responsible for bringing Freemasonry to England over a century before the founding of the United Grand Lodge of London. As Lord Chancellor, Francis Bacon would almost certainly have known of any affiliation James may have had with Freemasonry, and it is very likely that he was initiated himself. He would also have known that the Grand Master of Freemasons was said to sit on Solomon's seat. This explains all the references to Solomon in Bacon's written works and his flattering comparisons of James with this ancient king of Israel. It would appear, therefore, that the fictional 'House of Salomon' on the island of Bensalem was in reality no fiction at all. It was an oblique reference to a Masonic/Rosicrucian society that was already in existence in England. The likely identity of this organization is the subject of the next chapter.

CHAPTER EIGHT

REVOLUTION AND ENLIGHTENMENT

The defeat of Frederick, Count Palatine and king of Bohemia, at the Battle of the White Mountain in the winter of 1620 had serious repercussions throughout Europe. As the Austrians invaded Bohemia, the flower of that country's intelligentsia was either cut down or driven into exile. In Germany the Palatinate was invaded by a Spanish and Bavarian army under the command of the most famous general of his day, Ambrose Spinola. Heidelberg, formerly a great centre of learning, was sacked and its libraries despoiled. If the Austrians were hard on Bohemia, the Spanish and Bavarians were even worse in their determination to destroy the Palatinate. Yet these campaigns, as it turned out, were only the opening skirmishes of the Thirty Years War, which was conducted on both sides with grim savagery. This war was a great catastrophe for all of Europe but most especially for Germany, where up to a third of the population was killed either in the fighting or by the famines and diseases which followed in the train of occupying armies. In northern Europe it must at times have seemed that the flame of civilization itself, still less the delicate rosy flicker of enlightenment, was doomed to be extinguished. Yet this was not to be

– and the reason, once more, is to be found in England. For, though England too was to experience the unhappy event of a civil war and the repressive regime of Oliver Cromwell, throughout the 1620s and 1630s it was viewed as an oasis of calm amid the storms of religious hatred battering Europe. Indeed, English intellectual life not only survived but even grew stronger, in part at least because of an influx of refugee scholars and thinkers.

James I died in 1625. Never greatly loved by the English, who regarded him as uncouth, by the time of his death he was quite unpopular with all but a close clique at the court. Much of this unpopularity stemmed from his lack of support for his son-in-law Frederick during his time of need. The Protestant English could not understand how James could sit back and allow his own daughter to be driven from her homes in Bohemia and Heidelberg with hardly a murmur of disapproval. Still less could they appreciate the subtleties of a statescraft that in 1623 involved seeking an arranged marriage between his son and heir, Charles, and the Spanish Infanta Maria, the daughter of Philip III. This princess was not only a Catholic but a member of the family that had deposed Frederick and Elizabeth two years earlier. Such a union, were it to occur, could be expected to have devastating consequences for the Protestant cause, as any children born of the marriage would be brought up as Catholics. Thus English Catholics had every reason to hope and Protestants to fear that in the following generation Britain would be brought back under papal edict.

In the event, although a contract was signed, the marriage itself never actually took place; for although Charles, along with the duke of Buckingham, visited the court at Madrid with the intention of winning the hand of the infanta, the price demanded for such a marriage proved too high. Prince Charles was expected to convert to the Catholic faith immediately, which as far as the English were concerned was out of the question if he wanted to be their king. As a compromise, he promised that he would change the laws against Catholics within three years of his succeeding to the throne and that his children would be given a Catholic education up to the age of twelve. This, however, was not enough for the Spaniards, least of all the infanta herself, who was anyway not keen on the marriage.

Feeling slighted, Charles and Buckingham returned to England alone and set about their revenge. The following year, 1624, Charles was betrothed to Henrietta Maria, the daughter of King Henry IV of France, who was an arch-enemy of Spain. They married shortly after he ascended the throne in 1625, by which time, largely at Buckingham's instigation, England and Spain were once more at war. Even so, the British treated their young king with suspicion. When Charles asked Parliament to raise taxes so that he could better fight the war against Spain, the Commons refused to give him more than a paltry sum; rightly or wrongly, they suspected duplicity and trusted neither him nor Buckingham to use such money wisely in the interests of the Protestant English. Thus began a downward spiral that was to lead within a few years to a complete breakdown of relations between the king and the people of England.

In the meantime, in continental Europe ideas were moving apace. Francis Bacon's *Advancement of Learning* and *New Atlantis* had been deeply influential in the development of philosophy not just in England but throughout the Protestant world. As *The New Atlantis* shows, the trafficking of ideas was not all one way; it is clear from this treatise that Bacon had studied the Rosicrucian manifestos closely and used them in his exposition of a new utopian society. Indeed so similar to the Rosicrucian ideal of a philosophically led state are many of Bacon's ideas that many people believe him to have been the inspiration all along for the creation of the myth of Christian Rosencreutz. Certainly there are grounds for thinking that his New Atlantis with its 'House of Solomon' is to be understood as an allusion to the secret tomb of CRC as described in the *Fama*. Bacon himself never claimed openly to be the instigator of the Rosicrucian movement or even a member of a secret brotherhood; however, he had been an enthusiastic supporter of the alliance between Frederick of the Palatinate and the Princess Elizabeth, and had put on a masque at Gray's Inn in celebration of their marriage. In turn, the influence of his ideas on the Elector Palatine and his wife was profound. Under their rule Heidelberg developed as a working model of the sort of state Bacon was later to put forward as the ideal in *The Advancement of Learning*. Thus the stream of thought that Baconism represented in England was not merely sympathetic to Continental Rosicrucianism, in many ways it was identical with it. 'Rosicrucian' immigrants to England from Bohemia and the Palatinate were therefore to find in their place of refuge a better and in many ways more receptive environment than continental Europe in which to set about building the sort of utopian society of which they dreamed.

One scholar who did not escape the catastrophe now engulfing Germany was Michael Maier. Mention has already been made of one of his most famous works,

Fig. 25. The philosophic rose garden. (From Michael
Maier's *Atalanta Fugiens*.)

Atalanta Fugiens. Emblem 27 in this work would
appear to be a veiled reference to England, and more
especially London, as a place of sanctuary. It shows a
man standing before the bolted doorway of a rose
garden, emblematic of England whose flower has
always been the rose. Flowing from the garden is a
stream or moat in which the man stands ankle-deep as
he contemplates the padlocked door. These elements
make it clear that this rose garden is to be equated both
with the biblical garden of Eden (similarly locked after
the fall of Adam, and from which flowed four rivers)
and with the New Jerusalem, from which flows 'a pure

river of water of life, clear as crystal, proceeding out of the throne of God and of the lamb' (Rev. 22: 1). Behind the rose garden is a castle with cylindrical towers – reminiscent of Windsor, where the Knights of the Garter, one of whose symbols is also the rose of England, have their chapel. The enigmatic caption to this print is: 'He who tries to enter the Philosophic Rose-garden without a key is like a man wanting to walk without feet.'

That there were Rosicrucians active in England at this time is evidenced by the publication in 1629 of Robert Fludd's book *Summum Bonum*. This not only hints at the existence of a Rosicrucian school in England but publicizes it with an illustration that would have been understood by anyone with a knowledge of symbolism. At the centre of the picture is a very English-looking rose growing from a cross. Flying towards it is a bee and to the right of this is a beehive. The Latin caption to the picture is *Dat rosa mel apibus*: 'The rose gives honey to the bees.' As educated readers would have known, beehives symbolize places of learning and most especially esoteric schools. They are repositories of wisdom; the places to which the nectar of knowledge is brought back by the worker bees and where it is fermented to make honey. In this print the rose represents England and the hive with its bees the school of the Rosicrucians. Opposed to this, on the left-hand side of the picture is a framework trellis that carries a spider's web. In the context of the picture, this would seem to symbolize the Catholic powers of mainland Europe that in the 1620s were actively seeking to capture the Protestant bees to prevent them from joining the 'hive' in Britain.

As a Protestant island outside the jurisdiction of the

Catholic powers, Britain provided a safe haven for those Bohemian and Palatinate exiles who could escape across the Channel. One such émigré was Johann Amos Komensky, better known as Comenius, who arrived in England in 1622. Like many other Protestant intellectuals of his generation, he had been educated at Heidelberg University before going home to his native Bohemia. The last bishop of the Church of Moravia before its suppression by the Austrians, he was also an active member of a Protestant, philosophical and religious movement known as the 'Bohemian Brethren'. This was a mystical branch of the reforming movement going back to the time of Jan Huss, and it seems to have been the primary inspiration for the mythical Rosicrucian brotherhood described so cryptically in the *Fama* and *Confessio*.

In the years before war engulfed Bohemia and Germany, Comenius had been working on a system of Pansophia. Though his library was lost during the

Fig. 26. 'The Rose gives Honey to the Bees'.
(From *Summum Bonum* by Robert Fludd, 1629.)

troubles, his encyclopedia – probably the first book of its kind – was published in 1630 with the title *Pansophia prodromus*. Comenius was also ahead of his time when it came to the theory of education. Though he taught Latin and Greek, the most classical of classical subjects, he was not content with traditional teaching methods. He therefore devised a new system of instruction, based on the way children learn their own languages: through familiarity with objects and phrases rather than by studying formal grammar and syntax. This sort of forward thinking about educational technique was ahead of its time by several centuries and marked him out as a radical reformer. When Comenius crossed the Channel he brought with him an earnest attitude of scientific and mystical enquiry that was quite at home in the England of Francis Bacon.[1] His ideas on encyclopedism and teaching were to have a profound influence on the British.

Another important refugee was Samuel Hartlib, who came to England in 1628. For Hartlib, like many other European intellectuals, the developing reformist mood of society in England, if not exactly utopian, certainly represented a step in the right direction. Hartlib, and other 'Rosicrucian' thinkers like him, believed that a new age was dawning when governance would be founded on reason, and executive power, at present held in the hands of kings and their selected ministers, would be entrusted to democratically elected parliaments. This would be the citizens' guarantee of freedom and justice against the arbitrary whims of kings who were just as likely to be foolish as wise. In 1640 Hartlib wrote a book entitled *A Description of the famous Kingdom of Macaria*. A work of fiction in the genre of Francis Bacon's *New Atlantis*, it was addressed to the

232

English Parliament. In his book Hartlib heaped praise on this august institution, saying that it 'will lay the corner Stone of the world's happinesse before the final recesse thereof'. He could not have known it at the time, but these words would ring rather hollow a few years later when that same Parliament, reduced to a rump by Pride's Purge, would become itself an instrument of oppression. Even so, Britain's evolving model of democratic, parliamentary government was the way of the future and in due course it would be emulated across the globe.

Ironically, Charles I, who became king of England in 1625, had many qualities that were in harmony with the Rosicrucian ideal of a good ruler. He was a conscientious father and husband, appreciative of fine art, a lover of literature and a devout Christian. In less pressing times these virtues would have won him admiration. However, the mid-sixteenth century was a time of wars and revolution, and Charles was not an able politician. In him alongside his better features were also manifested all the worst traits of the Stuarts: vacillation, arrogance, weakness, deviousness and inconstancy towards friends. All too often, what he thought of as strength of mind was in reality simple stubbornness. Throughout his rule he was prone to taking up extreme positions regardless of all opposition. He did not believe in constitutional monarchy, but on the contrary had an absolute conviction that he had a divine right to govern his country as he saw fit. He failed to appreciate that while the crown itself might symbolize the majesty of God, the man wearing it was still only human and could properly govern only with the consent of the people. Unfortunately, he took a very narrow and literal interpretation of what it meant to be a king over 'Israel' in the line of David. In his eyes he was God's chosen instrument and it therefore followed that whatsoever he should decide was right for the country over which he ruled was beyond challenge. Such a tyrannical view of the role of a king might have worked for Henry VIII, who combined learning with a daunting physical presence; but a century later, such opinions seemed ridiculously out of place. Charles was no Henry; short on charisma, he was small in stature and retained a stammer all his life. He did not appreciate that, for all the rhetoric about God, Britain as Israel and the sanctity of monarchy, in reality the art of kingship depends on the love of the people or, failing that, on their fear.

In 1629 Charles dissolved Parliament, confining nine of its leading members to the Tower of London. But he still had need of money in order to fight wars – now not just against Spain but also in Germany. Without Parliament, which historically had vested in it the right to grant or withhold taxes, he now had to raise money by other means. The stealth taxes that he imposed – tonnage and poundage, fines for encroaching on royal property, and other even more underhand measures – further alienated people from all classes of society. Outside of England Charles was equally pig-headed. In Ireland he sought to impose a new form of feudalism, seizing whole estates, including those belonging to the City of London, in the name of the crown on the pretext that their charter deeds were not lawful. In Scotland he made the mistake of falling out of favour with the Calvinists by forcing on them high Anglican forms of worship that were not much different from the Roman Catholic. This led to riots and ultimately to rebellion.

To make matters worse, Charles was also duplicitous

in his foreign policy. In the late 1620s he discussed forming an alliance with King Gustavus Adolphus of Sweden, the champion of the Protestant cause in Europe. He even had King Gustavus, along with the Dutch prince of Orange, Henry Frederick von Nassau, elected to the august Order of the Garter. Part of what was at issue, of course, was how Frederick and Elizabeth, Charles's sister, should be restored to their rightful position in the Palatinate. For a time it looked as though an alliance of the Protestant powers of northern Europe might be a real possibility. Then, perhaps because these talks were not moving along fast enough, Charles went back on his word and instead of making a firm alliance with Sweden, he made peace with Spain. Taking this realignment a stage further, in 1630 he signed a treaty declaring that the English and Spanish together should make war on the Protestant Dutch. Under this new treaty the Netherlands were to be partitioned, with one part reverting to Spanish rule and the other being given to England. Needless to say this pact was totally at odds with public opinion in England, which supported the Protestant Dutch in their struggle for independence from Spain. Such a foreign policy, inimical to the proud traditions of Elizabeth I, was never going to win Charles friends at home and indeed played into the hands of his enemies. Nevertheless, Charles continued to support Frederick in his legal claims to be allowed to return to the Palatinate; and when, following Frederick's death in 1632, the claim and the 'pretender' title Count Palatine of the Rhine were taken over by his son, Prince Charles Louis, this prince too was duly elected to the Order of the Garter in place of his father.

In April 1641 Charles made a fundamental error: he

allowed his most loyal minister, Thomas Wentworth, earl of Strafford, to take the blame for failing to quell the Scottish rebellion which was by then gaining pace. The luckless minister was impeached by Parliament and Charles, albeit reluctantly, signed his death warrant. With that signature went his own credibility and honour. For, by treating this loyal minister and friend as a dispensable pawn that he could afford to sacrifice as he played the greater game, he left himself dangerously exposed. It was now only a matter of time before England too would rebel and he himself, like Strafford before him, would be taken to the executioner's block. The details of the English Civil Wars, the battles, sieges and retreats, do not concern us here. A more flexible king with better political judgement might have averted the disaster; but with Charles I on the throne the result was almost inevitable.

Charles I was executed for treason in Whitehall on 30 January 1649. To the very end he championed the right of kings to govern unimpeded by modern concepts of democracy. He assured the crowds gathered by the scaffold that he was not against the people having their freedom, but added: 'I must tell you that their liberty and freedom consists in having government . . . It is not their having a share in the government; that is nothing appertaining to them. A subject and a sovereign are clean different things.' Standing on the bare scaffold in his shirtsleeves and looking down at the block on which he was soon to stretch his neck, Charles had every reason to be scared. Yet history reports that he was remarkably composed on this most fateful of afternoons. Maybe he was contemplating his likely destiny amid the heavenly spheres. An educated man, he would have had ample time to study hermetic philosophy and it is very likely that he had read the following text which supports the notion that kings are higher beings than their subjects:

> And it comes to pass that other souls also are found to differ in quality; some are fiery and cold, some haughty and some meek, some skilful and some unskilful, some active and some inactive, and others differ in other ways. And these differences also result from the positions of the places whence the souls plunge down to be embodied. For those who have leapt down from a kingly zone reign upon earth as kings.[2]

As his head fell from his body, a groan rose from the crowd. For though Charles had been an unpopular king and had failed the people miserably, they had little stomach for regicide. Moreover, his death filled them with foreboding of what was to come: the protectorate of Oliver Cromwell.

In almost all ways Cromwell was the very antithesis of Charles I. A career politician from a modest background, he metamorphosed into the most formidable soldier of his generation. Under his command the parliamentarian troops, or New Model Army as they were called, became the best fighting force in Europe. As for Charles's 'Cavaliers', a rag-tag army of gentlemen equestrians and their retainers, though they won a few battles, in the long term they proved no match for the pike-bearing, breastplated 'Roundheads'. Yet, though reform of the monarchy was on his agenda, it had not originally been Cromwell's intention to execute the king. Indeed, if Charles had accepted that he must rule as a constitutional monarch through Parliament, he could have stayed on his throne and retained most if not all of his power. It was Charles's own reckless behaviour that was his undoing. For, in true Stuart fashion, he had sought to play his opponents one off against the other. His final and fatal move was his endorsement of a Scottish invasion of England after he himself had already lost to the forces of Parliament and was busy negotiating terms. Cromwell easily defeated the Scots at Preston and Charles was left with no other friends to hide behind. It was this act of treason, ostensibly against Parliament but really against the oligarchy now ruling Britain, that ultimately cost him his head.

Oliver Cromwell, the victor of the English Civil Wars, himself believed that he was the instrument of God's will, and may even have believed that it was his destiny to sit upon the throne. Like the Tudors he had Welsh connections, for his real family name was not Cromwell at all but rather Williams. His great-great-grandfather, Morgan Williams, had married the sister of Henry VIII's most ruthless minister, Thomas Cromwell. Like many of the Welsh gentry, Morgan could trace his line back to the pre-Norman kings of Glamorgan and through them back in time to the legendary Arthur, King of the Britons. Morgan's son Richard acted as his uncle Thomas Cromwell's agent and he it was who changed the family name from Williams to Cromwell. Even after the downfall of Thomas Cromwell, who was beheaded in 1540, the family, which had grown wealthy on the proceeds of looted abbeys and priories, continued to prosper. Though much of this wealth had been dissipated by the time Oliver came on to the scene, the Cromwells were still a major family in the county of Huntingdon. They were also fanatically Protestant.

238

According to Knight and Lomas, Oliver Cromwell was probably a senior Freemason.[3] For this reason, they say, he preserved Rosslyn Chapel from destruction at a time when the Puritans were defacing churches throughout the land. Cromwell seems also to have been a believer in Britain's special destiny as the latter-day Israel. Certainly this would explain why Sir Walter Scott, who was writing c.1800–32, makes reference to him in this context. In his novel *Woodstock*, set at the time of the English Civil War, he has Oliver Cromwell say: 'For surely he who hath been to our British Israel as a shield of help, and a sword of excellency, making her enemies be found liars unto her, he will not give over the flock to those foolish shepherds of Westminster, who shear the sheep and feed them not, and who are in very deed hirelings, not shepherds.'

Though the words put into Cromwell's mouth by Scott may be an invention, the sentiments they express are certainly in character. Having despatched the king and abolished the monarchy, Cromwell and his small band of fellow officers set about reforming Parliament. The House of Lords was also abolished, and the House of Commons, already reduced in December 1648 by Colonel Thomas Pride's purge of all royalist and Presbyterian sympathizers (Catholics were already excluded, of course), remained only as a 'rump' of Cromwellian members who could be trusted to rubber-stamp any edicts put before them. Thenceforth Britain was declared a 'Commonwealth' – a term first coined nearly a century earlier, though without such republican overtones, by Dr John Dee. It goes without saying that this friend of Queen Elizabeth, who throughout his life was a stalwart monarchist, would have been appalled by this parody of a British

Commonwealth. However, he would have approved of Cromwell's next act, which was to rebuild the navy into a formidable fighting force capable of projecting British power around the known world. This creation, alongside his New Model Army, was Cromwell's greatest military legacy and certainly the longest-lasting.

At the time of Charles I's execution Cromwell was, in theory at least, merely a member of the councils of state and of the army. In 1653 the officers of his victorious army framed a constitution that made him head of the Commonwealth. Like Julius Caesar nearly seventeen hundred years earlier he refused the title of king, perhaps feeling that he would be more compromised than exalted by it; instead he took the title of Lord Protector. Thenceforth, in nearly all things, his was the voice that mattered. With Parliament now reduced to a rump of obedient apparatchiks, Cromwell the dictator was free to do pretty much as he wanted. This was the form of government that held sway in Britain until 1660.

In 1657, towards the end of the Commonwealth period, John Evelyn, a friend and confidant of the future King Charles II, wrote in his diary for 10 August: 'Our vicar, from John xviii. 36, declaimed against the folly of a sort of enthusiasts and desperate zealots, called the *Fifth-Monarchy-Men*, pretending to set up the kingdom of Christ with the sword. To this pass was this age arrived when we had no King in Israel.'

The reference to 'no King in Israel' obviously refers to the period after the beheading of Charles I and before the crowning of Charles II, when there was no king of England. It is clear from this entry that during the time of the protectorate under Cromwell some people at least still regarded Britain as synonymous with Israel. John Evelyn, as we shall see later, was a pivotal figure at the time of the Restoration. The fact that he was aware of, and presumably one of those who believed in, the identity of Britain as Israel is therefore important.

The arrival of Comenius, Hartlib and other European intellectuals in London acted as a catalyst in the formation of a Rosicrucian society, which at first seems to have been based at Gresham College, which took on the role of 'beehive'. Throughout the period of the republican Commonwealth the professors of Gresham College continued to give free lectures in addition to carrying on with their private studies. The *Fama* and *Confessio* manifestos, which had announced that the secret Rosicrucian brotherhood was going public, had whetted the appetites of not a few Englishmen for such a project. The problem was that, even after the publication of the pamphlets and notwithstanding the work of such writers as Robert Fludd and Michael Maier, the brotherhood itself remained elusive. This, however, did not stop others from forming societies of their own which to a lesser or greater extent were Rosicrucian in their outlook in that they espoused the scientific method. One such grouping, with the obviously Rosicrucian title the Invisible College, began meeting at Gresham College on a fairly regular basis.

According to the testimony of John Wallis, the first informal meetings of the Invisible College were held in 1645 in London in the rooms of Gresham professor Samuel Foster. Theodore Haak, a German scholar from the Palatinate, seems to have been the instigator of these meetings, which also included John Wilkins. This influential prelate, later to become bishop of Chester, was close to the exiled Palatinate royal family. Indeed, he was chaplain to Prince Charles Louis, the son of Frederick and Elizabeth, who was to be restored as Elector Palatine under the terms of the Treaty of Westphalia in 1648.[4] Subsequent meetings of the Invisible College were to be held in Wilkins's rooms at Wadham College, Oxford. John Wilkins must have been a consummate politician, for despite his royal connections he was also in favour with Oliver Cromwell – to the extent that in 1656 he married the Protector's sister Robina. It follows that Cromwell, who took an active interest in Gresham College and its professorships, must have known about the Invisible College, and have approved of its aims; had he not, he would have suppressed it at birth.

Wilkins was not the only professor to keep his balance on the tightrope between royalist and republican loyalties. Another was Christopher Wren, whose meteoric advance in the 1640s does not seem to have been hindered by the fact that he came from a family with strong royalist connections. His uncle, Matthew Wren, bishop of Ely, was for eighteen years imprisoned in the Tower of London for refusing to recognize Cromwell's authority; his father, a former dean of Windsor and registrar of the Order of the Garter, had a slightly better fate but he too had been forced to flee his home at the time of the Civil War and had taken up residence with his son-in-law, William Holder. This move, however, turned out to be advantageous for the young Christopher, as Holder both encouraged him in his study of mathematics and provided him with useful contacts of many kinds, scholarly and esoteric.

Christopher Wren's was a precocious talent. Even at the age of fourteen he was engaged in scientific experimentation, using mathematics in inventing a sun-dial. The story is told by his son, Christopher Wren junior, in his memorial to his father, *Parentalia*:

He [Christopher Wren] continued also a peculiar instrument of use in Gnomonicks, which he explained in a treatise intitled *Sciotericon Catholicum*; the use and purpose of which was the solution of this problem, viz. 'On a known Plane, in a known Elevation, to describe such lines with the expedite turning of Rundles to certain Divisions, as by the Shaddow [*sic*] of the Style may shew the equal Hours of the Day.[5]

Still only fourteen years of age, Wren matriculated at Oxford, where he soon attracted the attention of his teachers:

In the year 1646 and 14th of his age, Mr Wren was admitted a Gentleman-Commoner at Wadham College in Oxford. He soon attracted the friendship and esteem of the two most celebrated virtuosi and Mathematicians of their time, Dr John Wilkins, Warden of Wadham, (afterwards Bishop of Chester) and Dr Seth Ward, Savilian Professor of Astronomy (afterwards Bishop of Sarum;) Which continued with intimacy and affection, during their lives. By means of Dr Wilkins, (who was Chaplain to his Royal Highness Charles Elector Palatine [Charles Louis, son of Frederick and Elizabeth], which resident in England) He had the honour to be introduced to the acquaintance, and favour of that Prince, a great lover & encourager of Mathematics and useful experiments.[6]

Thus from his youth Christopher Wren was

connected with the Rosicrucian tradition as represented by the Elector Palatine, Dr Wilkins and Dr Seth Ward (who was also a friend of Wren's brother-in-law, William Holder). Another friend from his days at Cambridge was a physician called Charles Scarburgh – a royalist who had extensive contacts in the academic world and was himself highly skilled in astronomy, navigation and mathematics, disciplines which in those days were more closely linked than they are today, and an early member of the Invisible College from the days when it held its meetings in the rooms of Samuel Foster at Gresham College. During his undergraduate days Wren acted as his assistant when Scarburgh was carrying out dissections of corpses, gaining thereby a good understanding of the anatomy of the human body and in particular of the way muscles worked.

Scarburgh encouraged Christopher Wren to make a Latin translation of a treatise on sundials written by William Oughtred. This must have appealed to the young man; as we have seen, making sundials had interested him from a very early age. However, Scarburgh's suggestion had a deeper motive: by thus flattering Oughtred, Wren gained favour with his many former students, who effectively made up the scientific establishment.

At Oxford, Wren studied astronomy under Dr Seth Ward who, at the suggestion of Scarburgh and Holder, had succeeded John Greaves in the post of Savilian Professor of Astronomy. It was during this time, so Wren junior tells us, that the Invisible College began holding its meetings at Oxford, with Christopher Wren among its members:

Some spaces after the conclusion of the Civil War Dr Wilkin's Lodging at Wadham College in Oxford was made the place of resort for virtuous and learned men, of Philosophical minds, where the first meetings were held which layed the Foundation of the Royal Society for Improving Natural Knowledge: the Principal and most constant of the Assemblies were Dr Seth Ward, the Bishop of Exeter; Mr Boyle; Dr Wilkins; Dr Wallis; Dr Willis; Sr. William Petty; Mr Matthew Wren [eldest son of Matthew, bishop of Ely and therefore Christopher's cousin]; Dr Goddard; Dr Bathurst; Dr Christopher Wren; and Mr Rook. Here they continued without any intermission till about the year 1658.[7]

The first Civil War ended with the beheading of Charles I in 1649, so these Oxford meetings must have begun some time in the early 1650s. In 1650 Wren received his Bachelor of Arts degree from Wadham College; in 1653 he received his Master's and was also elected into a fellowship at All Souls' College. We can therefore be certain that he was in Oxford at the time stated and, being a friend and associate of many of the other 'Invisibles', would have attended these meetings.

However, the Oxford professors were not the only ones to take an interest in the progress of the young Wren's career. It seems that it was as a result of a personal intervention by Oliver Cromwell, who was acting on the advice of his brother-in-law John Wilkins, that in 1657, at the still youthful age of twenty-five, Christopher Wren was appointed to the post of Gresham Professor of Astronomy. The Lord Protector would have been able to judge the young scholar for himself, for we know that Cromwell met Wren at least once.

This meeting was at the house of another mathematician, a Mr Claypole, who was married to the

Protector's favourite daughter. Wren used to dine regularly at Claypole's, where they would discuss matters scientific. It was on one of these occasions that Cromwell arrived unannounced and took his place at table. Over dinner the subject of Wren's uncle Matthew, then still in the Tower, was discussed.

From all of the above we can see that although today Wren is generally remembered as an architect, in his earlier years he was respected as something of an intellectual prodigy, a gifted mathematician and astronomer worthy to take on the mantle of such esteemed masters as Oughtred, Ward and Wilkins. Obviously influenced by the writings of Francis Bacon, who had died seven years before he himself was born, Wren decried the old logical system based on Aristotelianism, stating: 'Mathematical demonstrations being built upon the impregnable Foundations of Geometry and Arithmetick are the only truths that can sink into the Mind of Man, void of all Uncertainty; and all other Discourses participate more or less of Truth according as their Subjects are more or less capable of Mathematical Demonstration.'[8]

In his inaugural address at Gresham College, Wren laid out what was in effect a manifesto for a new scientific approach that he clearly hoped would reconcile religion with science. In this lecture, as an illustration of what he meant by this reconciliation, he presented a theory for how a miracle recorded in the Bible might actually have been achieved scientifically.[9] As Professor of Astronomy he was also interested in astrology, for in those days the two subjects still went hand in hand; indeed, one of his earliest writings was a Latin treatise on the zodiac. This interest seems to have extended to the supposed relationship between cities

246

and their ruling stars, for 'He depicted London as particularly favoured by planetary influences and "with so general a relish of mathematics and the liberal philosophia in such measure as is hardly to be found in the academies themselves".'[10] As we have seen, Rosicrucianism was intimately bound up with astrology – as witnessed by its interest in the new stars in Serpentarius and Cygnus that were thought to herald the birth of a new age.

Another important member of the Invisible College was John Evelyn, who during the 1640s had spent a good deal of time on the Continent, visiting Italy as well as residing for a time in Paris – where he probably developed his taste for gardening; his house at Sayes Court, Dartford, was recognized as having one of the finest gardens of the period. A king's man, he knew the royal family well, including the Palatine branch headed by the widowed Elizabeth of Bohemia. Although during the Commonwealth period Evelyn was in correspondence with the exiled Charles II, like other members of the Invisible College he managed to keep out of trouble through the long years of the Civil Wars and the protectorate. Like Elias Ashmole, also a founder member of the Invisible College, he was something of an antiquarian; it was he who persuaded the duke of Norfolk to present his priceless collection of sculptures (known as the Arundel marbles) to the University of Oxford, and the Arundel library to Gresham College.[11]

Charles, the heir to the now defunct throne, had been born in May 1630, the son of Charles I and his Catholic wife Henrietta Maria. When events began to slide towards civil war in 1641 he was only a boy of eleven; yet throughout his teens and twenties, first in

Civil War and then in exile, he behaved with courage and sagacity. In 1649 he wrote to Parliament, sending a signed, blank sheet of paper on which they were requested to write their demands in return for his father's life. They declined, and on 30 January 1649 Charles I was executed. One can only imagine the effect this must have had on the young Prince Charles, who now found himself king in name but pauper in practice.

In 1650 he went to Scotland. He had already, on his father's death, been declared king of the Scots; now, on 1 January 1651, he was formally crowned at Scone. Oliver Cromwell, the real power in the land, had no intention of allowing the son to take over from where the father had left off, and went in pursuit of the young king. Charles marched south and, though he and his men fought bravely, he was out-generalled and was defeated at the Battle of Worcester on 3 September. The young king was now a fugitive; from then until the time of his triumphant return in 1660, at the invitation of Parliament, he had to live the impoverished life of an exile. These experiences in his early life taught Charles to be a pragmatist. Though for a time, like his father before him, he tried to govern without Parliament, he was sensible enough to see that where matters of religion were concerned he needed to conform to what was required of him by the people: to be a Protestant king but not a Puritan.

During the period of his exile across the Channel, Charles spent much time in France, his mother, Queen Henrietta Maria, being an aunt of the young French king, Louis XIV. In France Charles had ample opportunity to admire the extraordinary architecture of the Louvre and other elegant palaces – the legacy of earlier rulers and proxy rulers such as his maternal grandfather,

Henry IV, his uncle, Louis XIII, and Cardinal Richelieu. Louis XIV, Charles's cousin, was to add to this architectural wealth by extending the Louvre and transforming the small château at Versailles, built by Henry IV, into the most magnificent palace Europe had ever seen. For the exiled Charles, who following his father's execution can have entertained little hope of ever going home, it must have been with mixed emotions that he contemplated the remarkable artistry of modern seventeenth-century French architecture and contrasted it with the largely dull traditionalism of England.

The young Charles also spent time with his aunt, Queen Elizabeth of Bohemia, the sister of his murdered father. She, following Frederick's untimely death in 1632, had been left a poor widow with a large family to support. While her brother had been king of England she had been able to rely on a small pension from him; with his death, her situation became more precarious. Fortunately, the English remembered her with affection as the queen they wished they had had: a Protestant Elizabeth willing to stand up to and fight Habsburg aggrandizement. Accordingly, Parliament continued, sporadically, to pay her pension even though it had executed her brother.

Elizabeth's family had divided loyalties with regard to the civil strife in England. Her eldest surviving son, Prince Charles Louis, was quite cold towards his mother, something of an intellectual and rather favoured the parliamentarian cause. On the other hand her third son, Prince Rupert of the Rhine, was a Cavalier and one of the most colourful characters of the age; her fourth son, Prince Maurice, accompanied Rupert in many of his campaigns. All three brothers were to become Knights of the Garter.

Prince Rupert had very mixed success as a royalist general. He was a good strategist, and it has been argued in some quarters that, given total freedom of action, he might have won the Civil War for Charles. This is probably overstating the case, for Rupert's rashness in following through cavalry pursuits rather than in concentrating on finishing off the enemy infantry cost the royalist forces a number of important battles. He was, however, more successful as an admiral and, with a larger fleet and a little more luck, could perhaps have won the seas for his cousin. In their seafaring exploits the brothers Rupert and Maurice mirrored those earlier, Tudor sailors, the Gilbert brothers, Sir Francis Drake and Sir Walter Raleigh. In a sad echo of the Gilbert tragedy, Prince Maurice was to die in an Atlantic storm with his brother unable to help him.

By 1660, after ten years of rule by first Oliver and then for a short time his son Richard Cromwell, the English had had enough of republicanism. General Monck, commander of the parliamentarian forces in Scotland but formerly a serving officer under Charles I, marched to London and persuaded the remnant of the Long Parliament to dissolve itself and call new elections. This, he and everybody else knew, would be the first step towards restoring the monarchy. Monck smoothed the way to make this possible without further bloodshed. On 25 May, at the invitation of the new Parliament, Charles II returned to London in triumph. The restored king and his friends were determined that they should not have to go on their travels again, and for the present at least he was very popular with the people.

Charles II was crowned the following year, on 23

April 1661. The choice of this date for so momentous an occasion was no accident: it was the Feast of St George, patron saint of England and of the Order of the Garter. The ceremony itself, carried out in Westminster Abbey, was one of the most magnificent occasions in London's history. Following the coronation, silver coins were thrown into the crowd and Edward Hyde, earl of Clarendon, read out a general amnesty. The very elaborateness of the festivities associated with this royal occasion was designed to emphasize the fact of the Restoration and how infinitely preferable a monarchy was compared with the drab uniformity of the protectorate.

Though Charles II forgave most of his former enemies – indeed, he had little choice if he wanted his restored administration to take root – he could not overlook the fact of his father's murder. Thus the bodies of Oliver Cromwell and two parliamentarian generals, Thomas Pride and Henry Ireton, along with that of John Bradshaw, who had been the presiding judge at the trial of Charles I, were ordered to be disinterred from Westminster Abbey and hanged at Tyburn, where Marble Arch now stands. To the enjoyment of the London crowd (though the smell must have been appalling) they swung there all day, from nine in the morning to six at night, before eventually being cut down and buried in a pit. The surviving regicides – those who had not given themselves up and been granted clemency – were put on trial. Ten of them were hanged, drawn and quartered the October before the coronation. Apart from this, and one or two other acts of retribution, the new regime dealt leniently with its former enemies. General Monck was rewarded for his work in bringing about this desired outcome by being raised to the peerage with the titles Baron Monck, earl of Torrington and duke of Albemarle. He was also made a Knight of the Garter, gentleman of the bedchamber, master of horse and commander-in-chief of the army, and was appointed lord lieutenant of Ireland (though he would not leave England) and given a pension of £7,000 per annum – at that time a sizeable income. Though Monck was the most obvious beneficiary of Charles's magnanimity, he was not alone; many other parliamentarians were allowed to keep lands and possessions that had formerly belonged to royalists.

At Charles's side on the return to Britain was his most loyal cousin, Prince Rupert of the Rhine. Now regarded as a hero, he was given rooms in St James's Palace where in his spare time he was able to carry out chemistry experiments and perfect the technique of mezzotint engraving for which he became famous. As a reward for his long years of service to the crown, he was given the titles duke of Cumberland and earl of Holderness. He was also a member of the Privy Council, where one can imagine that his close knowledge of European politics was of great value. Monck and he had served together before the war and now they were to do so again, this time as admirals in Britain's growing navy. Though he must have felt some sense of divided loyalty – he had, after all, fought in many wars alongside the Dutch – Rupert was successful in the Anglo-Dutch Wars which, being largely about trade, were fought at sea.

In 1661 Rupert's mother, the dowager queen of Bohemia, at last returned to England. By now old, and frail, she still possessed that spark of life that in her youth had made her famous as one of the great beauties of Europe. Though Charles had at first been against her return, perhaps feeling that the presence of his aunt might in some way inhibit him from the pleasures of office, once she had arrived he treated her with dignity. He gave her a small pension out of the royal purse and she, in the absence of Charles's own mother Henrietta Maria (then resident in France), was able to enjoy the role of surrogate 'queen mother'. For the elderly Elizabeth, whose many misfortunes had clouded what should have been a charmed life, this was but a brief Indian summer. She died at Leicester House on 13 February 1662, close to where her portrait now hangs in the National Portrait Gallery. Her state funeral, which took place in Westminster Abbey, in many ways marked the end of a period of history. If her marriage to Frederick V, Count Palatine, had seemed emblematic of the Rosicrucian enlightenment with all of its promised blessings, so her return to the land of her nativity marked the start of a new venture. From now on, what had been whispered behind closed doors and posited in terms of secret symbolism was to explode outwards. Under the protection of kings and guided by the Royal Society, the new science born of Rosicrucianism would soon establish England as Europe's pre-eminent power and London as the capital city of the world.

CHAPTER NINE

THE COVENANT OF THE ARK

King Charles II was in many ways the very opposite of his father. A tall man, over 6 feet in height, he had the imposing bearing that the former king had so lacked. He was also very good-humoured and not at all pompous in his dealings with those of lesser rank. Whereas Charles I was very proper in his behaviour, the son enjoyed going to the theatre and more especially the company of desirable actresses. The most famous of these was Nell Gwynn, but there were many others who caught his eye; indeed, not since the time of Henry VIII had an English king been quite such a one for the ladies. Provided they gave him pleasure, his mistresses – some of whom were almost like wives – could be high-born ladies or whores. Many of them, such as Barbara Castlemaine and Louise-Renée, duchess of Portsmouth, bore him children. Unfortunately, though his wife, Catherine of Braganza, was not wholly un-attractive, she proved unable to have children. Thus Charles II was denied legitimate offspring. However, unlike Henry VIII he did not make the mistake of causing a scandal by divorcing his Portuguese queen in quest of an heir. Rather, he accepted that if his wife were barren then his brother, the duke of York, should ultimately succeed to the throne. For himself, he was content that Catherine should enjoy all the status and protection to which she was entitled – just as long as he was allowed to indulge himself in a little pleasure on the side.

Yet amid all this frivolity there was a serious side to Charles that was concerned with the advancement of learning in the Baconian sense of the word. After the death of Oliver Cromwell and the restoration of the king, British intellectuals breathed a sigh of relief and came out of hiding. It was no longer necessary for Rosicrucians to meet in secret. The Invisible College no longer needed to be invisible; it could come out into the open and announce its existence publicly to the world. Soon the meetings of the 'Invisibles' were once more being held at Gresham College in the heart of London.

On 28 November 1660 Christopher Wren, by now Gresham Professor of Astronomy, delivered a lecture at the college, at the end of which a memorandum was drawn up recording as present Lord Brouckner, Mr Boyle, Mr Bruce, Sir Robert Moray, Mr Rooke, Mr Wren and Mr Hill. It was there proposed that a new college should be founded for the promotion of 'Physico-Mathematicall Experimentall Learning'. This college, which at that time had no premises of its own, was to be funded by a subscription from its members of ten shillings per annum with an extra charge of one shilling per week. The appointed chairman was John Wilkins and a list was drawn up of forty-one people (presumably mostly members of the existing Invisible College) thought likely to want to join.

It was clearly intended right from the start that this new college should seek royal patronage, for when the proposed members next met, on the following

Wednesday, Sir Robert Moray was able to inform them that the king gave his approval to such a scheme. Moray was an important man to have on board, for he was a representative of the Scottish establishment as well as having the king's ear. Under Charles I he had served as quartermaster general of the Scottish army, and he was a close friend of Charles II. In his book *Parentalia*, Christopher Wren junior eulogizes this former friend of his father's:

> Sr. Robert Moray, one of his Majesties Privy Councillors in Scotland, was an excellent Mathematician and well versed in Natural Philosophy and Chemistry. He was among the first, who modeled, instituted and promoted the Royal Society and was elected President . . .
>
> A character so parallel in all pointes to that of Sr. Christopher Wren, naturally produced a most friendly and inviolable attachment to each other. He died suddenly at Whitehall, and being particularly in the King's favour, was at his Majesties own charge, bury'd in Westminster Abbey in the year 1673.[1]

At a subsequent meeting, it was decided that the membership of the new college should be restricted to fifty-five, to which number should be added a few supernumerary professors from Oxford, Cambridge and the Royal College of Physicians. On 6 March 1661 Sir Robert Moray was indeed elected president and it was decided that he should occupy that seat until such time as a royal charter incorporating the society should be granted. In the event this took another year or more to organize, but in the meantime the king himself, as well as his cousin Prince Rupert, joined as active members. The charter of incorporation eventually passed the Great Seal on 15 July 1662, the college being given the title of The Royal Society of London for improving Natural Knowledge. This was soon shortened to the more easily remembered Royal Society, the name by which it continues to be known to this day. Lord Brouckner was elected the first official president after the society's incorporation and he is shown dressed in flowing Roman robes on the frontispiece of Thomas Sprat's *History of the Royal Society*.

From the start the Royal Society stood against Aristotelianism. That it took inspiration from the works of Francis Bacon is evidenced by his being depicted on this frontispiece on the other side of the bust of Charles II from Lord Brouckner. The inscription beneath Bacon's feet makes it clear that he has been placed on the frontispiece because he proposed the great instauration that would overthrow the tyranny of Aristotelianism. According to Joseph Glanvill, one of the founder members, the Royal Society's earliest remit was 'to defend against the attacks of the Aristotelian traditionalists, to enlarge knowledge by observation and experiment'.[2] These are sentiments that had been expressed in the Rosicrucian manifestos of some fifty years earlier. Haak, Hartlib, Comenius, Evelyn, Ashmole, Wilkins, Wren and others were quite familiar with the Continental Rosicrucian movement and its teachings that enlightenment could be obtained through scientific investigation of the natural world. Through them the underlying philosophy of the enlightenment, which had previously inspired the courts of Heidelberg and Prague, was passed back from the European continent to England. Even so, Rosicrucianism was not the only influence inspiring the

Fig. 27. 'The fame of the Royal Society'. (From *History of the Royal Society* by Thomas Sprat.)

creation of first the Invisible College and then the Royal Society. Sprat's book, published in 1667, was the officially sanctioned memorial to the founding of the society. It is clear therefore that, though the Royal Society was intended to be Rosicrucian in its attitudes, there was another, deeper and more nationalistic understanding at work in all of this, which was connected with England's perceived destiny. The *Fama*, the call to arms of the Rosicrucian movement, concludes with the words *Sub umbra alarum tuarum, Jehovah* – 'Under the shadow [hence protection] of your wing, O Jehovah'. By the British, and maybe some others, this was seen as applying in a very direct way to them. For Britain was believed by many to be a holy land that was especially blessed by God as the place appointed for the re-gathering of the scattered tribes of Israel.

The Royal Society is, and always has been, an avowedly scientific organization. Even so, many of its founder members had as much interest, if not more, in the Holy Scriptures as in the new empirical methods of enquiry. Christopher Wren, for example, wrote a treatise on Noah's Ark and Isaac Newton, a younger man who was elected to join the Royal Society in 1672, wrote a number of books on such diverse subjects as biblical chronology, the meaning of the Book of Revelation and the true shape of King Solomon's Temple. Indeed, it is said that Newton wrote far more on the subject of religion than on science, even though it is the latter work for which he is now mostly remembered.

Though the Royal Society was created as a tangible expression of the Baconian ideal of a 'House of Salomon', many of its members brought with them other ideas and systems of belief. One of these would

259

appear to have been Freemasonry, which in the course of the late seventeenth and early eighteenth centuries was remoulded into the form in which we know it today. At the time of the early Stuart kings – James I, Charles I and Charles II – speculative Freemasonry, if we may use the term, would seem to have been restricted to a fairly narrow circle of architects and courtiers. These 'masons' were not engaged in the rough trade of dressing and laying blocks of stone, but rather studied and worked with compass and ruler designing, planning and building edifices in accordance with the ancient canon of measures. For such work a knowledge of mathematics and in particular geometry was absolutely essential. Thus one of the emblems and signs used by Freemasons is the symbol of Euclid's forty-seventh proposition, better known to non-masons as Pythagoras' theorem. A master mason was therefore, by definition, a master geometer. This was not a new idea of the late seventeenth century but went back for many centuries before. In Michael Maier's classic *Atalanta Fugiens*, Emblem 21 depicts a master mason carrying out geometric measurements in accordance with the canon of proportions. That this was secret knowledge allied to alchemy is made clear from the wording accompanying the drawing: 'Make a circle around man and woman, then a square, now a triangle, make a circle, and you will have the Philosopher's Stone.'

The connections between Freemasonry and the Royal Society are clearly apparent. Among the earliest recorded initiated Freemasons are Sir Robert Moray, who was made a master mason at some time in 1641, and Elias Ashmole, who was initiated in a lodge in Warrington, Lancashire, on 16 October 1646.[3] The definitive birth date of Freemasonry as a universal philosophical movement, rather than as a secret society of architects preserving ancient secrets, is said to be the founding of the United Grand Lodge of England in London in 1717. However, even before this time there was certainly a closed organization of practising stone-masons operating throughout Britain. These 'Freemasons' – freemen who travelled around the country building churches, cathedrals and palaces as the need arose – were organized into operative craft lodges both to maintain standards of workmanship and to preserve the secrets of their trade from outsiders. Within what were essentially trade guilds, the

Fig. 28. Emblem 21 from Michael Maier's *Atalanta Fugiens*.

Freemasons were organized into three levels of the craft: apprentice, journeyman and master mason. To reach the higher grades, candidates had to train and then pass some sort of examination (or 'initiation') to show that the level of skill required had been attained. Each grade of masonry had its own secret passwords, handshakes, symbols and insignia, so that masons of the same grade or higher – especially those from different lodges – could recognize that an applicant for a particular job was properly trained up to that level. We may also assume that, at least when working on a specific project, these 'jobbing masons', the equivalent of today's bricklayers, were directed by architects. These architects, who may or may not have been skilled as stonemasons themselves, would have been artists of the first order. For it was they, not the craftmasons, who designed the cathedrals and palaces of Europe.

The London building boom of the late seventeenth century made it possible for a time for a relatively large number of masonic lodges to thrive in the capital. With the end of the boom and the dispersal of the large workforce that had been needed, the lodges found themselves short of members. This is why they amalgamated to form the first Grand Lodge. Yet even this was not enough to halt the decline: for the lodge to continue, it found it necessary to bring in new members who were not themselves practising Freemasons in any trade sense. These new members – the 'speculative Freemasons' – might be bankers, shopkeepers, judges or petty bureaucrats. They joined the Freemasons not through any wish to change career, but because they had an interest in the symbolic aspects of the old craft and a wish to meet up with men of like mind. Thus the new Grand Lodge of 1717 was different from the old craft lodges in that the majority of its members did not (as their successors today do not) actually work in the building trade. It is a curious irony that the very process of democratizing Freemasonry and making its initiations available to interested parties outside the trade in fact marked its decadence. Most of the new Freemasons who joined in the hope of discovering ancient secrets were actually profoundly ignorant of the real meaning behind symbolic architecture. Consequently they were not in a position to understand that the three degrees leading to the title of master mason were in reality just the beginning of an involvement in some very esoteric matters indeed.

That there is more to Freemasonry than the three degrees, and that this was known to at least some of those involved in setting up London's Grand Lodge in 1717 is borne out by evidence contained in the Kirkwall Scroll. As we have seen, this large tapestry dates from the fifteenth century and is currently kept at a masonic lodge in Kirkwall on the island of Orkney. It would seem therefore to confirm that, as an esoteric tradition, Freemasonry goes back at least to the mid-fifteenth century. Kirkwall was part of the fiefdom of the Sinclairs who after the Battle of Bannockburn were intimately connected with the preservation of the secret knowledge of the Knights Templar. In 1454 Sir William Sinclair, who was responsible for building Rosslyn Chapel, was created earl of Orkney. The Kirkwall scroll would seem to date from around this time, indicating that the 'Scottish Rite' Freemasonry that it exemplifies owes as much if not more to the Knights Templar than to the medieval craft-masons who built the cathedrals of Europe. How this came about is very interesting and, as will be seen, this link with the Templars explains much about the rebuilding of London in the seventeenth century.

The headquarters of the masonic Templar tradition would appear to have been transferred to London at the time of James I. As this was done in the utmost secrecy, we can only take an informed guess that this was so. However, it does seem significant that the first initiated Freemason of whom we have a record is Sir Robert Moray (or Murray), who was initiated into the Scottish Lodge of Edinburgh on 20 May 1641.[4] Sir Robert Moray may or may not have been related to the earlier earls of the same name, but, like them, he was certainly a Scottish royalist of importance. It seems significant, therefore, that this earliest of recorded Freemasons was also elected as the first president of the Royal Society, and that it was through him that the society received its royal charter. This if nothing else would appear to confirm that there was at least some sort of link between Freemasonry and the Royal Society prior to 1717, the two organizations sharing members and being different facets of the same 'Rosicrucian' movement. As the seventeenth century gave way to the eighteenth, however, the destinies of the Royal Society and the Freemasons became separated. The first became a purely scientific organization and the latter, which till then had been an essentially secret society, reorganized itself and went public under the banner of the United Grand Lodge of England. However, even then one of the most important secrets of Freemasonry, the connection between the Scottish Rite and the Knights Templar, remained closely guarded.

As we have seen, at the time of Robert the Bruce, the kings of Scotland became closely associated with the legacy of the Knights Templar following the order's suppression by the pope. Among Robert's companions of arms at the Battle of Bannockburn were the first Earl Sinclair and also Thomas Randolph, who was later created earl of Moray for his services to the Scottish cause. Like Sinclair, Thomas Randolph was closely associated with the Knights Templar and may well have been one himself. This was all the more important in that, following the death of King Robert, he became one of the regents of Scotland. It was almost certainly during the time of this regency, from 1329 to about 1351, that steps were taken to conceal the identity of the surviving Templars and their traditions within the guise of Freemasonry.

The connection between the Knights Templar and the building trade is not as surprising as it may at first seem. In its heyday the order had functioned as the bankers of Europe at a time when banks, as we know them today, simply did not exist. Templar preceptories operated outside the jurisdiction of kings and princes, and they did not have to pay taxes. Although individual knights took an oath of poverty, the order itself was exceedingly wealthy. As a result they were able to finance many of the great building projects of the middle ages, including the construction of the Gothic cathedrals of France and England.[5] This meant that, as commissioning patrons, the Templars had a close relationship with the guilds of stonemasons. Indeed, the latter's lodges must very frequently have held their meetings within the protected environment of the knights' preceptories. Moreover, some of the knights – who had a great deal of experience in build-ing castles in Palestine – were themselves master architects.

Although the avowed purpose of the order was the

protection of pilgrims, it secretly had a very different aim: one known to King Baldwin II of Jerusalem and to very few others. For when the first nine Templars (still then called Poor Knights of Christ) had arrived in Jerusalem in 1118 they were given a royal welcome. Far from being offered accommodation in some flea-bitten hostel in a poor quarter of the city, they were given custody of the Temple Mount itself and housed in its largest building: what had been (and now is again) the Al-Aqsa Mosque.

The reasons for this preferential treatment – certainly in comparison with their rival order the Knights Hospitaller, who enjoyed no such privilege – is not hard to discern. Then as now, the northern end of the Temple Mount was dominated by the Mosque of Omar or 'Dome of the Rock' as it is known. It was believed then (and is generally held now) that the large rocky eminence over which this mosque stands was the very rock on which Abraham had tied his son Isaac in preparation for his sacrifice.[6] Solomon built his temple on top of Mount Moriah to provide a permanent lodging place for the Ark of the Covenant, and it seems likely that he did so in such a way that its *adytum*, or Holy of Holies, covered this rock. Thus the Ark would have been placed on top of this selfsame rock.

The Ark of the Covenant was a small wooden chest, overlaid with gold, into which were placed the slabs of stone on which were inscribed the Ten Commandments. How the Ark was to be made is described in the Book of Exodus:

And they shall make an ark of shittim [acacia] wood: two cubits and a half shall be the length thereof, and a cubit and a half the breadth thereof, and a cubit and

266

a half the height thereof. And thou shalt overlay it with pure gold, within and without shalt thou overlay it, and shalt make upon it a crown of gold round about. And thou shalt cast four rings of gold for it, and put them in the four corners thereof; and two rings shall be in the one side of it, and two rings in the other side of it. And thou shalt make staves of shittim wood, and overlay them with gold. And thou shalt put the staves into the rings by the sides of the ark, that the ark may be borne with them. The staves shall be in the rings of the ark: they shall not be taken from it. And thou shalt put into the ark the testimony that I shall give thee. And thou shalt make a mercy seat of pure gold: two cubits and a half shall be the length thereof and a cubit and a half the breadth thereof.

And thou shalt make two cherubims of gold, of beaten work shalt thou make them, in the two ends of the mercy seat. And make one cherub on the one end, and the other cherub on the other end: even of the mercy seat shall ye make the cherubims on the two ends thereof. And the cherubims shall stretch forth their wings on high, covering the mercy seat with their wings, and their faces shall look one to another; toward the mercy seat shall the faces of the cherubims be.

And thou shalt put the mercy seat above upon the ark; and in the ark thou shalt put the testimony that I shall give thee. And there I will meet with thee, and I will commune with thee from above the mercy seat, from between the two cherubims which are upon the ark of the testimony, of all things which I will give thee in commandment unto the children of Israel. (Exod. 25: 10–22)

According to the Bible, the Israelites carried the Ark

with them when they entered the promised land of Canaan. Except for a short period when it fell into the hands of the Philistines, causing the people of Ashdod to develop haemorrhoids, according to some translations, it was kept safely in a tent. After the death of King David, who established Jerusalem as the capital of Israel, his son Solomon set about building a permanent home for the ark: the Temple of Jerusalem. It was this temple that was destroyed by the Babylonians, rebuilt by King Herod and again destroyed by the Romans.

The Ark continued to reside inside the Temple of Solomon until the time of the sack of Jerusalem. However, in the Bible it is not mentioned in the list of booty taken from Jerusalem c.586 BC by Nebuchadnezzar, the king of Babylon. The implication is that it had either gone missing before this date or been destroyed along with the temple. Though there is a theory that it had been removed from the Temple to Abyssinia by an illegitimate son of Solomon and the Queen of Sheba, this seems hardly credible. With the amount of security surrounding Solomon's Temple, even to attempt to steal the Ark would have been not just dangerous but virtually impossible. This is not to say that there could not have been at least one copy made of the Ark, and that this found its way to Ethiopia in the way suggested. What seems more likely is that at some time prior to the sack of Jerusalem the Ark itself – the one made by the Israelites at the time of Moses, and not a copy – was hidden in some secret chamber beneath the Temple itself.

One theory, not without its own logic, is that the real reason for the crusades was not the securing of the holy places for Christian pilgrims, desirable as this was no doubt felt to be, but to retrieve the Ark from its hiding place on the Temple Mount. Twenty years after the 'liberation' of Jerusalem by the crusaders, it might have been felt that the time was right to make a serious search for this lost relic of old Israel. Certainly the grant to the Templars of jurisdiction over the Temple Mount was an extraordinary privilege for a brand-new knightly order. A possible reason for such an action could be a belief that the Ark of the Covenant might still be found hidden somewhere among the ruins of the Temple. In this case the secret purpose in forming the order of the Knights Templar, indeed their whole raison d'être, was that they should secure the Temple Mount from prying eyes and carry out secret investigations. That such a search was carried out is almost certain, and it is not beyond the bounds of possibility that the Ark was actually found, brought out and secretly moved to Europe. If so, then this would surely have been the chief treasure of the Templars and one that they would have guarded with their lives.

Given free range over the Temple Mount, the Poor Knights of Christ had the freedom to do what many archaeologists today would love to do as well: to survey the ruins of what they believed to have been King Solomon's Temple. The Templars were in possession of the site of the Temple Mount from 1118 until 1187 when, following his great victory at the Horns of Hattim, Saladin retook Jerusalem for Islam. During this period of nearly seventy years they had ample time to examine the remains on the Mount, as well as to open up certain subterranean chambers known as Solomon's Stables.[7] It is rumoured that during these excavations they actually found the Ark of the Covenant, buried some fifteen hundred or more years earlier. Louis Charpentier, who has made a study of this subject, writes: 'If the nine [Templars] wished to live by themselves, it was necessarily because they were engaged, not on the roads but in the Temple itself, in some secret activity. What activity? It can only be a question of searching for something hidden . . . What could be so important, sacred, precious, dangerous? Unless it was the Ark of the Covenant and the Tables of the Law?'[8]

Assuming that the Ark really was found by the Templars, and that it remained in their possession thereafter until the order was suppressed by the pope in the early fourteenth century, the implication is that it was still in the possession of those Templars who escaped. If this is so, then it seems likely that it was taken to Scotland for safe keeping by the refugee Templars who sought sanctuary with Robert the Bruce – in which case it is more than likely that even today the Ark of the Covenant is in the hands of the Templars' successors: the Freemasons.

If this is true (and it has to be admitted that this line of argument contains many maybes, ifs and mights), the whereabouts of the Ark today is still a closely guarded secret. Nevertheless, the legend of King Solomon's Temple continues to influence modern-day Freemasonry in a most profound way. Masonic halls are intended to represent Solomon's Temple and the three stages of initiation of candidates, taking them up to the level of master mason, are supposedly modelled on ancient traditions going back to his time.

Confirmation that the Templars may have discovered some great secret concerning Solomon's Temple and passed this on to the Freemasons is implied by Thomas Harding's article about the Kirkwall Scroll in the *Daily Telegraph* of Saturday, 10 July 2000. What is very significant – indeed, exciting – about this Scroll is that on one part of it is a picture that bears a striking similarity to the coat of arms used by the Grand Lodge of London. (Compare plates 16 and 17, showing the Kirkwall Scroll and the coat of arms of the Grand Lodge.) It is a complex design which only a highly initiated Freemason could fully interpret. However, some of its elements can be understood by anyone with a knowledge of the Bible and in particular of the story concerning the building of King Solomon's Temple.

The dominant feature of the Scroll is a semicircular archway supported by two columns, reminiscent of those raised by Solomon before the porch of his Temple: 'And he set up the pillars in the porch of the temple: and he set up the right pillar, and called the name thereof Jachin: and he set up the left pillar, and called the name thereof Boaz' (1 Kgs 7: 21). To Freemasons the twin pillars, Jachin and Boaz, that Solomon placed before the entrance to his temple hold a further significance. Something of this hidden meaning is explained in a booklet of *Old Charges* that was issued by a leading Freemason called J. Roberts in 1722. This booklet, originally printed in the form of several newspaper articles, is the first account of masonic history to have been openly published. It predates the first edition of Anderson's *Constitutions of the Freemasons* (of which more will be said in the next chapter) by several months and claims to have been drawn from a very old manuscript explaining the origins of Freemasonry in remote antiquity. Like Anderson's *Constitutions*, it links the origins of Freemasonry with the mythical history of humankind as contained in the book of Genesis. According to this version of history, prior to the Flood certain information was recorded on two indestructible pillars, one of marble (that could not be destroyed by fire) and the other of brick (that could not be destroyed by drowning it in water). After the Flood one of these pillars was found by 'Hermames' (i.e. Hermes) and because of this he was able to teach the antediluvian sciences to post-diluvian humankind.

The source of these ideas concerning the twin pillars is unknown, as the documents on which Roberts claimed to be drawing have long since disappeared. However, this does not mean they never existed; they may, like the Kirkwall Scroll, be closeted away in the library of the Grand Lodge itself or on some remote Scottish island. What is of interest is that what he says about the recording of information on pillars has a resonance with another ancient 'Book of Hermes'. This writing is today known as the *Kore Kosmu*, or 'Virgin of the World', and it is contained in the *Hermetica*, the collection of writings from Greco-Roman times which was brought back to Florence from Greece at the time of Cosimo de' Medici. In the *Kore Kosmu* there is a reference to the writings of Hermes being inscribed on pillars which may very well have been the original in-spiration for Robert's account: ' "They", said Hermes, "will get knowledge of all my hidden writings, and dis-cern their meaning; and some of those writings they will keep to themselves, but such of them as tend to the benefit of mortal men, they will inscribe on slabs and obelisks." '[9]

Thus we can see that the pillars depicted on the Kirkwall Scroll could just as well represent these earlier ones associated with Noah and Hermes as those later placed before Solomon's Temple. This alternative certainly makes sense, as the pillars on the scroll are not free-standing like those before Solomon's Temple; on the contrary, they support an arch – possibly symbolic of the 'Royal Arch' mentioned in certain higher-degree ceremonies of Freemasons today. Closer inspection reveals that this arch, which embraces a cloudy sky with the sun shining, itself symbolizes a rainbow. This would appear to be a reminder of the biblical story of Noah, in which God placed the rainbow in the sky as a reminder of his covenant that there should never again be such a flood.

In religious terms the 'Noetic Covenant' is especially important because it is universal; it is acknowledged by the Jews that even the Gentile nations – those not descended from Abraham – are equal beneficiaries of this contract between God and humanity. However, the Noetic is only the first of a number of such covenants recorded in the Bible, most of which concern the Israelites as God's chosen people and the rights of the House of David to provide kings to rule over them. It is therefore not surprising that beneath the arch on the Kirkwall Scroll is depicted the symbol of the most important of these later contracts: the Ark of the Covenant. This is shown framed by two figures with the wings of angels. The pose of these figures indicates that they are clearly meant to represent the golden cherubim that Solomon placed inside the inner sanctuary or 'oracle' of his temple to protect the Ark of the Covenant:

> And within the oracle he made two cherubims of olive trees, each ten cubits high. And five cubits was one wing of the cherub, and five cubits the other wing of the cherub: from the uttermost part of the one wing unto the uttermost part of the other were ten cubits. And the other cherub was ten cubits: both the

cherubims were of one measure and one size. The
height of one cherub was ten cubits, and so was it of the
other cherub. And he set the cherubims within the inner
house: and they stretched forth the wings of the
cherubims, so that the wing of one touched one wall,
and the wing of the other cherub touched the other
wall; and their wings touched one another in the midst
of the house. And he overlaid the cherubims with gold.
(1 Kgs 6: 23–8)

There can be no doubt that the winged figures guard-
ing the Ark are intended to be cherubim, for they stand
with wings touching as described in the Bible. Yet there
is a difference. The cherubim as depicted on the
Kirkwall Scroll (and on the coat of arms of London's
Grand Lodge) are a species of bull-sphinx, their upper
bodies being manlike while their lower quarters are
those of oxen. This detail is not included in the biblical
account and could be evidence that the Knights
Templar really did find the Ark of the Covenant, along
with statues or images of its cherubic guardians. This
could account for the masonic understanding that the
cherubim were really bull-sphinxes, in many ways
similar to those found in ruins throughout the Middle
East.

Whether or not the Templars did take the Ark to
Scotland, it is certainly true that Freemasons continue
to revere the story of Solomon's Temple and that the
coat of arms of the United Grand Lodge indicates an
interest in the Ark of the Covenant. As the Latin motto
that goes with these arms is *Aude, Vide, Tace*, meaning
'See, Hear, Keep Silent', it is not surprising that these
matters are not discussed openly outside of the society
itself. However, the natural corollary to all this interest

274

in King Solomon's Temple is that at some time the Freemasons should attempt to rebuild the Temple, preferably in Jerusalem but, failing that, in some other location of their own choosing.

As we have seen, King James I, in his rebuilding scheme for Aldersgate, indicated his belief that London was to be equated with Jerusalem, the capital of ancient Israel. Strange as it may seem, the evidence is that in the late seventeenth century an attempt was made physically to transform London into a version of the New Jerusalem. This seems to be the great secret at the heart of a building scheme masterminded by Sir Christopher Wren; one so extraordinary that it deserves careful examination. The logic behind this scheme was that the lions of England and Scotland were to be equated with the lion of Judah, and as such indicated that Britain was now God's especial kingdom: Israel. The old Jerusalem had failed to keep to God's covenants but London, having been purged of its sins by cleansing fire, would take its place as the 'New Jerusalem'. Where once it had been a warren of fetid streets, it was now to be rebuilt out of white Portland stone to show that it was indeed the city of light. In London, the New Jerusalem, there was to be a great instauration of the covenants between God and man. King Solomon's Temple, emblemized and mythologized by Francis Bacon, would be rebuilt, and it would be linked to the imperishable throne of David that, as the Stone of Scone, underpinned the coronation throne. This seems to have been the secret plan of England's fraternity of Rosicrucian Freemasons. The man charged with the realization of this plan was, as we shall see in the next chapter, himself almost certainly a Freemason of the highest order: Christopher Wren.

CHAPTER TEN

FROM AUGUSTUS TO SOLOMON

Prior to the seventeenth century it was generally accepted that the city of London owed its foundations to Brutus and his Trojan companions. It was taken for granted that the historian Nennius, writing around AD 800, knew what he was talking about when he said that Julius Caesar fought a pitched battle against the Britons outside Trinovantum. It was assumed that this was the same Battle of the Ford (over the Thames) which Caesar himself recorded in his journals. Similarly, the story of London's foundation as told by Geoffrey of Monmouth in his *History of the Kings of Britain* was also treated with respect. Nobody disputed that Ludgate had been first built by King Lud, that Billingsgate took its name from a King Belin or that the head of Bran the Blessed was once buried under the White Hill at the Tower of London. That these legends were unprovable was no hindrance to their acceptance, for at the end of the day what is history but a collection of stories from the past?

The story of how and when Christianity came to Britain had been a matter of debate for centuries. According to Gildas, who lived in the sixth century, the first missionaries arrived in 'the last year of Tiberius

Caesar', which gives a date of AD 36 or 37. How this came about was also a matter of conflicting stories. According to many early writers the 'apostle to Britain' was Joseph of Arimathea, who brought the Holy Grail to Glastonbury. Writers of the seventeenth century were for the most part sceptical about this, but they were enthusiastic supporters of another legend: that the apostle Paul visited London and had preached at the spot where his cathedral was later to be built. For obvious reasons this version of history seems to have been popular in London. In his book *Parentilia* Christopher Wren junior quotes a contemporary of his father's, Edward Stillingfleet (1635–99), who was both a historian of some note and a former dean of St Paul's:

> The Christian Faith without doubt was very early received in Britain; and without having recourse to the monkish tale of Joseph of Arimathea and other legendary fictions, there is authentick testimony of the Christian church planted here by the Apostles themselves, and in particular, very probably by St Paul.

Wren junior goes on to quote from Rapin's *History of England*, book 1, to justify this assertion (Rapin was a Protestant Frenchman whose *History* was published in English in the early eighteenth century):

> It is very certain the Apostle [Paul] from his first imprisonment at Rome to his return to Jerusalem had spent eight years in preaching in diverse places, but more especially in the Western Countries. We know he designed for Spain and it is not improbable, but for his earnestness to convert the Britons might have carried him to that island. This opinion may be strengthened

by the evidence of Venutius Fortunatius, who says the same thing, speaking of the travels of St Paul in his poem on the life of St Martin.

Transit et Oceanum, vel qua facit Insula Portum Quasq. Brittanus habet terras, quasq. ultima Thule.
(And he crossed the ocean, take your choice which island port he made for, the land held by Britain, the ultimate Thule.)

As the seventeenth century advanced, so a re-assessment of British history began. Whereas John Stow (*c.*1525–1605), an antiquarian active during the reign of Queen Elizabeth, had been inclined merely to repeat the traditional accounts handed down from earlier generations, with the advent of the new science of archaeology people began to question the validity of traditional history. William Camden (1551–1623), a contemporary of Francis Bacon, belonged to this new generation of historians. One of the foremost intellectuals of his age, he numbered among his friends Isaac Casaubon and Archbishop Ussher, famous for his calculation that the world began in 4004 BC. The new history being pioneered by Camden was not afraid to be critical of the legendary past. For him, and for others who followed in his footsteps, the really interesting history of Britain began with the invasions of the Romans and the introduction of their civilization into what had previously been a barbaric land. This was wholly in accord with the new fashion for the Roman architecture, which owed nothing to Brutus, King Lud, Belinus or any of the other 'Welsh' kings of Britain. As the seventeenth century wore on, so these fabled kings and their even more fabulous city of 'New Troy' gradually faded from memory to be all but lost in the collective unconscious of the nation. Instead, London was celebrated as a daughter of Rome; a city which had even in those far-off times rivalled its mother in size of population, prosperity and all things civilized. Following the Great Fire of 1666 it was intended that the new London which rose from the ashes should challenge the Rome of the Catholic Church as the fulcrum of Christian Europe. The movement propelling this new vision of London as the pre-eminent city of light, a beacon to the world, was Freemasonry.

Like Continental Rosicrucianism, English Freemasonry in the seventeenth century was still a secret society. Thus, while the evidence of masonic activity is all around us in the form of buildings and monuments, written records of the actual beliefs and practices of early Freemasons are not so freely available. Our best source on the early history of Freemasonry in England comes from the following century: the 1738 edition of the *Constitutions of the Freemasons*, written by Dr James Anderson. This book, which is an update of an earlier but less complete edition of 1723, gives a wide-ranging chronology of English Freemasonry. Unfortunately, the reliability of the text is somewhat blighted by the fact that the earliest parts of the 'history' cannot be taken literally. For example, who would today believe that Saxon kings such as Hengest and Aethelstan (still less Adam and Noah) were 'Freemasons' in any formal sense of the word? It is clear that the earlier part of Anderson's account is to be read as mythology wrapped up as history and given a suitably Anglo-Christian slant. This being so, it might be tempting to dismiss Anderson's history in its entirety – were it not that from the time of James I onwards the tone of his account changes. One feels reasonably

Fig. 29. Frontispiece from *Constitutions of the Freemasons* by James Anderson (1723).

confident that as regards the history of Freemasonry from 1603 onwards Anderson, who had access to all the records, knew what he was writing about. Moreover, he was an experienced genealogist, used to ferreting out just this sort of information.[1] Thus the 1738 edition of Anderson's *Constitutions* has to be the starting point for any serious enquiry into the history of Freemasonry.

Highly pertinent to our present theme are Anderson's lists of Grand Masters, Deputy Grand Masters and Grand Wardens of England. Careful analysis of these lists indicates that whatever written records they may or may not have been based upon, the Freemasonry described is closely connected with the Stuart court. Though there may have been English craft lodges associated with Scottish Rite Freemasonry from before 1603, Freemasonry would appear to have been brought to London at the time of James I.

> James I. Stuart, now the first King of all Britain, a Royal Brother Mason, and Royal Grand Master by Prerogative, wishing for proper Heads and Hands for establishing the Augustan Stile here, was glad to find such a subject as Inigo Jones: whom he appointed his General Surveyor, and approv'd of his being chosen Grand Master of England to preside over the Lodges.
>
> 1618. William Earl of Pembroke was chosen Grand Master and being approved by the king, he appointed Inigo Jones his Deputy Grand Master.[2]

That James I himself took a keen interest in architecture is not in doubt: witness his rebuilding of Aldersgate so that it would convey the message that he was king over Israel. Thus it is not impossible that he was indeed a 'Grand Master by Royal Prerogative' as Anderson claims. In Britain he was certainly the most important artistic patron of his time, and he undoubtedly took a great interest in the building of Whitehall Palace. Inigo Jones, who is listed by Anderson as England's first 'Deputy Grand Master', was active as an architect during the reigns of both James I and Charles I. He is the first great English architect whom we know by name, and in 1612 the king did indeed appoint him Surveyor-General of Royal Buildings. It is not inconceivable that Inigo Jones was also, with the king's approval, elected as Masonic Grand Master of England with authority to preside over the English lodges.

James was not the first to approve of Jones; his talents had first been spotted some years earlier by William Herbert, third earl of Pembroke – the man who in 1618, according to Anderson, was to become second Grand Master of England's Freemasons. With the earl's help Jones, the humble son of a cloth-worker, was able to visit Italy. He was already an outstanding draftsman, but while in Italy he came into contact with neoclassical architecture: what Anderson refers to as the 'Augustan Stile'. This style of architecture, inimical to the Gothic, owed its inspiration to the ancient Romans and before them the Greeks. In 1452 an old collection of textbooks, written by a Roman architect called Vitruvius, had been discovered. Vitruvius had lived in the latter part of the first century AD at the time of the Emperor Augustus, and in his book he explained the canon (i.e. the rules or laws) governing architecture. This architectural canon owed its origins to ancient Egypt, where exact laws of proportion governed everything from the setting out of temples to the correct form for statues.

These laws had been further refined subsequently in Greece. The Greek canon, which was later adopted by the Romans, covered such matters as the appropriate use of the three orders of architecture, Doric, Ionian and Corinthian; the correct proportions for rooms; the appropriate ratios (according to the order being used) for the diameters of pillars compared with their height; and rules for what we would now call *feng-shui*: the orientation of buildings and elements within them in such a way as to optimize their 'energy'.

During the Renaissance the books of Vitruvius were very highly regarded and they influenced deeply the work of contemporary Italian architects. One of the greatest of these, very largely responsible for this classical revival in Italian architecture, was Andrea Palladio (1518–80). Turning his back on the pointed Gothic arch and the elaborate tracery of the late medieval age, Palladio exulted in the classic simplicity of imperial Rome at its height under Augustus. He built many churches and country villas in northern Italy, notably in Vicenza. The textbook which he sub-sequently wrote, *I quattro libri dell'architettura* (The four books of architecture, 1570), was the first serious work on architectural principles since the days of Vitruvius. Palladio's book was widely read throughout Europe and it made the 'Augustan style' absolutely de rigueur for any architect or patron who wanted to seem forward-thinking. Inigo Jones, who saw many examples of classical as well as neoclassical buildings while travelling in Italy, subsequently published an English translation of Palladio along with notes of his own. Consequently he was regarded as the foremost English authority on the neoclassical or Augustan style.

Prior to his return to England in 1612, Jones built

palaces at Rosenborg and Fredericksborg for the Garter knight King Christian IV of Denmark. As his reputation as an architect grew, so it was inevitable that James I would ask him to do the same at home. Accordingly, Jones returned to England and designed the neoclassical Palace of Whitehall, which has unfortunately since been largely destroyed by fire. What remains of this palace – most especially the Banqueting House (built between 1619 and 1621) – reveals what a huge influence Jones had on subsequent British architects such as Christoper Wren, Nicholas Hawksmoor, John Vanburgh and John Nash.

During the course of the building of Whitehall Palace, most of which took place during the reign of Charles I, Inigo Jones still occupied the office of Surveyor-General. In this role he hired and supervised the teams of operative masons involved in this building project. Thus it can be said that whether or not he was actually a 'Grand Master' or 'Deputy Grand Master' in the masonic sense of the word, he was certainly the most senior British architect of his day and thus de facto the practising 'grand master' of his age. Since Inigo's buildings were strikingly classical in conception and quite unlike anything seen in England since Roman times, it is no exaggeration on Anderson's part to say that it was he who introduced the Augustan style into England.

In Anderson's list of Grand Masters and their deputies, Inigo Jones is followed by his first patron, William Herbert, the earl of Pembroke. This was the elder of the two sons (the other being Philip Herbert) of the famous countess of Pembroke to whom the poet Spenser dedicated his *Ruines of Time*. The two brothers were also, of course, the nephews of the countess's brother, Sir Philip Sidney. Thus William Herbert, Inigo Jones's patron, was heir, so to speak, of the mystical Elizabethan tradition, represented by Sir Philip Sidney and his mentor, Dr John Dee. Like Sir Francis Bacon, whom he would have known well, William Herbert achieved high office, rising to become Lord Chamberlain of the Royal Household and Lord Steward. He was also very prominent in academic circles. In 1624 he was made chancellor of the University of Oxford and Broadgates Hall was renamed Pembroke College in his honour. Given these privileged connections, it is not at all unlikely that he was chosen as Grand Master of whatever English Freemasonry then existed.

During the Civil War and the Commonwealth period that succeeded it, architecture went into a steep decline. The post of Surveyor-General was suspended and Inigo Jones, who was regarded by parliamentarians with disdain, was fined. He died in poverty in 1651 and with his passing serious English architecture went into hibernation. Consequently the 1650s saw little building work – but this was to change once the king returned in 1660. Yet for all the merriment of the Restoration, the 1660s were trying years for Londoners. Between 1664 and 1665 a Great Plague swept through the capital and took the lives of about a sixth of the population. The fire of 1666, which destroyed filthy slums and rat-infested warehouses as well as churches, was looked upon by many as an act of God. In this light, the near-complete destruction of London was viewed as a cleansing of the land so that a new and better city might rise in its place.

The Great Fire of London gave Charles II a perfect opportunity to show not just London but the world just what an enlightened monarch could do for his people: he would rebuild London in the Augustan style. The man chosen to carry out this scheme was, of course, Christopher Wren. His son writes:

After the most dreadful conflagration of London in the fatal year 1666, Dr Christopher Wren was appointed Surveyor-General and Principal Architect for rebuilding the whole city; the cathedral church of St Paul, all the parochial churches (in number fifty-one, – enacted by Parliament, in lieu of those that were burnt or demolished) with other publick structures; and for the disposition of streets, a charge so great and extensive, incumbent on a single person, dispos'd him to take to his assistance Mr Robert Hook Professor of Geometry in Gresham College, to whom he assign'd chiefly the business of measuring, adjusting and setting out the ground of the private street houses to the several proprietors; reserving all the Publick-works to his own peculiar care and direction.

On 6th Mar 1667/8 he received his Majesties Warrant under the Privy-Seal (in confirmation of a deputation from Sr John Denham Knight of the Bath) to execute the Office of Surveyor General of the Royal Works: upon whose decease in the same month, his majesty was pleased to grant him Letters Patent, under the Great-Seal to succeed in that employment. Dr Wren had confer'd on him the Honour of Knighthood in the year 1674.

In 1684 Sr Christopher Wren was constitute by Patents under the Great-Seal, the Principal officer by the state of the Comptroller of the works of the Castle of Windsor, and of all Mannors, Lodges, etc. in the Forrest thereof in the room of Hugh May esq. deceas.

> In 1698 He was appointed Surveyor-General and
> Commissioner of Works and Repairs of the ancient
> Abbey church of St Peter in Westminster.[3]

There can be no doubting that Christopher Wren was a genius of the first order, one of the greatest intellects of his time. That we possess so many fine churches in London today is largely attributable to his extraordinary ability to work on numerous projects at once. Perhaps the only other single architect in the last thousand years to have personally made such an impression on a great city was Sinan, born in 1489. He, a Turkish soldier by profession, turned his hand to architecture and designed the Blue Mosque, the Suleimaniye Mosque, and many other fine buildings in Istanbul. So capable did he turn out to be that Ottoman architecture became synonymous with his style of building. As an architect Wren was certainly in Sinan's class, for the City of London of the late seventeenth and eighteenth centuries was very much a product of his handiwork. Even so, the question arises: was he working alone or was he, like his friends Elias Ashmole and Sir Robert Moray, also a Freemason?

For over a century this question has been the subject of lively debate. Following Wren's death in 1723 and for the best part of the ensuing two centuries it had always been assumed, even by Freemasonry's opponents, that he was a member of the brotherhood. However, in the early twentieth century this assumption was challenged and evidence of his membership was demanded. To set the minds of his brother masons at rest on this apparently vexing point, in 1917 a mason named Revd F. de P. Castells published a pamphlet entitled *Was Wren a Mason?* In this the author presented three clear points of evidence which, taken together, ought to have put the matter beyond question.

The first line of evidence presented by Castells was a reference in a newspaper called the *Postboy*, the second issue of which was published shortly after Wren's death. It gives details of his interment on 5 March 1723, describing Sir Christopher Wren as 'that worthy Freemason'. Castells goes on to inform us that on 9 March, four days after the interment, another newspaper, called the *British Journal*, used precisely the same words in reporting the same event. At the time no one challenged the assertion, printed in both these newspapers, that the late Christopher Wren had been a Freemason. This would suggest that the idea of his membership of the brotherhood was, if not common knowledge, at least considered to be unremarkable.

The second piece of Castells' evidence was drawn from John Aubrey's *Natural History of Wiltshire*. The original manuscript of this work was written while Wren was alive and is now in the Bodleian Library in Oxford. There is in addition a hand-written transcript, which Aubrey made himself for the use of the Royal Society. At the time Castells was writing this was preserved at Burlington House, where the Royal Society had its headquarters from 1857 until its twentieth-century move to a new home close to Trafalgar Square at 6 Carlton House Terrace. Though the *Natural History of Wiltshire* is, as the title would suggest, devoted to an entirely different subject from architecture, there are two paragraphs in the form of a diary entry which refer to Wren:

24. Church of the Holy Sepulchre in Jerusalem, covering what are believed to be the sites of the execution and burial of Jesus Christ.

25. The Dome of the Rock, the wheel-shaped mosque covering the spot where it is believed Abraham nearly sacrificed his son and where the Adytum of King Solomon's Temple was later sited.

26. The Al-Aqsa Mosque on the Temple Mount of Jerusalem, covering part of the site of Herod's Temple and where the crusading Templars once had their headquarters.

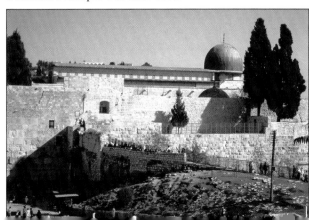

27. Inigo Jones's Banqueting Hall, part of Whitehall Palace and the first major British building to be constructed in the once fashionable Augustan style of Vitruvius.

28. Sir Christopher Wren, mathematical genius, founder member of the Invisible College and Royal Society, masonic Grand Master and chief architect of the 'New Jerusalem'.

29. The mallet (in the background) believed to have been used by Sir Christopher Wren to lay the foundation stone of the new St Paul's Cathedral.

30. John Evelyn's Kabbalah-plan for the rebuilding of London as a sacred city.

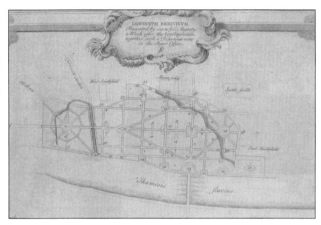

31. John Evelyn's later and less obviously hermetic plan for rebuilding the city of London.

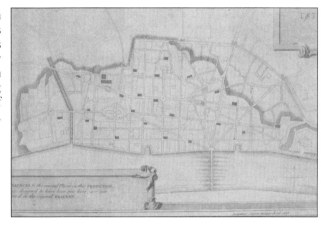

32. Christopher Wren's proposed plan for the rebuilding of London which for economic reasons was never properly realized.

33. Wren's deeply symbolic Great Model for the rebuilding of St Paul's Cathedral, which was deemed unacceptable by the clergy (*left*).

34. Model of the Jerusalem Church of the Holy Sepulchre as originally built by the Empress Helen, mother of Constantine the Great (*right*).

35. St Paul's Cathedral, the most significant Augustan-style building in Britain and itself a model of the cosmos.

36. St Paul's Cross, near the spot where the apostle himself is said to have preached to the people of London.

37. The southern pediment of St Paul's Cathedral, featuring a phoenix, symbolic of rebirth from the ashes.

38. The sun on the summer solstice crossing in the east behind the Monument to the Great Fire. It casts a significant shadow.

39. Symbolic plaque by Gabriel Cibber on the base of the Monument.

40. The London Temple Church, which once belonged to the Knights Templar. Today it is a 'royal peculiar', though used as a chapel by lawyers.

41. Inside the Temple Church, which was modelled on the Holy Sepulchre and bears the same relation to St Paul's as that building does to the Dome of the Rock.

42. Nelson's Column in Trafalgar Square, the same height as the Monument and therefore casting significant shadows on the solstice.

43. Statue of Lord Nelson, England's greatest hero of the nineteenth century, standing atop his column and looking down Whitehall towards the coronation seat.

44. A symbolic banner of the British Israel movement featuring angels, the royal coat of arms, the garter, the coronation seat with the Stone of Destiny, the cross of Edward the Confessor and the roses of England.

1691 after Rogation Sunday Mdm, this day [May the 18th being Monday] is a great convention at St Paul's Church of the Fraternity of Accepted the Free Masons: where Sr Christopher Wren is to be adopted a Brother: and Sr Henry Goodric ... of ye Tower, and divers others. There has been Kings, that were of this sodalite. – Sr William Dugdale told me many years since, that about Henry the third's time, the Patents Pope gave a Bull or diploma to a Company of Italian Freemasons Architects to travell up and downe over all Europe to build Churches. From these are derived the Fraternity of Adopted-Masons.

'Free-Masons'. They are known to one another by certayn signes and Marks and Watch-words; it continues to this day. They have severall Lodges in severall Counties for their reception: and when any of them fall into decay, the brotherhood is to relieve him, etc. The manner of their Adoption is very formall, and with an Oath of Secrecy.[4]

It does not seem that Aubrey himself was a Freemason, so he no doubt heard all of this from Sir William Dugdale, one of whose daughters was married to Elias Ashmole. We know from other sources that Ashmole, who among many other accomplishments wrote the first, definitive history of the Order of the Garter, was initiated into speculative Freemasonry on 16 October 1646. He was fifteen years older than Wren and, like him, a founder member of the Royal Society. As he lived until 1692, after the events described by Aubrey, it is quite possible that it was he who told Sir William Dugdale about the special meeting that was to be held on Monday, 18 May 1691. However, the real purpose of this 'adoption' meeting – to which we shall turn shortly – seems not to have been understood by Aubrey. Not being a Freemason himself, he was not told everything and does not seem to have realized that Christopher Wren was already not only a mason but the Deputy Grand Master of England.

The third of Castell's proofs comes from the 1738 edition of Anderson's *Constitutions*. Carrying on from the appointment of Charles I as 'Royal Brother and Grand Master by Prerogative', Anderson tells us that:

> When Grand Master Pembroke demitted AD 1630, Henry Danvers Earl of Danby succeeded in Solomon's chair by the King's Approbation.
> Followed by Thomas Howard Earl of Arundel 1634?
> Grand Master Beckford.
> Inigo Jones again (died 26th June 1652)
> (Restoration Charles II)
> Henry Jermyn Earl of St Albans Grand Master.
> Sir John Denham his Deputy Grand Master.
> Sir Christopher Wren ⎱ Grand
> Mr John Webb ⎰ Wardens
> Thomas Savage Earl of Rivers succeeded St Albans as Grand Master 24th June 1666
> Sir Christopher Wren his Deputy.
> Mr John Webb ⎱ Grand
> Grinling Gibbons ⎰ Wardens
> Master Rivers demitted AD 1679
> Succeeded by George Villiers.[5]

Throughout most of the seventeenth century there seems to have been an arrangement that, if there were a suitably available royal or noble candidate able and willing to fill the post, then 'Solomon's Chair' would be occupied by him in preference to a lowly architect. In these circumstances a real architect would be appointed as a subordinate deputy. Thus it was that Inigo Jones, who had been Grand Master of English Freemasonry under James I, later occupied the position of Deputy Grand Master to a succession of nobles – the earls of Pembroke, Danby, Arundel and finally of Bedford – before eventually, towards the end of his life, once again becoming Grand Master himself.

Anderson's list is almost a roll-call of important architects, their assistants and patrons for the mid- to late seventeenth century. Henry Danvers, earl of Danby, like his predecessor William Herbert, earl of Pembroke, was a Garter knight at the time of Charles I. Thomas Howard, earl of Arundel and later duke of Norfolk, was a scion of what is still the most eminent Catholic family in England. Like many other Howards, his political career was something of a roller-coaster, involving both high office and imprisonment in the Tower of London. In 1641, having presided over the trial of Strafford, he retired to Padua in Italy. Thus his mastership, if genuine, cannot have amounted to very much in terms of financing building projects, and after 1641 would have had to have been carried out in exile. However, he may still have held the position of Grand Master in an honorary sense, rather like a modern chancellor of a university. Thomas Howard is most famous for the large collection of Roman and Greek statues that he collected and sent back to England. Many of these were either lost or destroyed during the Civil War, when Arundel Castle was looted by the parliamentarians; however, some survived and were later presented to Oxford University by his grandson, Henry Howard. After the Great Fire of London, Arundel House was for a time the home of the Royal

Society, to which Thomas Howard's library was donated by Henry at around the same time he gave the statues to Oxford University. Given Thomas Howard's love of Italy and all things Italian, we can be sure that he was enthusiastic about the Augustan style and would have done his best to encourage its adoption among British architects.

John Webb, who is listed as one of two Grand Wardens during the mastership of Sir John Denham, was perhaps the best trained architect of his day, having trained under Inigo Jones. He should have been Grand Master had not political considerations intervened. The other Grand Warden was Sir Christopher Wren, which implies that he was already a Freemason soon after the Restoration of Charles II. Although Wren was not appointed to the post of Surveyor-General of the King's Works until 1669, he was already a member of the commission for the repair of St Paul's Cathedral in 1663, three years before the Great Fire. In that year Wren presented a model of his first serious architectural project: the Sheldonian Theatre at Oxford. This building is thoroughly classical in style, being based on a plan of the Theatre Marcellus in Rome. Round-arched windows and doorways are a major feature of the building, giving it a look immediately recognizable as 'Augustan style'.

During the time of these aristocratic Grand Masters, real architects, such as Wren and Webb, got on with their work. So too did Grinling Gibbons, a Dutchman whose woodcarvings adorn many of Wren's churches, and Gaius Gabriel Cibber, a Danish sculptor from Flensburg. According to Anderson they also were Grand Wardens at one time or another, which would suggest that even in the seventeenth century

Freemasonry was an international movement.

In 1666, the year of the Great Fire, the earl of St Albans died and was succeeded as Grand Master of English Freemasons by Thomas Savage, earl of Rivers. According to Anderson, Christopher Wren (by now the King's Surveyor) was appointed his deputy, his colleagues John Webb and Grinling Gibbons being Grand Wardens. These three continued to hold these ranks during the Masterships of the next two occupants of Solomon's Seat: George Villiers, duke of Buckingham, and Henry Bennet, earl of Arlington. When the latter died in 1685 he was succeeded for a short time by Wren himself, Gabriel Cibber and Edward Strong being his Grand Wardens. For three years between 1695 and 1698 Wren went back to the subordinate position of deputy to Grand Master Charles Lennox, duke of Richmond and Lennox, before being once more elected Grand Master himself. He then seems to have continued in the role of Grand Master for most if not all of the rest of his life.

On the face of it, Aubrey's reference to Wren attending a convention at St Paul's in 1691 and there being adopted as a 'brother' stands in flat contradiction to Anderson's claim that at this time Wren was himself Grand Master. However, Aubrey was not himself a Freemason and, according to the Revd Castells, did not realize the significance of what really happened at St Paul's on that day. By that time work on rebuilding the cathedral, which had begun in earnest in 1675, was well advanced. To carry out this work and indeed to rebuild fifty-two of the eighty-seven London churches destroyed by the fire, Wren had had to employ a veritable army of master masons, journeymen and apprentices. These were drawn from all over England

and probably the Continent as well. These operative masons, who would have been real craftsmen and not speculative Freemasons, met together in lodges, the most famous of which was a hostelry called the Goose and Gridiron, where the masons employed by St Paul's held their meetings.

According to Castells, quoting from Prestin's *Illustrations of Masonry*, 'Wren presided over the old Lodge of St Paul's during the building of the cathedral. The same lodge is said to have owned the mallet used in laying the foundation stone.' He goes on to say: 'In the edition of 1792, Preston stated that the said mallet was a gift of Sir Christopher Wren himself and that "during his presidency he presented the lodge three mahogany candlesticks, which were still in use at the time of writing".' It would appear to have been a meeting of this St Paul's lodge, called by Preston 'Lodge number 1, "the Lodge of Antiquity, formerly called of Old St Paul's", that was attended by Wren in 1691 and reported on by John Aubrey in his *Natural History of Wiltshire*.' Wren's mallet – or what is believed to have been his mallet – is now in the possession of the United Grand Lodge of London.

A charge has been laid against Wren that towards the end of his life he neglected his duties as Grand Master and allowed the London lodges to go into decline. Certainly it is true that he came in for criticism over what was perceived to be the slow progress of the rebuilding of St Paul's. In 1697 an Act of Parliament suspended payment of half his salary until such time as the work should be completed. The construction was finished in all but a few details in 1710, so in 1711 he petitioned for payment of the residue. He was still the most senior architect in the land but by now, at the age of seventy-nine, he was no longer running the project. In 1718 he was deprived of the title of Surveyor-General and forced to retire, his post being taken over by an incompetent successor, William Benson. The following year Wren was charged with mismanagement of the St Paul's project. To this outrageous slur on his character he replied with sincere humility that he had 'endeavoured to doe his Majesty all service I was able, with the same integrity and zeal which I had ever practised ... as I am dismissed, having worn out (by God's mercy) a long life in Royal service, and having made some figure in the world, I hope it will be allow'd me to die in peace.'[6] His wish was granted five years later, when on 25 February 1723, at the grand age of ninety-one, he passed away quietly at his house in St James's Street.

It is against this background, with the building of St Paul's complete and Wren himself under attack by mean-minded critics, that we have to consider the birth of the Grand Lodge. According to Anderson, this came about in 1717 with the amalgamation of four existing craft lodges: the St Paul's Lodge that met at the Goose and Gridiron alehouse in St Paul's Churchyard; the lodge from the Crown alehouse in Parker's Lane; the lodge from the Apple Tree tavern in Charles Street; and the lodge from the Rummer and Grapes tavern in Westminster. These four lodges are supposed to have been the only ones then in existence in the south of England and to have met together at the Apple Tree tavern, where they voted for union. The result of this union was the formation of the United Grand Lodge of England with a Mr Anthony Sayer voted Grand Master for the following year. Though there are other Grand Lodges in existence throughout the world – most especially in America – the London group is generally regarded as the parent body of all modern Freemasons. The chief difference between this lodge and those that preceded it (other than size) was that it allowed for the recruitment of speculative Freemasons, i.e. men who though not themselves involved in the building trade nevertheless went through its initiation ceremonies in symbolic fashion. This obviously widened the field for potential members, turning the old masonic craft guilds into a broad-based society.

Yet according to some commentators at least, the formation of Grand Lodge and the birth of modern, speculative Freemasonry was not so much a progressive movement as a symptom of decline. The London building boom of the late seventeenth century had slowed the decline of medieval craft masonry, which was a national problem, by making it possible for a relatively large number of lodges to thrive in the capital. With the end of the boom and the dispersal of the large workforce that had been needed to build so many churches all at once, the lodges found themselves short of members. This seems to have been why they amalgamated to form the first Grand Lodge. Yet even this was not enough to halt the decline: they also found it necessary to bring in new members who were not themselves practising masons in any trade sense. These new members might be bankers, shopkeepers, judges and bureaucrats. These men joined the Freemasons not through any wish to change career but because they had an interest in the symbolic aspects of the old craft and a wish to meet up with like-minded men for philosophical discussion.

Thus the new Grand Lodge of 1717 was different from the old craft lodges in that the majority of its members did not (as their successors today do not) actually work in the building trade. Consequently most twenty-first-century Freemasons are ignorant of the real secrets of Freemasonry, which are not as obvious as they may first appear. As William Stirling, himself a Freemason of the late nineteenth century, wrote:

In the traditions and ritual of modern Freemasonry, we have the remains of those philosophical doctrines, which at one time guided the practice of architecture. Whatever uncertainty there may be as to the precise secrets of the old operative masons, it is evident that the rites which are said to have been formulated for the first time in the eighteenth century, were not a brand new invention. For it may be asserted – and this is confirmed by many contemporary evidences – that the establishment of the present forms of initiation and instruction was the attempt of certain mystics of that time, to preserve the ancient secrets of architecture from sinking into the oblivion which was rapidly overtaking the lapsed craft of operative Freemasonry. And the new dilettante masons seem to have been sufficiently instructed in the mystical traditions, still existing at that time, to compose the degrees in accordance with the old system, so they may be taken as tolerably reliable expositions of the ideas which governed the practice of their predecessors.

. . . The disuse of symbolical architecture, however, does not seem to have come about till after the time of Sir Christopher Wren, for it is known that he was the master of an operative lodge, and that Freemasons were employed in building St Paul's, the last of the old cathedrals . . .

The coming to light of all sorts of mystical

knowledge that had been carefully concealed in previous times, is one of the noticeable features of the seventeenth and eighteenth centuries. But it is a mistake to suppose that for this reason these centuries were peculiarly given to mysticism, on the contrary, the appearance in the seventeenth century of Rosicrucian, Hermetic, and Masonic Societies was a sign of decadence, and the premonition of the final extinction of the esoteric traditions of antiquity. As long as the secret doctrines of masonry were received as the vital inspiration of the craft, no one heard anything about them, and the same thing applies to theology itself. In fact the mysteries, which in the past were only spoken in secret and never written, became faintly heard when their power had practically ceased.[7]

From what Stirling writes we may deduce that Christopher Wren was a Grand Master of a different order from those who came after him; and that there is much that he both knew and did which is not common knowledge among ordinary Freemasons today.

In the seventeenth century more and more people became convinced that Britain had a special role in the world: a destiny which they believed was linked to the holy covenants established between God and man at the time of Abraham, Isaac, Jacob, Moses, David and Solomon. The idea that St Paul came to Britain and preached in London chimed with the concept that the British themselves (or at least some of them) were descended from the lost tribes of Israel. It seemed obvious that Paul – and possibly other apostles such as Joseph of Arimathea – had come to Britain because they knew it was the land where the lost tribes were gathering. It was God's wish that the Britons be now converted to Christianity so that they could fulfil their destiny in Christ.

These speculations were to find their ultimate expression two hundred years later in the Victorian age with the formation of the British Israel movement. They are pivotal to our understanding of the symbolism implicit in the structure of the new cathedral of St Paul's that was built under the supervision of Sir Christopher Wren. It is because he was a high initiate from before the time of Freemasonry's decadence that William Stirling describes St Paul's as 'the last of the old cathedrals'. This, however, is not an entirely accurate description, for Wren's cathedral was really emblematic of something else: the Temple of Solomon.

CHAPTER ELEVEN

BUILDING NEW JERUSALEM

In 1666, with almost every building in the square mile of the old City of London razed to the ground, King Charles II turned to his colleagues of the Royal Society for assistance. As it was widely believed that the narrow streets with their overhanging wooden houses had been responsible for the fire, the king was keen that the whole area should be levelled and that the city be rebuilt in brick and stone. This offered a unique opportunity to get away from the past and to develop a new, modern street plan. In the event, unfortunately, owing to difficulties arising out of land ownership and a general lack of funds to see through such grand designs, the city was rebuilt along the old streets; however, plans for a new, grid-based city were drawn up and a close examination of these reveals the hidden, esoteric influences that pervaded the thinking of the time.

Among the members of the Royal Society whom Charles consulted was his old friend John Evelyn. Evelyn, who had experience of laying out formal gardens, seems to have approached the task of designing a whole city with some alacrity and also a great deal of imagination. Within weeks he had produced several alternative schemes (see plates 30 and 31). The most audacious of these almost completely did away with the old higgledy-piggledy street plan that had grown up over the centuries. In its place he proposed a city of wide boulevards, the houses and churches being built of either brick or stone. Closer inspection of Evelyn's plans, however, reveals that what he had in mind was not simply a grid system but something much more significant. He more than anyone seems to have had in mind the idea that the new London should be an esoteric city: a 'New Jerusalem'.

By the late seventeenth century science, in a form we would recognize today, was beginning to find its feet. However, growing side by side with this culture of rationalism there still clung the vine of mysticism. The fruits of this vine were philosophy – not the modern creation of Descartes, Erasmus and Spinoza but something older and more potent: hermeticism. The prime method of study was, of course, alchemy, and men such as Elias Ashmole, Robert Boyle and even Isaac Newton paid attention to their athanors. There were, however, other methods of studying what is known as the 'perennial philosophy' and one of the most intriguing of these was Kabbalah.

The origins of this philosophy, an esoteric outgrowth of Judaism, are lost in the mists of time. According to Z'ev Ben Shimon Halevi, a modern-day teacher of Kabbalah, there is a tradition that it was imparted by Melchizedek, the priest-king of Salem (Jerusalem), at the time he blessed Abraham (see Gen. 14: 18–20). According to Halevi, it was preserved as an oral teaching and passed down from master to pupil until finally being written down, perhaps in the first centuries after Christ. This is about the same time as the Egyptian *Hermetica* were penned; and, as the Kabbalah has much in common with certain of those writings, it is tempting to think that, in the form we have it, this system of Jewish mysticism was actually composed by members of the Jewish community of Alexandria. Later on Kabbalistic schools flourished in Spain, where there was a large Jewish community up until the end of the fifteenth century. It was probably here that the original teachings of Kabbalah were first set down in a short book called *Sepher Yetzirah* (or 'Book of creation'). Lengthy commentaries were added to this in the form of the *Zohar*, a work on mystical Judaism that was written in Spain during the thirteenth century.

During the late medieval period Jews were increasingly unwelcome in much of western Europe. They had been expelled from England en masse in 1290 by order of King Edward I; after that date any who remained in the country had to convert to Christianity or face persecution. The same thing happened in France in 1306 (where a mass expulsion of Jews took place at the same time that the king was busy suppressing the supposedly heretical order of the Templars) and in Spain in 1492. A perhaps unexpected side-effect of this last persecution was to bring the Jewish Kabbalah to the attention of Christian scholars, often via the medium of Jews who converted. At the time of the Italian Renaissance, in the late fifteenth and early sixteenth centuries, the study of Kabbalah became extremely popular with such Hermeticists as Pico della Mirandola and Cornelius Agrippa von Nettesheim. In their books, which were read throughout Europe, a 'Christian' Kabbalah was developed. This not only insulated them from charges of heresy but it also made the subject more acceptable to their readers. Among these readers was Dr John Dee, who was not only enthusiastic about

Kabbalah in theory but put it into practice in his angel magic.

That the Kabbalah was studied intensively in England during the sixteenth and seventeenth centuries there can be no doubt. The English Rosicrucian author Robert Fludd, who was writing in the early half of the century, had much to say on the subject. By the time of Charles II the study of Kabbalah (sometimes written Cabala) was almost commonplace among English intellectuals. For this reason the word 'Cabal', meaning secret or exclusive, was used to describe Charles's inner circle of ministers: Clifford, Arlington, Buckingham, Ashley-Cooper and Lauderdale, the first letters of whose names spell out the word. In was in this climate that Evelyn, himself clearly interested in esoteric matters, drew up his plans for London.

At the centre of Kabbalistic philosophy is a diagram known as the 'Tree of Life', which is based upon the teachings given in the *Sepher Yetzirah*:

> Yah, the Lord of hosts, the living God, King of the Universe, Omnipotent, All-Kind and Merciful, Supreme and Extolled, who is Eternal, Sublime and Most-Holy, ordained and created the Universe in thirty-two mysterious paths of wisdom by three Sepharim . . . They consist of a decade out of nothing and of twenty-two fundamental letters.[1]

The 'decade out of nothing' is conceived of as ten spheres or *sephiroth*, and these are arranged in three columns according to a set pattern. They are joined to one another by twenty-two pathways, one for each letter of the Hebrew alphabet. An eleventh, 'hidden' sphere represents knowledge. The resulting pattern of relationships is the major object of study for Kabbalists.

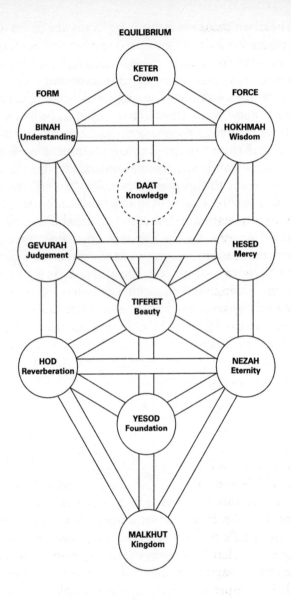

Fig. 30. The Kabbalistic tree of life.

There are many ways of interpreting the Tree of Life diagram, and indeed it has been the life's work of many Kabbalists. However, at root the ten *sephiroth* represent the heavenly spheres, which in ancient times were believed to revolve around the earth carrying the sun, moon, stars and planets with them. These spheres, which were really a metaphor for the orbits in which the heavenly bodies travelled, were thought of as being transparent and therefore glass-like. It was believed that at birth the soul journeyed down through these invisible spheres, like taking steps down a ladder, on its way to incarnation. After death it was thought that the soul would leave the body and have to make the return journey, laboriously climbing its way back to heaven. Thus the heavenly spheres or *sephiroth* were like way-stations linking the heaven to earth.

When we compare the Tree of Life diagram with Evelyn's plan for the rebuilding of London, it is immediately apparent that he had this diagram in mind when designing his proposed new layout for the city. Like Wren, he planned an eight-spoked wheel at the west end of Fleet Street by the church of St Dunstan's-in-the-West. The axis leading east from its centre would have major intersections at St Paul's, the Lord Mayor's House and the fountain in Gracechurch Street market place, and another eight-spoked wheel at the church of St Dunstan's-in-the-East. North-east and south-east of the Gracechurch Street fountain would be Bishop's Gate and the Fish Market respectively. These would link St Paul's with St Dunstan's by means of a kite-shape remarkably similar to the upper portion of the Tree of Life diagram used by Kabbalists. In fact, if the Tree of Life is superimposed over the city plan it becomes clear that this was deliberate, for the positions of the major intersections are all marked by *sephiroth*. This fact was brought to the attention of the author in December 1992 by Robert Bauval.[2]

The idea of using the Kabbalistic Tree of Life diagram in the city plan of London doubtless reflects Evelyn's own esoteric interests and also those of his circle. However, there are biblical references that he may also have had in mind and to which he may have been secretly alluding. The key passage occurs in the last chapter of the Book of Revelation and is a reference to the building of the New Jerusalem:

> And I John saw the holy city, new Jerusalem, coming down from God out of heaven, prepared as a bride adorned for her husband.
>
> And I heard a great voice out of heaven saying, Behold, the tabernacle of God is with men, and he will dwell with them, and they shall be his people, and God himself shall be with them, and be their God . . .
>
> And he said unto me, It is done. I am Alpha and Omega, the beginning and the end. I will give unto him that is athirst of the fountain of the water of life freely . . .
>
> And he shewed me a pure river of water of life, clear as crystal, proceeding out of the throne of God and of the Lamb.
>
> In the midst of the street of it, and on either side of the river, was there the tree of life, which bore twelve manner of fruits, and yielded her fruit every month: and the leaves of the tree were for the healing of nations. (Rev. 21: 2–6, 22: 1–2)

On Evelyn's plan for the new City of London, the head point or crown *sephirah* (Keter) was to be the church of St Dunstan-in-the-East, whilst the root or

306

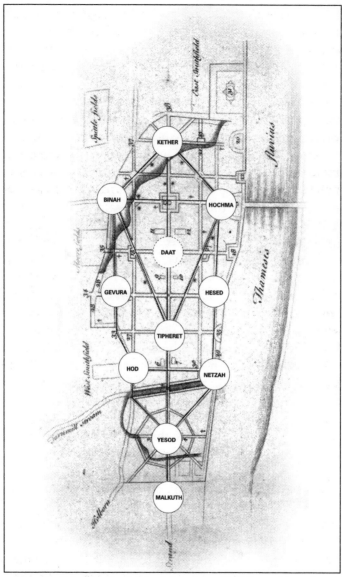

Fig. 31. John Evelyn's plans for the rebuilding of London showing the *sephiroth*.

base of the tree (Malkhut) was to be its complement, St Dunstan's-in-the-West. The road running between these two churches was to be the main axis of the city and either side of it are the subordinate thoroughfares. Heaven and earth would therefore be symbolically linked by the churches dedicated to this former archbishop of Canterbury who was responsible for building the first known English Christian church at Glastonbury. The hidden Dunstonian reference in the plan was also entirely appropriate in that he had promoted the building of churches in London, and stood for observance of the law and the value of education. These were all matters close to the hearts of seventeenth-century thinkers such as John Evelyn.

Many of the other positions on the map also seem to have had symbolic meaning. The fountain in Gracechurch Street market place was clearly intended to represent the hidden, eleventh *sephirah* of Daat or knowledge. It therefore represents the fountain of knowledge that irrigates the whole, and it is perhaps not accidental that it lies close to the site of Gresham College, home at that time to the Royal Society. The great cathedral church of St Paul's was to be linked with the *sephirah* Tipheret, whose meaning in Hebrew is 'beauty'. In many ways this is the most important *sephirah*, as astrologically speaking it represents the sun. This would be appropriate for a cathedral, the spiritual heart of the city and therefore an analogue of the sun itself.

Evelyn's Kabbalistic plan for the rebuilding of London was probably intended more as an intellectual exercise in the possible rather than as a serious blueprint to be worked from. At the same time or perhaps shortly afterwards he presented to the king a second, more practical though less obviously esoteric scheme. This involved a grid layout of east–west boulevards and north–south streets to create Roman-style city blocks. The main point of focus of this plan was the northern entrance to London Bridge, from which roads radiated in all directions. Evelyn's third plan was something of an amalgam of the other two. In the event none of these schemes was approved.

The man upon whom the burden of reconstructing London fell most heavily was, of course, Christopher Wren. Seldom in the history of Britain has there been such a marriage of man and moment as when this young professor of mathematics took on the task of rebuilding the capital city of what was already growing into an empire. As we shall see, Wren was able to embed into the very structure of his masterpiece, the new St Paul's Cathedral, the very essence of the British Israel philosophy. To cover the cost of the rebuilding of St Paul's and the many other London churches, a tax was imposed on coal entering the City; thus it was that the hearths of London were made to pay for the sacrilegious damage wrought by unruly fire.

Wren's preferred plan for rebuilding London was to be a compromise between Evelyn's Kabbalistic scheme and the street plan as it already existed. The main design feature of all Wren's plans was to be a system of major boulevards, mostly running east–west, criss-crossed by north–south streets, thereby producing a structure of city blocks (see plate 32). A large civic centre was to be constructed (where the Royal Exchange now stands), and from this was to radiate a wheel of ten streets. Another, eight-spoked, wheel and a perfect octagon of infill streets was to be built about halfway down Fleet Street. This he copied directly from Evelyn's Kabbalistic plan. A major west–east avenue would run from this centre through Ludgate, pass to the south of St Paul's Cathedral and proceed eastwards to terminate near the Tower of London. A second avenue would run north-east from Ludgate, bypass St Paul's on its northern side, go through the civic complex at the Royal Exchange and terminate at Aldgate. These two roads, with their point of focus at the ancient Ludgate, were intended to be the major east–west thoroughfares of Wren's proposed city. The main boulevard running from south to north would begin at Queen's Hithe docks, cut through the two avenues and terminate at Bishop's Gate.

Had Wren been able to rebuild the city to this scheme, the new London would have been an excitingly modern city, more akin to present-day Washington than anything of its time. As it was, the pressure to build quickly, coupled with problems relating to land ownership and compensation, made such a radical scheme impractical. The best that could be done was to pass a law making it illegal to build houses and churches out of materials other than brick or stone.

The greatest element of the project facing Wren was, of course, the rebuilding of St Paul's Cathedral. Prior to the Great Fire this church had been a Gothic edifice of gigantic proportions. This building had been constructed during Norman times, between 1085 and 1155, to replace an earlier Saxon church built in 607. In 1255–83 a new choir had been added to the Norman church, making it, at over 600 feet, the longest Gothic church in Europe.[3] Prior to an earlier fire in 1561 it featured a central tower and spire 534 feet in height – taller by far than that of even Salisbury Cathedral (404 feet).[4] Standing as it did on Ludgate

Hill, the medieval cathedral must have absolutely dominated the skyline of London, its enormous length and skyscraping spire making it the ancient equivalent of today's Canary Wharf.

Old St Paul's had, however, even for some years prior to the fire of 1666, been in serious need of renovation. The spire, damaged in the fire of 1561, had been deemed beyond repair and had never been rebuilt. During the Civil Wars the cathedral had suffered the fate of many of England's great buildings and been requisitioned for civilian and military use. Part of it had been used as a stable, and the fabric of the building itself had been allowed to fall into disrepair. Following the Restoration of Charles II and with it a return to power of high churchmen as opposed to Puritans, steps were taken to rectify the situation and to see what could be done to refurbish the old building.

At that time Christopher Wren was already engaged on his first major, architectural project, the Sheldonian Theatre at Oxford, the foundation stone of which was laid in 1664. From June 1665 to the following May he was in Paris, where he was able to inspect personally the many architectural works then in progress, including Bernini's extension to the Louvre – the only time he was able to view personally the work of contemporary European architects. It seems likely that he undertook this trip because the recently returned king had spoken to him of modern French architecture in such glowing terms that he felt impelled to see these marvels for himself. Certainly the impressions he took home from France were to affect his thinking greatly. Everywhere he went he would have seen how the neo-classical 'Augustan style' derived from the works of Vitruvius was in the ascendancy. In Paris he saw the Church of the Sorbonne by Jacques Lemercier and the Church of Val-de-Grâce begun by François Mansart but finished off by Jacques Lemercier. Both of these buildings were domed and had main entrances fronted by double colonnades – features he would later adopt in his designs for St Paul's.

Wren must already have been asked by Charles to produce some recommendations for the repair of St Paul's, for on his return to England he almost immediately presented a report on how the old building should be renovated. Alas, barely three months later the cathedral was a gutted shell. Wren's plans for a simple restoration, involving casing the inside of the nave with smooth stones and placing saucer-domes within its vaulting, was now redundant. Worse still, it soon became clear that even what was left of the cathedral would have to be demolished. What was called for was a total rebuild, the only question being how it was to be done: by replacing the old Gothic building with something similar or by rebuilding in a more modern style?

In 1668 Wren was given personal responsibility for the rebuilding of St Paul's. His initial ideas were modest to say the least, his brief having been to keep costs down to a minimum. To this end he produced plans for a simple church consisting of a rectangular building attached to a square surmounted by a dome. A model of this was made, part of which still exists. However, this first proposal did not meet with universal approval, partly because the dome, which was not at the centre of the church, was deemed to be in the wrong place but also because the design was not considered to be grand enough. Wren's reply to his critics was to produce a new scheme, called the Great Model. If the first model had been simple, this proposal went to the opposite extreme and seems to have embodied a hidden mysticism altogether different from anything before seen in England.

Wren's Great Model, which still exists today and can be viewed in the basement of St Paul's, shows a decidedly eastern influence (see plate 33). Uniquely for a British cathedral, it featured an enormous dome. In choosing this feature, Wren was undoubtedly influenced by the designs of the French churches he had seen in Paris; however, what he had in mind was on a much grander scale than the relatively small churches of Lemercier and Mansart; it was more in the tradition of St Peter's in Rome and the Hagia Sophia Cathedral of Constantinople – prototype of all the mosques built by Sinan. There is a further implied connection with possibly the most famous of all domed churches: the Church of the Holy Sepulchre in Jerusalem.

The ground plan of the Great Model, which was very carefully conceived to conceal a kabbalism all of its own, shows further, clear connections with Jerusalem. In the first place, the positioning of pillars within the proposed building emulates a Jerusalem Cross – the symbol of the crusader state (see figure 32). The second reference, equally obvious once it is seen, was to the Dome of the Rock (Mosque of Omar) in Jerusalem. This building, which is eight-sided, covers a rocky outcrop of Mount Moriah, where King Solomon's Temple once stood and where, according to the traditions of both Jews and Arabs, Abraham had prepared his son Isaac ready to be sacrificed to God. Like the Dome of the Rock, the new St Paul's was to be based on a wheel of eight sides. Thus, just as the Dome of the Rock stood at the centre of Old Jerusalem and crowned the area where the Holy of Holies of Solomon's Temple had

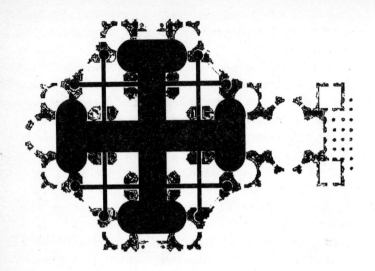

Fig. 32. Ground plan of the Great Model of St Paul's
Cathedral, showing Jerusalem Cross.

once stood, so St Paul's stood at the heart of London:
symbolically the New Jerusalem.

To emphasize the Christian nature of the proposed
building, Wren introduced another element: the novel
feature of concave walls to join the arms of his
Jerusalem Cross design. These concave walls were to be
based on circles with the same diameter as the central
area supporting the dome. They therefore emulate the
pattern of the quintessence, the fifth point at the centre
of four. This design can be read as symbolically equivalent to the frequent depiction of Christ as the *logos*
surrounded by four circles containing symbols for the
four evangelists, Matthew, Mark, Luke and John, who
take the Gospel to the four corners of the world. The

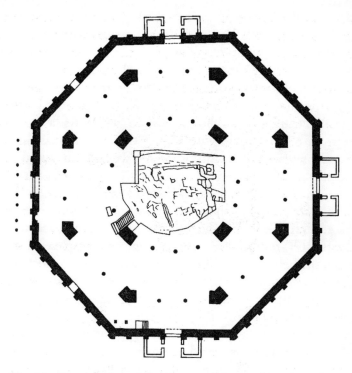

Fig. 33. Ground plan of the Dome of the Rock in Jerusalem, showing its eightfold geometry.

apostle to the Gentiles, of course, was St Paul, traditionally said to have preached the Gospel in London. St Paul's Cross, which stood outside the cathedral (in a slightly different place from where it stands today), was a traditional meeting place – and also, like Hyde Park Corner today, a place where sermons could be preached and anyone could address the public. Wren's new design for St Paul's emphasized its role as the point from which the *logos* or Word of God was to be preached – as the heart from which

Britain–Israel, like the original evangelists, would take Christ's message out to all the nations in the four corners of the world.

In the event, Wren's Great Model for the rebuilding of St Paul's was also turned down, both as too radical a departure from traditional English tastes and as being impractical for the holding of services. As a compromise he came up with a third design, and it is this, with some modifications, that we see in today's cathedral. Bowing to the practical religious needs of the clergy, this new building included a nave and choir. It was also given the shape of a cross, in accordance with tradition. However, the way the design was executed was still radically different from anything seen in Britain before – so different, indeed, that for most of the time it was being built the new cathedral was kept under wraps lest it should excite criticism. The building as constructed was also markedly different from the plans submitted to the clerics and approved by the king. Though Wren discarded the concave walls and the Jerusalem Cross design of the Great Model, he none the less retained what he must have regarded as the most important element – a gigantic dome over an octagon, in emulation of the Jerusalem Dome of the Rock (see plate 25).

Further to stress the identification of the new church with Jerusalem's monuments, Wren changed the axis of St Paul's so that it ran from roughly 8° north of east to the same south of west. This put it directly in line with the old Temple Church (see plate 40). Since the dissolution of the Knights Templar in 1307 this church has had a special status as a non-diocesan chapel under the direct jurisdiction of the monarch as head of the Church of England. It is, in part, a round church, and like many others belonging to that ill-fated order it was modelled on the Church of the Holy Sepulchre in Jerusalem, which has a rounded nave west of the choir (see plate 24). So, just as the Dome of the Rock lies to the east of the Holy Sepulchre, so the new St Paul's was aligned with the latter's analogue, the Temple Church in London. Further still, this alignment equated Ludgate Hill, where a British temple had stood from at least the time of the Romans and probably before, with Mount Moriah, where Abraham was stopped by an angel from sacrificing Isaac and where Solomon later built his Temple. Seen in this light, the Cathedral of St Paul's symbolizes the new Temple of Solomon, serving God and 'Israel' in their new home of Britain.

Following the Great Fire it was decided by Act of Parliament that a permanent memorial to the event should be raised at Fish Street, close to where the blaze started in Pudding Lane.

And the better to preserve the memory of this dreadful Visitation, Be it further enacted, That a Colume or Pillar of Brase or Stone be erected on or as neere unto the place where the said Fire so unhappily began as conveniently as may be, in perpetuall Remembrance thereof, with such Inscription thereon, as hereafter by the Maior and Court of Aldermen in that he halfe be directed.[5]

Again, King Charles approached Wren, asking him to produce a proposal for a suitable monument.

Wren worked on this project with Robert Hooke who, as well as occupying the chair of Gresham Professor of Geometry, was by then curator of experiments at the Royal Society. In 1675 the pair produced a series of drawings and even a scale model in wood showing possible alternative designs for this monument. These were inspected by Charles before being passed on for further comment to the City Lands Committee, the most senior committee of the Corporation of London. As Wren and Hooke worked closely together on this project, it is impossible to say whose input to the final design was the more important. Suffice it to say that all of the designs were variations on a theme and were intended to be symbolic expressions of the belief that the reborn London was a city especially chosen and blessed by God and nature alike.

What all of the designs had in common was that the main body of the Monument should be in the form of a single Doric column of such a size and dimension that it could accommodate within it a spiral staircase so that visitors could climb to an enclosure and enjoy a view over the city of London. What differed from design to design were, first, the style of the pillar, and, second, what should crown it. Among the early designs proposed for the latter element was a statue representing the presiding goddess of London, holding aloft her sword and supporting a shield. We may deduce from these features that in Wren's view she was to be equated with Minerva (Athene), whose prowess as a warrior was matched only by her intelligence and diligence. This design would have been in harmony with the doctrines of Vitruvius, for according to him the Doric order of architecture was virile in both its simplicity and its symbolism: 'The temples of Minerva, Mars, and Hercules, will be Doric, since the virile strength of these gods makes daintiness entirely inappropriate to their houses.'[6] An alternative design for the pinnacle was a phoenix rising from a fiery urn – emblematic both of London's resurrection from the ashes and of the Egyptian mysteries. A third design was for a flaming ball, which can be interpreted as the 'egg' of the phoenix, again symbolizing renewal.

After showing these designs to the king and getting his approval, Wren submitted them to the City Lands Committee accompanied by the following letter:

In pursuance of an order of the Committee for City Lands, I doe herewith offer the several designes wich some monthes since I shewed his Majestie [Charles II] for his approbation; who was then pleased to thinke a large ball of metall gilt would be most agreeable, in regard it would give an ornament to the town, at a very great distance; not that his Majestie disliked a statue; and if any proposal of this sort be more acceptable to the City, I shall most readily represent the same to his Majestie. I cannot but commend a large statue, as carrying much dignitie with it; and that which would be more vallueable in the eyes of forreiners and strangers. It hath been proposed to cast such a one in brasse, of twelve foot high, for £1000. I hope (if it be allowed) wee may find those who will cast a figure for that money, of fifteen foot high, which will suite the greatnesse of the pillar, and is (as I take it) the largest at this day extant; and this would undoubtedly bee the noblest finishing that can be found answerable to soe goodly a worke, in all men's judgements.

A ball of copper, nine foot diameter, cast in several pieces, with the flames in gilt, may well be done, with iron, copper and fixing, for £350; and this will be most acceptable of any thing inferior to a statue, by reason of the good appearance at a distance and because one may goe up into it, and upon occassion use it for fireworks.

A phoenix was at first thought of and is the ornament in the wooden modell of the pillar, which I caused to be made before it was begun; but upon second thoughtes, I rejected it, because it will be costly, not easily understood at that highth, and worse understood at a distance; and lastly dangerous by reason of the sayle the spread winges will carry in the winde.

The balcony must be made of substantiall well forged worke, there being no need, at that distance, of filed worke; and I suppose (for I cannot exactly guess the weight), if may be well performed and fixed, according to a good designe, for fourscore and ten poundes including painting. All which is humbly submitted to your consideration. Christopher Wren, July 28, 1675.[7]

In the event a fluted, Doric column was chosen as the design for the pillar, to be surmounted by an urn with the flaming ball emerging from it (see plate 38).

Reading Wren's submission to the committee, we can see that the flaming ball had been his own favoured option all along. He made this seem preferable to all others in terms of cost, looks and safety. His inclusion of the expensive statue (nearly three times the cost of the ball) was undoubtedly done to make the ball seem cheap in comparison. The aldermen of London could scarcely begrudge £350 for a gilded copper ball when they were being spared £1,000 or more for a cast statue. From this we can see something of Wren's talents not just as an architect but as a salesman for grand artistic projects.

The building of the Monument to the fire of London

was finished in 1677. Though on first impressions it is the simplest of structures – a viewing pillar capped with a flaming urn – further investigations reveal that it carries far greater meaning. Around the base of the pillar, facing in the four cardinal directions, are four large panels. Three of these carry Latin inscriptions which tell of the burning of London and of its renovation. In translation, the beginning of the inscription on the north panel reads as follows:

In the year of Christ, 1666, on 2nd September; at a distance eastward from this place of 202 feet, which is the height of this column, a fire broke out in the dead of the night, which the wind blowing devoured even distant buildings and rushed devastatingly through every quarter with astonishing swiftness and noise. It consumed 89 churches, gates, the Guildhall, public edifices, hospitals, schools, libraries, a great number of blocks of buildings, 13,200 houses, 400 streets. Of the 26 wards, it utterly destroyed 15 and left 8 mutilated and half-burnt. The ashes of the City, covering as many as 436 acres, extended on one side from the Tower along the bank of the Thames to the church of the Templars, on the other side from the north-east along the walls to the head of Fleet-ditch.[8]

The south panel tells of the rebuilding of the city:

Charles the Second, son of Charles the Martyr, King of Great Britain, France and Ireland, defender of the faith, a most gracious prince, commiserating the most deplorable state of things, whilst the ruins were yet smoking provided for the comfort of his citizens, and the ornament of his city; remitted their taxes, and

321

transferred the petitions of the magistrates and inhabitants of London to the Parliament; who immediately passed an Act, that public works should be restored to greater beauty, with public money, to be raised with an imposition on coals; that churches, and the cathedral of St Paul's should be rebuilt from their foundations, with all magnificence; that the bridges, gates and prisons should be new made, the sewers cleansed, the streets made straight and regular; such as were steep levelled and those too narrow made wider; markets and shambles removed to separate places. They also enacted, that every house should be built with party walls, and all raised of an equal height in front, and that all house walls should be strengthened with stone or brick; and that no man should delay building beyond the space of seven years. Furthermore, he procured an Act to settle before hand the suits which should arise respecting boundaries, he also established an annual service of intercession, and caused this column to be erected as a perpetual memorial to posterity. Haste is seen everywhere, London rises again, whether with greater speed or greater magnificence is doubtful, three short years complete that which was considered the work of an age.[9]

According to the inscription on the Monument itself and all official publications, it was deliberately given the height of 202 feet as this was the distance from its position to the Pudding Lane bakery where the fire started. Yet the location of the Monument was clearly not chosen solely because the fire began in a house nearby. During the reign of Charles II and for hundreds of years previously, the main approach to London from the south was across London Bridge. Prior to the

322

building of Westminster Bridge between 1739 and 1750, this was the only fixed crossing of the Thames in the London area. Its economic importance was therefore huge, and we can imagine that during the middle ages large numbers of people crossed back and forth between Southwark and London every day. On the south side of the bridge was the Church and Priory of St Mary, while on the north was the Church of St Magnus the Martyr, which was rebuilt by Christopher Wren in 1705. Coming off the bridge, travellers would proceed north up Fish Street on their way to the centre of the City. To them the Monument would stand out like a sentinel, both guiding and inviting them as they made their way into London. From the public balcony at the top of the pillar, which could be reached by climbing its 311 spiralling stairs, they would have been able to enjoy a spectacular view over a new London panorama dominated by the great dome of St Paul's Cathedral. Looking at the Monument today, the modern visitor can have little idea of the impact that it must once have had on travellers entering the City of London. At the time it was built it would have dominated the skyline like some lonely minaret. This aspect of the Monument is now lost, as not only is it huddled behind quite tall buildings that from most angles make it difficult to see, but since Wren's time London Bridge itself has been rebuilt and moved up river. This means that it no longer feeds into Fish Street but instead leads to King William Street and from thence into Gracechurch Street, the main northern axis of London.

Not all the churches burnt down by the fire were rebuilt. The actual site occupied by the pillar and the square that at the time surrounded it was originally the location of an ancient church dedicated to St Margaret.

The placing of the urn on top of a tower seems to relate to the legendary history of London as told in Geoffrey of Monmouth's *History of the Kings of Britain*. Fish Street is, of course, so named because fishermen would draw up at Billingsgate wharf and unload their catches for sale in the nearby market. As we have seen, Billingsgate supposedly takes its name from a king called Belin. Close to the gate was said to have been built a tower of remarkable height on top of which, after Belin had died and been cremated, a golden urn containing his ashes was placed. Monument Street runs down to old Billingsgate, thereby indicating the connection between Wren's urn and that of the old king Belin, who according to Geoffrey had once sacked Rome.

After he died on 23 February 1723, Sir Chistopher Wren was buried in a simple, unostentatious tomb in St Paul's Cathedral. Later, his son Christopher Wren junior placed a Latin epitaph on the wall above his grave: *Lector si monumentum requiris circumspice* (Reader, if you seek a monument look around you). A close examination of this monument – St Paul's Cathedral itself and the rebuilt City of London – indicates that there was much that Wren knew but evidently did not reveal to anyone outside a very small clique of associates. For his handiwork at St Paul's and elsewhere shows that he was a master not just of mathematics and architecture but also of hermetic symbolism. In rebuilding London he was putting into practice the hermetic dictum of 'as above, so below', and quite literally building a New Jerusalem.

CHAPTER TWELVE

PHOENIX RESURGAT

Right from the start there was a feeling that the Great Fire of London had been God's judgement on England for its sins. For royalists, it was tempting to think that the city's acquiescence in the beheading of Charles I was being punished; for Puritans, it was clear that the excesses of the new Stuart court had sorely tried the patience of a benevolent God. Conveniently for some, one Robert Hubert confessed to deliberately starting the fire in the royal bakery of Thomas Farriner in Pudding Lane. Though he was of unsound mind and almost certainly invented the story, Hubert was nevertheless found guilty of the felony and executed. In memory of the terrible event – and perhaps also to draw away public suspicions that fellow members of the Royal Society, who as we have seen were very quick to produce plans for a new city and cathedral, had had anything to do with its occurrence – the king issued a royal proclamation calling for a general fast and penitential commemoration to be held throughout the country, and for alms to be collected in all churches and parishes for the benefit of the poor. A day of repentance in memory of the event was to be observed each year on 2 September. This tradition continued – at least in

London – right up until the middle of the nineteenth century, by which time it had ceased to have much meaning.

When Christopher Wren set to the work of rebuilding St Paul's, he and his workmen were faced with a daunting task. The gutted remains of the building had been calcined by the fierce heat so that the existing walls had to be demolished in their entirety before new building work could begin. The many tombs and monuments that had once graced the cathedral were all damaged if not destroyed – with the sole exception of the effigy of John Donne, the celebrated poet and former dean of St Paul's who had died not long before the fire. Because his effigy had been standing upright, it fell through the burning floor unharmed into the crypt below.

When Wren came to lay out the foundations for the new building, he had first to mark the proposed centre, the point where the nave, choir and transepts would meet underneath the proposed new dome, from which all other measurements would be taken. Accordingly, he picked up the first piece of broken rubble that came to hand and used this to mark the position on the ground. Legend has it that when he examined this piece of rock more carefully he discovered it was part of a broken tombstone, which had carved on it the single Latin word *Resurgam*: 'I will rise again.' Thereafter this word, so pregnant with hope for a new beginning, became the motto for the resurrection of both St Paul's and London.

A symbol for resurrection, used by Christians but of much more ancient origin, is the phoenix – the mythical bird which, according to legend, deliberately immolates itself in its own nest so that its young might be reborn from its ashes. This symbol seemed thoroughly appropriate for the new cathedral as it rose out of the ashes of the old. Accordingly it was used as the main design element, in conjunction with the motto *Resurgam*, for one of the chief sculptures of the cathedral: the pediment relief over the south portico (see plate 37). This sculpture was carved by Caius Gabriel Cibber, who worked closely with Christopher Wren on a number of projects. As we saw earlier, he is listed in the 1738 edition of James Anderson's *Constitutions of the Freemasons* as having been elected in 1685 (along with Edward Strong) as one of the two Grand Wardens of the Freemasons. These were senior positions in the brotherhood which Christopher Wren and John Webb had occupied some twenty years earlier. It should therefore come as no surprise to discover that the phoenix, far from being a simple device symbolizing resurrection, has a much more complex and indeed more interesting history that links it with Freemasonry.

The origins of the phoenix legend lie in ancient Egypt and to the cult once practised at Heliopolis. Here there was a temple dedicated to the father of the gods, whom the Egyptians called Atum-Ra. The Greek historian Herodotus was shown this temple when he made his famous trip to Egypt in the fifth century BC. He recorded a local legend that once in every five hundred years the phoenix (called by the Egyptians the *bennu* bird and equated with a grey heron) would fly to Egypt from Arabia. It would bring with it the embalmed body of its parent, wrapped up to look like an egg. This it would deposit in the temple of the phoenix at Heliopolis, where it would catch fire. The ashes would then be buried in the temple, and from these another phoenix would arise.

There were other variants on this story, all of them to do with renewal and the cycles of time. According to other authorities the phoenix would make its visits even less frequently: once in every 1,471 years (the Sothic cycle) or even once in every 13,000 years (the half-precessional cycle). What these cycles have in common is that they are all concerned with astronomy and calendrics. This is scarcely surprising as the priests of Heliopolis, or Awen (or On, as it is called in the Bible), were 'watchers'; their task was to observe the risings and settings of stars. It is therefore safe to assume the phoenix legend was concerned with time cycles.

We can only speculate on what the coming of the phoenix symbolized for the ancient Egyptians, but it seems most likely that it was connected with the cult of Atum-Ra. His temple at Heliopolis, the ruins of which still exist, was one of the most important places in Egypt and at one time was home to a sacred pillar. This pillar, which was almost certainly crowned by the Benben stone – probably an oriented meteorite – represented the phallus of Atum-Ra himself.[1] Later, during the Middle Kingdom period (*c.*1991–1786 BC), long after this original pillar had been removed, the first obelisk was raised at the same temple. The purpose of obelisks remains obscure, but this one must have been connected in some way with the phoenix legend. For reasons that will become clear, it seems to have functioned as a species of sundial.

As we have seen, in 1637–8, during the reign of Charles I, a Gresham professor named John Greaves made a trip to Egypt. He went there ostensibly to study an eclipse of the moon, but at the same time carried out a survey of the pyramids. Given that he was a skilled astronomer, he cannot have failed to notice that Cairo stands exactly on latitude 30° north. He would easily have been able to work this out (if he didn't know it already) from the altitude of the North Star. Now, the position of the Cairo area at 30° north has a very particular effect as far as sundials are concerned. Because the axis of the earth is inclined in relation to its orbit, the effect of the planet's annual peregrination around the sun is to give us seasons. If we imagine the sky around us is like the inside of a hollow sphere, with the earth standing at its centre, then the ecliptic, the pathway through the stars along which the sun seems to progress in the course of a year, can be imagined as an invisible circle. There is a second circle, the celestial equator, which corresponds to our own earth's equator as projected on to this sphere. These two circles, the ecliptic and the celestial equator, intersect at two positions in the sky.

The sun appears to move along the ecliptic at a perceived speed of roughly 1° per day, thereby making a complete circuit of 360° in a year. The ancient Egyptian year was 360 days long, the extra 5 days to make 365 being considered extra-calendrical. The sun reaches the crossing points between the circles of the ecliptic and the celestial equator on two days in the year: these are the equinoxes, one marking the first day of spring and the other the first day of autumn. As we all know, in the northern hemisphere the sun rises on the eastern horizon, culminates in the south and sets on the western horizon. During the spring and summer months the sun rises north of east and sets due north of west. During the autumn and winter months it rises due south of east and sets due south of west. Only on the days of the equinoxes does it rise exactly in the east and set exactly in the west. This is because on

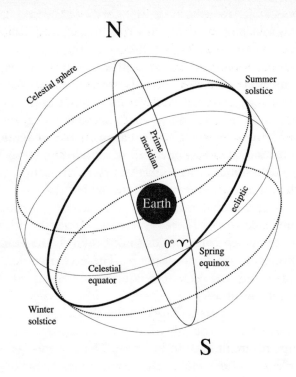

Fig. 34. The celestial sphere with ecliptic and equator.

these days it is actually lying on the celestial equator.

For an observer standing on the earth's equator, the celestial equator appears to be a great loop in the sky running from due east, passing through the zenith point (directly overhead at elevation 90° above the horizon) and terminating exactly in the west. Now, while the loop of the celestial equator, regardless of the observer's position, always begins in the east and ends in the west, the more northerly the latitude (N°) of the observer, the lower the angle in the sky that the sun attains as it culminates in the south. If the altitude of the sun at the equator is the zenith point (90°), its highest altitude (A°) at a more northerly latitude will be given by the equation:

$$A° = 90° - N°$$

In Cairo and its suburbs (an area which includes Heliopolis and Giza), N° = 30°. This means that on the equinoxes the sun will culminate in the south at an altitude above the horizon of exactly 90° − 30° = 60°.

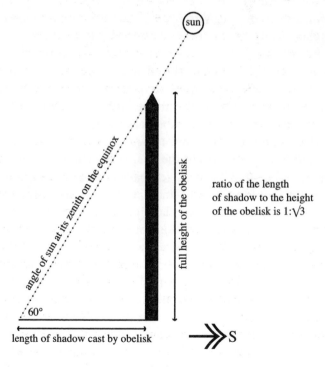

Fig. 35. The obelisk at Heliopolis casting a noontime shadow on the equinox.

What this means in practical terms is quite interesting from a geometric point of view and produces a result which may have been observed by John Greaves. The length of a shadow cast by an obelisk depends on the elevation of the sun: the higher the altitude of the sun in the sky, the shorter will be the shadow cast by any object – such as an obelisk. With the sun at an altitude of 60°, as it is at midday on the equinox in Cairo, the length of the shadow (L) may be determined by an exact equation: $L = H/\sqrt{3}$, where H is the height of the obelisk. (See figure 35.) Now, the proportion $1:\sqrt{3}$ is that of the width:length of the *vesica piscis*, the basis for much of the Vitruvian canon of measure and a relationship that appears to have been very important in the design of churches and chapels during the middle ages. This means that the obelisk at Heliopolis could actually have been used to generate this proportion directly from the angle of the sun on the day of the equinox. This must have been known to the Egyptians, who made use of the *vesica* and were the most renowned geometers of the ancient world. The fact that the $1:\sqrt{3}$ proportion was generated by the sun's shadow at the equinox would have indicated to them that Heliopolis was very special. It would have confirmed that this was indeed the city of the sun, as the sun god himself generated shadows with this divine proportion.[2]

The connection between the obelisk of Heliopolis and the *vesica piscis* symbol would very likely have been understood by John Greaves, who was after all both a professor of geometry and an astronomer. It would therefore be surprising if he had not mentioned this to his colleagues after his return to England in 1649. The knowledge of the way the obelisk at

Heliopolis cast shadows giving the 1:√3 relationship may have been passed on in notes to Christopher Wren, who took over the position of Gresham Professor of Astronomy in 1657. This may have been the inspiration that led Wren secretly to incorporate a similar code into the design of the Monument. For strangely enough, the location of London is similarly significant in astronomical terms.

The key to this code is given in a sculptured plaque by Caius Gabriel Cibber, commemorating the Great Fire, on the west face of the plinth (see plate 39). On the face of it this is simply a rather baroque allegorical representation of what happened in the aftermath of the fire and how King Charles II offered his support to the desolated city. On the plaque London is shown as a female figure. She is worn out, dishevelled and in a state of great distress. She has almost dropped the sword of London – that which is shown in the upper left quadrant of the London coat of arms – and she is on the point of collapse. The depiction of London in this way harks back to the Bible, where at a time of distress Jerusalem is similarly allegorized. 'How doth the city sit solitary, that was full of people! how is she become as a widow! She that was great among the nations, and princess among the provinces, how is she become tributary!' (Lam. 1: 1). However, unlike Jerusalem, London is not without friends in her hour of need. On Cibber's plaque the figure of winged Time and another female figure, probably representing Minerva, the presiding goddess of Britain, help the stricken London to her feet. Minerva points towards the sky with a wand, the termination of which is a hand. With this she invokes the blessings of heaven. These are represented by two more goddesses who sit in the clouds, one of them pouring out a cornucopia of good fortune and the other holding a palm branch signifying peace. These two goddesses probably represent the influences of the beneficent planets: Jupiter (Wealth) and Venus (Peace). These influences will counteract those of the maleficent planets – Saturn (Judgement) and Mars (Destruction) – that have obviously taken their toll of poor London.

These expected 'blessings from heaven' would have had a further meaning for those who believed the British were descended from the lost tribes of Israel. According to the Bible, the leading tribe of northern Israel was that of Ephraim, the son of the Joseph who had been sold into slavery by his brothers and later became the vizier of all Egypt. Joseph had married the Egyptian daughter of Potiphera, the 'chief of the watchers', who was the high priest of On (also called Awen), the biblical name for Heliopolis. Joseph's sons Ephraim and Manasseh were especially blessed by his own father Jacob, and on their seed were promised the blessings of heaven. Each of the twelve tribes of Israel was linked to a sign of the zodiac. England is often symbolized by the cartoon character 'John Bull' and indeed to anyone who knows anything about astrology the English character is very Taurean. Ephraim, the leader of the ten lost tribes of Israel, inherited from Joseph the insignia of the bull as his tribal standard. In the Bible, God's blessings on Abraham, Isaac and Jacob were inherited by Ephraim and Manasseh. Thus in the eyes of those who believed Britain to be the reincarnation of Israel, the cornucopia being poured out from heaven could signify this blessing being now passed on to London, the new capital city of the Israelites.

Also shown on Cibber's plaque, close to 'London's' left leg, is a beehive. We have seen in an earlier chapter that while beehives can symbolize industry and thrift, they also have a more esoteric significance. In the ancient world the beehive was used as a symbol for a secret brotherhood or esoteric school. Like bees, the 'brothers' would go out from their 'hive' (symbolic of a college, school or monastery) to gather the nectar of knowledge. This they would bring back to be fermented inside the hive to produce the honey of wisdom with which young bees could be fed. This idea is of very ancient origin. In Egypt the pharaoh had a bee-name, signifying that he was head of the hive. In Syria there was a well-known collection of stories called *The Bees* that was revised by a thirteenth-century Nestorian archimandrite called Mar Salomon. This book, like many others from the east, would almost certainly have found its way into the libraries of western Europe at the time of the Renaissance.

The importance of the bee as a symbol of esotericism would have been known to scholars of the late seventeenth century. In 1653 the tomb of King Childeric I (d. 481), one of the Merovingian kings of France, was discovered in the Ardennes. Among other treasures Childeric's tomb was found to contain some 300 golden bees, each exquisitely made. These bees were taken by the Austrians but were later returned to France, and in 1804 Napoleon had them affixed to his own coronation robe.[3] In this context it seems more than likely that the hive shown on the Monument is symbolic of Gresham College, where first the 'Rosicrucian' Invisible College and later the Royal Society used to hold their meetings. As we have seen, the bee and beehive are used as Rosicrucian symbols in the title page of Robert Fludd's book *Summum Bonum* (see figure 26). Gresham College was just such a 'beehive', where the nectar of scientific knowledge was being collected and turned into the honey of enlightenment. It was an important resource in the rebuilding of London. Significantly, it survived the fire unscathed and its buildings were made available to be used by, among others, the Royal Exchange.

To the right of Cibber's plaque are shown other forces coming to the aid of the stricken figure of London. These include King Charles II and his brother James II (then duke of York), who are shown dressed as Roman patricians. The former is garlanded like an emperor, presumably as an allusion to the superiority of the 'Augustan style' to which he, Wren and other intellectuals of the time were attracted. The king and the duke of York stand on top of a small staircase that covers a culveted sewer. Lying in the sewer is a grotesque figure, with pendulous breasts and snakes for hair, breathing out vile odours. This old hag would seem to represent the now conquered plague which had ravaged London the year before the fire. The vile odours of London, which were believed to have caused the pestilence, are now to be confined to sewers where they can do no harm.

On the plaque Charles and James are accompanied by a party of assorted symbolic attendants. Standing behind them are figures representing Justice (wearing a crown) and Fortitude (controlling a lion). Immediately to Charles's right is Liberty (holding aloft a hat) and Architecture (with the tools of the architect's trade, the compass and set-square). Leading the royal procession is Science. He is shown as a Mercury or Hermes figure, wearing a winged cap with Cabiri, fertility gods, dancing upon it. That he is the most important figure of all is indicated by the fact that the crown of his cap

336

Fig. 36. Cibber's plaque on the Monument.

337

is exactly in the centre of the plaque. Hermes was, of course, the patron of hermeticism or the initiatory tradition. On the plaque he carries in one hand an open scroll bearing what look like the plans for the new city. In the other he holds forth a statue of the many-breasted goddess Diana (Cybele) of Ephesus. She stands on a plinth, and emanating from her hands are what look like flows of water or subtle influence directed towards the foot of her column-plinth at exactly 30°. This figure of the goddess is very similar in form to an image of her on the frontispiece to a book called *Actorum Chymicorum Holmiensum* by a Swedish alchemist called Urbani Hierne. This was published in Stockholm in 1712 and it shows the goddess Cybele/Diana with her arms stretched out in similar fashion. That the image is meant to be Cybele is in-dicated first by the multiple breasts but also because she is attended by two lions.

According to Geoffrey of Monmouth, Brutus met Diana in a dream while sleeping in her temple on one of the Greek islands. It was she who told him that he should take his people beyond the Mediterranean and that they would find an uninhabited island of their own: 'Brutus, beyond the setting of the sun, past the realms of Gaul, there lies an island in the sea, once occupied by giants. Now it is empty and ready for your folk. Down the years this will prove an abode suited to you and your people; and for your descendants it will be a second Troy. A race of kings will be born there from your stock and the round circle of the whole earth will be subject to them.'[4] The inclusion of the Diana figure on the plaque would seem to be a secret reference to this prophecy. It both affirms London's identity as successor city to Troy and reminds the viewer of

Fig. 37. Cybele/Diana. (Frontispiece from *Actorum Chymicorum Holmiensum* by Urbani Hierne, 1712.)

Diana's prophecy that one day Britain will rule the world. There is, however, more to it than this.

The patron goddess of the pre-Roman Britons was called Ave or Awe. Her symbol was the broad arrow or 'Awen symbol', which was drawn as /|\. As we have seen, this symbol is said to represent the three vowels O I V (in the old Latin script the letter 'V' has the sound value of 'U') that in the druidic tradition formed the unpronounceable name of God. The Awen symbol also represents the shadows cast by an upright stone at

different times of day at the solstice. In Welsh the word
Aven or Awen means 'the muse'. Ave was the great
muse of the druidic tradition, who springs from sunlight just as Athene sprang from the head of Jupiter. For
this reason the Romans identified Awe with their own
goddess Minerva, who in turn was equivalent to the
Greek Athene.

In this context it is important to note that on Cibber's
plaque the lozenge shape made by the statue of the
goddess with her outstretched arms and flows of water
out of her hands depicts the *vesica piscis*. This is so for
a specific reason. As noted in chapter 11, the height of
the Monument (202 feet) is supposed to have been
chosen because that was the distance from it to the
baker's shop in which the fire started. However, there
was in fact an esoteric reason for Wren's selecting this
height for a tower which could as easily have been sited
two feet closer to the baker's shop and been given a
height with the round number of 200 feet. Closer
inspection of the number 202 would seem to indicate
that this height of tower was chosen for the length of
shadow it would cast at the solstice.

The City of London lies at latitude 51° 30' north,
and this is something rather special, astronomically
speaking. We can imagine a curved line running
upwards from the eastern horizon, to the zenith point
of the sky and back down to the western horizon. At
the spring and autumn equinoxes, the sun will rise
exactly in the east and set exactly in the west at the
point where this line intersects the horizon. Between
those two dates, that is to say during the spring and
summer months, the sun will rise north of east and set
north of west. This means that it will cross the line linking the east and west with the zenith at an angle above

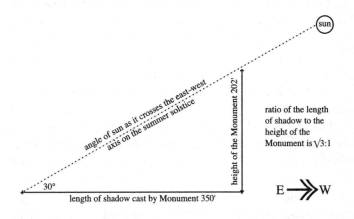

Fig. 38. The shadow cast by the Monument, generating the proportions of the *vesica piscis*.

the horizon. The closer to the summer solstice we get, the greater will be this angle of altitude of the sun as it crosses the line. Because London's latitude is 51° 30′, the sun will cross this line on the summer solstice at an altitude close to 30°.[5] It will do so in the east in the morning, at around 9.22 a.m. (summer time), and in the west in the afternoon, at around 4.42 p.m. This means that, looking eastwards in the morning and westwards in the afternoon of the summer solstice, to an observer standing at just the right distance from the Monument, the sun will appear to sit on top of it (see plate 38).

Now, just as at Heliopolis, the ancient city of On or Awen, the length of shadow cast by a pillar or obelisk exhibits the proportions of the *vesica piscis*, so too will the shadow of this London obelisk, the Monument to the Great Fire. If we imagine a triangle whose base is the shadow and vertex is given by the height of the Monument, this will have a base angle of almost exactly 30°. By simple geometry it can be seen that the length of the shadow cast by the Monument will then be √3 times its height. As the height of the Monument is 202 feet, the length of the shadow will be almost exactly 350 feet (349.87426 feet, to be more precise).

This is a very interesting proportion, which must have been well understood by Christopher Wren. As Keith Critchlow pointed out in his article in

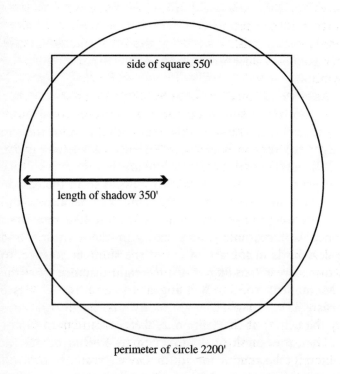

Fig. 39. Squaring the circle, using the shadow from the Monument.

Glastonbury: A Study in Patterns, the 1:√3 relationship was used in the laying out of the Lady Chapel at Glastonbury Abbey. It is also discussed in Caesariano's edition of Vitruvius as the appropriate proportional relationship for the laying out of churches such as Milan Cathedral. The fact that this relationship could be generated in London by a shadow cast by the sun in a sense consecrates the city to Awe or the virgin goddess. This, it would seem, is why on Gabriel Cibber's plaque a statue of the goddess Diana is held by Mercury, the god associated with measurement: she gives him the sacred proportions of the *vesica piscis*. A further identification of Diana/Cybele with Awe, the pre-Roman British goddess of wisdom, is indicated by her standing on an upturned 'broad arrow' or Awen symbol.

As if the connection between the Monument to the Great Fire, the sun at the summer solstice, the *vesica piscis* and the symbol of Awen were not enough, there is even more sacred geometry associated with this tower. If the length of the shadow cast by the sun at 30° of altitude is used as a radius (r), then a hypothetical circle can be inscribed on the ground. The perimeter (P) of this circle is given by the equation $P = 2\Pi r$, where Π = 22/7 approximately. As r has the value of 350 feet, P = 2 × 22/7 × 350 feet = 2200 feet. We can now construct a square of equal perimeter to this circle, with a base length of 550 feet. Using this square base we can construct an imaginary pyramid, whose height is given by the length of shadow, i.e. 350 feet (see figure 40).

The angle of slope of this pyramid will be 51° 51′, which is the same as that of the Great Pyramid of Giza. As the Great Pyramid of Giza has a base length of 440 royal cubits, each cubit being 21 Egyptian inches, it

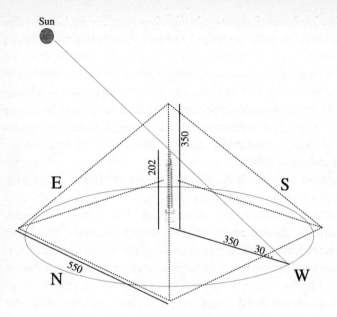

Invisible pyramid of side 550 and height 350 implied by length of
shadow cast by the Monument on the summer solstice with the sun in the east.

Fig. 40. Generating an invisible pyramid in harmonic
proportion with the shadow.

therefore has a side of 440 × 21/12 Egyptian feet = 770
Egyptian feet. Ignoring for a moment the slight difference in measure between the English foot and the
ancient Egyptian foot (about 0.38 English inches), it
can be seen that the length of side of the hypothetical
pyramid divided by that of the Great Pyramid
of Giza will be 550/770. It therefore follows that the
imaginary pyramid that can be drawn in harmonious
proportion to the Monument will be a 5/7 scale replica
of the Great Pyramid of Giza.

All this may seem rather abstract and removed from

the simple furnishing of a monument to the Great Fire, but it has to be remembered that Sir Christopher Wren was one of the world's leading astronomers. Indeed, as Professor of Astronomy at Oxford he would probably have been appointed the first Astronomer Royal had he not been so preoccupied with rebuilding London. He is also recorded as having been interested in sundials from the age of fourteen and he was well known as an extremely skilled mathematician. Given these peculiar circumstances, it would be strange indeed if he had not noticed that a pillar 202 feet high would cast a shadow of very nearly 350 feet when the sun was at an altitude of 30° and that this generated the *vesica piscis* shape which, according to Palladio, is the most important relationship in architectural geometry.

The Monument is, of course, only one of many buildings constructed by Wren in London after the Great Fire. Impressive as it is, it was only a sideshow compared with his greatest monument, St Paul's Cathedral. It follows that if he was really serious about incorporating a secret gnosis into his architecture that linked symbolic geometry with astronomy, then we should expect to find evidence for it in St Paul's; and indeed, there is strong evidence for just such a supposition.

As we have seen, the new St Paul's was designed to embody as complete a break with the past as possible. Wren's preferred plan was that of the Great Model, a basilica-style building making no concessions to Anglican tastes. In the event he was forced to modify his scheme and to build something that, while Augustan in style – with rounded arches, Corinthian pillars and Vitruvian proportions – nevertheless retained such traditional elements of a Gothic building as a nave, choir, transepts and a high altar at the eastern end of the building. The major change, and indeed the cathedral's most noticeable feature, was the incorporation of a great dome over the central crossing. Undoubtedly part of the reason for building such a dome was to make an architectural statement that this building was of equal importance to the pope's basilica of St Peter's and therefore that London, now the capital of the Protestant world, was on a par with Rome. However, there was more to it than simple one-upmanship, which as the dome of St Paul's is smaller than that of St Peter's was a game already lost. What seems to have been more important than size and to have been Wren's real motivation was a more esoteric symbolism of numbers, geometry and astronomy.

All this was based on the teachings of Vitruvius, who in his textbook for architects had lain out the principles which need to be followed if a building is to work in a correct manner:

1. Architecture depends on Order (in Greek ταξισ), Arrangement (in Greek διαθεσισ), Eurythmy, Symmetry, Propriety, and Economy (in Greek οικονομια).
2. Order gives due measure to the members of a work considered separately, and symmetrical agreement to the proportions of the whole. It is an adjustment according to quantity (in Greek ποσοτησ). By this I mean the selection of modules from the members of the work itself and, starting from these individual parts of the members, constructing the whole work to correspond. Arrangement includes the putting of things in their proper places and the elegance of effect which is due to the adjustments appropriate to the character of the work. Its forms of expression (in Greek ιδεαι) are these: groundplan, elevation, and perspective. A

groundplan is made by the proper successive use of compasses and rule, through which we get outlines for the plane surfaces of buildings . . .

3. Eurhythmy is beauty and fitness in the adjustments of the members. This is found when the members of a work are of a height suited to their breadth, of a breadth suited to their length, and, in a word, when they all correspond symmetrically.[6]

Christopher Wren, like all good architects, was aware that a church is not just a room or suite of rooms in which people congregate; rather, it is a type of machine. The function of such a machine is the transformation of human energies – the raising of consciousness from the mundane to the beatific so that the person may more properly relate to God. This is a matter of atmosphere; the psychic/spiritual energies present in a building are profoundly affected by colour, light and music, and also by the symphony of proportions: what Vitruvius calls 'eurhythmy'. St Paul's Cathedral is a profoundly eurhythmical building in the sense that the geometry of the parts relates to that of the whole. However, there is even more to it than a harmony of proportions. Wren was well aware that in the classical world temples were usually designed as microcosms of the macrocosm: that is to say, as models of the greater universe. The dimensions of a temple were deeply symbolic and had to reflect the relationship of sun, earth, moon and stars. As William Lethaby, a former surveyor of Westminster Abbey, observes:

The commonplaces of poetry, in which the world is likened to a building, 'heavenly vaults', or 'azure domes', 'gates of the sun' and the rest, are survivals of a time when the earth was not a tiny ball, projected at immeasurable speed through infinite space, one, among other fireflies of the night, but was stable and immovable, the centre of the universe, the floor on which the sky was built. The whole a chamber lighted by the sun, moon, and stars . . .

In all of this there is enough to dispose us to receive evidence of a cosmic symbolism in the buildings of the younger world, and we shall find that the intention of the temple (speaking of the temple *idea*, as we understand it) was to set up a local reduplication of the temple not made with hands, the World Temple itself – a sort of model to scale, its form governed by the science of the time; it was a heaven, an observatory, and an almanac. Its foundation was a sacred ceremony, the time carefully chosen by augury, and its relation to the heavens defined by observation. Its place was exactly below the celestial prototype; like that it was sacred, like that strong, its foundations could not be moved, if they were placed foursquare to the walls of the firmament, as are still our churches – and was it not to be like the heavenly sanctuary, that Solomon built the temple without the sound of a tool?[7]

Applying this mysticism to St Paul's (or indeed any other domed church), it can be seen that the dome represents the great vault of space, the celestial sphere, which is apparently moved by God himself. Lethaby makes this comparison:

If we may take it as proved that the architectural dome was known and first reared in Chaldea . . . by a people who saw in the sky a solid hemisphere, and much given to nature symbolism in their buildings; may not the design and daring construction of the cupola be attributed to the form of the heavenly dome, and the desire that the 'ceiling' of the temple should still recall the ceiling of the great nature temple?

There is such a clear and constraining congruity between them that to describe a dome seems to call for the simile to the firmament: St Paul's, for instance—

'Whose sky-like dome
Hath typified, by reach of daring art,
infinity's embrace' (Wordsworth).[8]

The connection between the dome of St Paul's and astronomy is made clear by the heights above ground of its various components. From ground level to the top of the cross is 365 feet, which is the same as the number of days in the year. However, the distance to the top of the cross from the floor level of the cathedral itself is only 355.5 feet. This too is symbolic as it is approximately the length of the lunar year, i.e. of 12 lunations. Thus, in a symbolic way, the cross on the pinnacle of the dome marries together the cycles of sun and moon: it harmonizes the male (solar) and female (lunar) influences.

The height to the 'Golden Gallery', which is at the very top of the dome itself, is 280 feet. This number, too, is very interesting, as it links the church, symbolically speaking, with the Great Pyramid of Giza, which has a height of 280 royal cubits. It is also very pertinent astronomically speaking. As we have seen, the slope of this pyramid is such that the perimeter of its base (4 × 440 = 1760 royal cubits) is the same as a circle drawn using its height as a radius: $2 \Pi r = 2 \times (22/7) \times 280$ = 1760 cubits. Pyramids of this kind have a slope of 51° 51'. On the right day and at the right time, the sun would have an altitude of 51° 51' and would therefore seem to sit exactly on top of the pyramid when viewed by an observer standing at its base. It just so happens that because the Great Pyramid is located close to the 30° north line of latitude, at the time it was built (*c*.2450 BC) the sun would achieve this altitude of 51° 51', in the morning in the east and again in the afternoon in the west, at a time when it was stationed in the zodiacal sign of Leo. The length of the shadow cast by the top of the pyramid would be exactly the same length as the distance from the centre of its base to its edge, i.e. half a base length. It would appear, therefore, that the Great Pyramid was connected with the worship of the leonine aspect of the sun-god Atum-Re.[9]

It is a peculiarity of the location of London, at 51° 30' north, that in Wren's time (and for a century or so before) the sun at the time of its Regulus conjunction (*c*.18 August) would culminate in the southern sky at an altitude of roughly 51° 51'. This means that although St Paul's is not a pyramid as such, it would perform the same sort of function where the sun is concerned. The length of the shadow cast by the great dome of St Paul's, which is 280 feet above ground level, will correspond to that cast by a Π pyramid of the same height. This means that as the sun culminated in the south at the time of the Regulus conjunction, so the shadow cast by the top of the dome from the level of the Golden Gallery would be approximately 220 feet from the centre of the crossing of the aisles underneath the centre of the dome. The shadow cast by the dome would be quite visible cast in the churchyard on the north side of the cathedral. In this way London, like Jerusalem at the time of Solomon, was seen as being

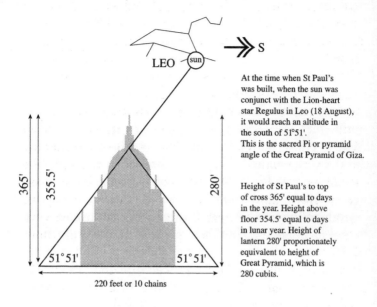

At the time when St Paul's was built, when the sun was conjunct with the Lion-heart star Regulus in Leo (18 August), it would reach an altitude in the south of 51°51'. This is the sacred Pi or pyramid angle of the Great Pyramid of Giza.

Height of St Paul's to top of cross 365' equal to days in the year. Height above floor 354.5' equal to days in lunar year. Height of lantern 280' proportionately equivalent to height of Great Pyramid, which is 280 cubits.

365'

355.5'

280'

51°51'

51°51'

220 feet or 10 chains

Fig. 41. The sun over an invisible pyramid on St Paul's, generating the π angle of 51°51'.

consecrated as the new 'City of the Lion' or Ariel; it was the New Jerusalem.[10]

As we have seen, at the end of the 1630s Professor John Greaves visited Egypt and made the first modern survey of the Great Pyramid. Among other accomplishments he accurately measured the dimensions of the King's Chamber, showing that it was twice as long as broad. Using Greaves's data, Sir Isaac Newton was able to determine the unit of measure used by the ancient Egyptians. He found that the King's Chamber had a width of 10 and a length of 20 royal cubits – each cubit being about 20.62 British inches in length. This, it turns

351

out, is in accordance with the architectural principles laid down by Vitruvius and known as the Augustan style. For Vitruvius writes: 'The length of a temple is adjusted so that its width may be half its length . . .'[11] Christopher Wren knew his Vitruvius and it therefore comes as no surprise that when he built St Paul's he constructed this sanctuary in accordance with Augustan principles. This can best be seen in the ground plan. The overall length of the building (excluding the porch at the west end and the apse at the east) is exactly twice its greatest width (the distance between the outer walls of its north and south transepts). Furthermore, the width of the north–south transepts is exactly half their combined length. Thus, whether viewed from the main entrance in the west, or from the north, or from the south, St Paul's, as built, is also in accordance with the architectural principles laid down by Vitruvius.

There is yet more to this complex building. The building of Solomon's Temple is a central mystery at the heart of Freemasonry, so it would be surprising if it had no influence on the rebuilding of St Paul's. The story of how Solomon recruited Hiram, king of Tyre, and his principal architect, Hiram Abif, is told in the Bible in the first Book of Kings. The dimensions of King Solomon's Temple are very precisely given: 'And the house which king Solomon built for the Lord, the length thereof was three-score cubits, and the breadth thereof twenty cubits and the height thereof thirty cubits.' Thus the temple was three times as long as it was wide, not twice, as was the Vitruvian ideal. Christopher Wren got over this contradiction by making the central area of the great church a square with a side length exactly a third of the length of the cathedral as a whole. In this way the building symbolizes Solomon's Temple as well as obeying

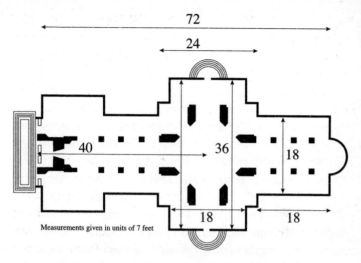

72

24

40 | 36 | 18

18 | 18

Measurements given in units of 7 feet

Fig. 42. Ground plan of St Paul's Cathedral.

the canon of Augustan style architecture as laid down by Vitruvius.

St Paul's was finished around 1710, when Christopher Wren's son, Christopher junior, was hoisted up in a basket to place the great stone cross on top of his father's creation. Wren senior died thirteen years later, in 1723, at the age of ninety-one. By this time Great Britain, which as a political entity did not exist until the Act of Union of 1707, was well on its way to being a world power. Two hundred years of peace and prosperity lay ahead, and those who believed in the nation's identity with Israel had much to be pleased with.

CHAPTER THIRTEEN

THE RISE AND FALL OF BRITISH ISRAEL

Queen Mary II died in 1694 and her husband King William III in 1702. As they were childless, the crown passed to Mary's Protestant sister Anne. Unfortunately, the death in 1700 of her only surviving child, William, duke of Gloucester, meant that she too had no direct heir. Meanwhile the line of the Catholic Stuarts – those descended from James II by his second wife, Mary of Modena – flourished. With the death of Anne in 1714 the crown should, by right of primogeniture, have passed to her younger half-brother, James Francis Edward Stuart, known to the English as 'the Old Pretender'. This, however, was not to be. Having invited William to depose his father-in-law, James II, English Protestants were not about to hand the crown back to James's Catholic descendants. Anticipating this eventuality, an Act of Settlement was passed through Parliament in 1701. This declared that on Anne's death the throne should pass to the line of Princess Sophia, the youngest daughter of Queen Elizabeth of Bohemia. To reinforce the likelihood of this desired outcome, in 1707 an Act of Union was passed through both the Scottish and English parliaments that for the first time brought together the legislatures of the two countries. This meant that, theoretically at least, the 'Old Pretender' was delegitimized as heir to the throne of Scotland as well as that of England. Princess Sophia died on 8 June 1714; Queen Anne on 1 August the same year. Thus it was that Sophia's eldest son 'German George', elector of the petty principality of Hanover and grandson of Queen Elizabeth of Bohemia, became King George I of Great Britain.

The position of George I was vastly different from that of James I a century earlier. Having gained the throne by virtue of an Act of Parliament rather than by right of birth, he was in effect the first modern, constitutional monarch. From now on kings and queens of Great Britain would be essentially figureheads for the elective Parliament that raised taxes, passed laws and decided policy. However, the king's position, though now largely ceremonial, did have its perks in the form of castles, palaces and, above all, prestige.

The Hanoverian succession did not please everyone, least of all the Scots. George I could not speak English and had little interest in Britain except as a source of revenue and power. Nevertheless, the Jacobite rebellion of 1715, which sought to put the Old Pretender on to the throne in his place, failed. So too did a second rebellion in 1745, led by the charismatic 'Young Pretender', Charles Edward Stuart, during the reign of George II. Both these rebellions had begun in Scotland, where, despite the Act of Union and the fact that the majority of Scots were Protestants, there was still a strong sentimental attachment to the Stuarts. The defeat of the Young Pretender effectively brought an end to any hopes the Scots entertained that the Jacobites might regain the throne of Britain. The throne of Scotland as well as England was destined to remain in the custody of the house of Hanover.

Despite these birth pangs, the dawning of the eighteenth century saw British power in the ascendant. The victories of John Churchill in the War of the Spanish Succession (1701–14), as a result of which he was ennobled as the first duke of Marlborough, established Britain as the leading military power in western Europe. Meanwhile the country's growing maritime strength enabled it to build up its colonies in America. Though most of these were subsequently lost in the American War of Independence (1775–83), Britain held on to Canada and the West Indies and thereby remained a force in the western hemisphere. In the course of the eighteenth and nineteenth centuries it also obtained new colonial possessions in Australia, New Zealand and Africa to add to its considerable territories in India and the Far East. A revolution in agricultural practices followed by the industrial revolution saw British productivity outstripping all competitors. Dr John Dee's vision of a great, world-encompassing empire was beginning to be realized in practice.

These changes in British fortunes were reflected in the development of London. Throughout the eighteenth and nineteenth centuries the city grew at an alarming rate. In 1841 the population of Greater London, including the suburbs, was 2,235,344. By 1881 this had jumped to 4,766,661, making London far and away the largest city in the world and the first megalopolis of the modern age.[1]

The development of Victorian Britain as the first great power of the industrial age went hand in hand with the growth of the British Israel movement. As we have seen, as far back as the late middle ages there had been a belief, at least in royal circles, that the British were descended from the lost tribes of Israel. During the nineteenth century these ideas were to be developed from amorphous traditions into a systematized creed. The first prophet of what, to his critics at least, seemed like a new religion was a Scot from Kilmarnock named John Wilson. He commenced his work of evangelizing the nation in 1837 – the same year that Queen Victoria ascended the throne. The following year he began lecturing at the Witness Hall in Aldersgate Street, London. Two years later, in 1840, he published a book, *Our Israelitish Origin*, based on these lectures. It was hugely successful and in 1874 the 'Anglo-Israel Association' was founded, holding its meetings in Wilson's house near St Pancras.

Wilson's message, that the British were descended from the lost tribes of Israel and that this could be proved from the Bible, was in tune with the mood of the period. Britain was by now the pre-eminent economic power not just in Europe but in the world. A cosy relationship existed between motherland and colonies such that Britain imported raw materials and exported manufactured goods at advantageous prices. The continuing economic boom that this reciprocal arrangement generated – though not necessarily to the benefit of those who worked in the cotton fields, sugar plantations and rubber forests of the colonies, or the sweatshops, coal mines and foundries of Britain itself – led to the growth of a large middle class. These people, merchants, lawyers, bankers and civil servants, were literate, with disposable income and time to spare. Many middle-class men were Freemasons – a much more influential movement at that time than it is today – with an interest in and regard for ancient mysteries. They were also keen readers of the Bible and were only too ready to be told how they were descended from God's own chosen people.

The British Israel torch lit by Wilson was eagerly taken up by another evangelist for the cause, Edward Hine. A younger man than Wilson, he attended the latter's lectures in his youth and wrote what was to become a best-seller on the subject: *Forty-seven Identifications of the British Nation with the Lost House of Israel, Founded upon 500 Proofs*. This remarkable book, which went into enormous detail in analysing the Bible for texts supportive of the identification of the descendants of the lost Israelites with both the Celts and the Anglo-Saxons, sold over 416,000 copies. To put matters on a firmer footing, Hine also began to publish a monthly journal entitled *Life from the Dead*. This was followed by a further magazine, *Leading the Nation to Glory*, the name of which was later changed to *The Glory Leader*.

As well as proselytizing in Britain, Hine lectured in America and Canada, where he found equally keen audiences. This led to the setting up of various 'identity' societies in those countries as well. In the United States in particular, the idea of 'manifest destiny' was already written into the constitution. The discovery that this new nation was none other than the most recent incarnation of the tribe of Manasseh (Britain was identified as the tribe of Ephraim, Manasseh's brother) did not strike people as incredible; rather, it was regarded as an explanation for God's providence in first of all giving North America to the British and then causing the United States to separate from the motherland. To these American 'Israelites' it was clear that God wanted the two kindred tribes of Ephraim and Manasseh, descended from the sons of the same patriarch Joseph, to enjoy separate identities. In accordance with prophecy (Gen. 48: 19), the one (Manasseh) was destined to become a 'Great Nation' (the United States), while the other (Ephraim) would become a 'Company of Nations' (the British Empire, later the Commonwealth).

Another prominent British Israelite was Charles Piazzi Smyth, then the Astronomer Royal for Scotland. He too had attended some of Wilson's lectures and was convinced of the truth of what he heard because it chimed with another passion of his: pyramidology. The origins of this movement, which for a time ran in parallel with British Israelitism before being virtually taken over by it, go back to the work of John Greaves and his 1638 survey of the pyramids of Giza. As we have seen, from Greaves's data on the measurements of the King's Chamber Sir Isaac Newton had been able to work out that the ancient Egyptians must have made use of a particular unit of measure that he called the 'profane cubit' but which is now more generally referred to as the 'royal cubit'. This cubit he worked out as being equivalent to 20.62 British inches, which implied it was 21 Egyptian inches – each Egyptian inch being only slightly shorter than the modern-day British unit. The implication of this discovery was that British units of measure owed their origins not to the Romans but rather to the Egyptians: the 'fathers' of geometry.

Newton further proposed that the Egyptians had also used a longer measure of 25 inches, which he called a 'sacred cubit'. Evidence for this was not as obvious as for the other unit, and from the start it was treated with some scepticism. However, the idea was revived in the 1860s by John Taylor, editor of the *London Magazine*.

Himself a skilled mathematician, he computed that the perimeter of the Great Pyramid was exactly 36,653.76 British inches, which could compute to 36,600 pyramid inches – each pyramid inch being slightly shorter than the British measure. To Taylor this implied that the Great Pyramid had been intended to be a species of calendar, with each 100 inches of its perimeter representing one day. On this analysis a full circuit of the pyramid symbolized 366 days, or approximately a whole year. Though the Royal Society rejected his paper on the subject, Taylor published his results in 1864 in a booklet entitled: *The Great Pyramid: Why Was It Built? & Who Built It?*

Like others of his time, John Taylor was deeply influenced by the Bible and the apparent need to attribute knowledge relating to measures to divine influence. He died the same year that his book was published but his mantle was quickly taken up by Charles Piazzi Smyth, who had been in correspondence with him for some months prior to his death. Shortly afterwards Piazzi Smyth made his own survey of the pyramids, finding further proof that the Great Pyramid was designed not just as a calendar but as an almanac of the ages. He believed that the lengths of its internal corridors, as measured in pyramid inches, mapped out the course of world civilization, with each pyramid inch representing one year. The role of Britain as 'Israel' was read into the measures of mute stones, especially the Great Step at the top of the pyramid's Grand Gallery. Summing up how the Grand Gallery symbolized the Christian era and the ascent of true Christians to the light represented by the messiah, Smyth felt able to write in all seriousness:

And who are more particularly, the great national body of these rising, improving, and we may trust approved Christians?

Some will claim the Church of one nation, and some another; some will argue for spiritual Israel, whether spread among Teutonic people, or mainly confined to the British Isles and America. And who shall decide amongst them?

None but the Great Pyramid itself. Advance we, therefore, to the great step of 1813 A. D. (i.e. at 1,813 Pyramid inches from the North, or Christian nativity, beginning) of the Grand Gallery, and inquire *there* what is signified.

The step marks there, by that date, the most energetic advances made by Great Britain in its latter-day spread of the Bible, and its latter-day preaching of Christianity to all the world . . .

What manner of people, then, ought not we of Great Britain now, of Israel in ages past, to be at this juncture of our eventful history; saved above all nations by the providence of God in a manner we have never deserved, and for divine purpose in the future, respecting which nothing but the glorious Scriptures of Inspiration can give us any sufficient or saving idea; a halcyon time, when Ephraim shall be united once more with Judah, and both shall be on the Lord's side.[2]

Today, given the prevailing scepticism of modern society concerning the existence of God, it is difficult to appreciate the powerful influence the idea that they were really Israelites in disguise had on Britons of the mid- to late nineteenth century. For very many people this was a plausible explanation for the extraordinary providence shown by God to Victorian Britain which gave them a standard of living to be envied throughout the world. It also gave them a sense that building the empire was a national duty, for in this way, in accordance with God's wishes, the Gospel could be carried to all corners of the world.

Smyth's choice of 1813 for the start of his 'great step' had as much to do with his appreciation of recent history as with pyramid measurements. In 1789 revolution had broken out in France as it had done in England a century and a half earlier. This, however, was not to remain a domestic affair and the new government of France soon found itself at war with Austria and Prussia. In 1792 Louis XVI and his Austrian-born wife, Marie Antoinette, were taken to the guillotine and beheaded, to the horror of George III, then king of Great Britain. The fear that such an insurrection might spread across the Channel and once more plunge Britain into revolution and civil war concentrated minds in London and brought Britain into the conflict as well. The arrival of Napoleon on the European theatre of war for a while tipped matters in favour of the French republicans. For some years Britain, without a toe-hold on the Continent, could only fight at sea. However, victory at the Battle of Trafalgar in 1805 made Britannia ruler of the waves and turned the tide decisively against Napoleon. His rash invasion of Russia in 1812 made his ultimate defeat almost inevitable, as in the winter of that year his *Grande Armée* was all but destroyed in the snowy wastes of Ukraine. This meant that by 1813 Britain, revolutionary France's implacable enemy throughout the long Napoleonic Wars, was left as the most powerful nation-state in Europe. Finishing off Napoleon, first in 1814 and then again, more convincingly, at the Battle of

Waterloo in 1815, was all but a formality. In the eyes of the British they had done their duty for Europe and ensured the defeat of dangerous republican forces.

In the nineteenth century 'doing one's duty' was a virtue much admired. One of its prime exemplars was Horatio Nelson, victor of the Battle of Trafalgar, whose courage in the face of adversity made him a national hero. The fact that he was handicapped by the loss of both an arm and an eye in earlier battles did not deter him. Dressed in full regalia so that his men should know he was present and sharing their ordeal, he had insisted on walking the poop deck of his flagship, *Victory*, during the battle. A lucky shot from a French marksman severed Nelson's spinal cord. He was taken below decks, where he died in the arms of Captain Hardy. Shortly before his passing he uttered the words 'Kismet, Hardy', which is often mistranslated as 'kiss me, Hardy' but actually referred to his belief in destiny – *kismet* in Arabic. However, these were not Nelson's last words, which are recorded as having been: 'Thank God I have done my duty.' He, for one, evidently saw his own death at the moment of victory as his destiny. His one consolation was that he had fulfilled the task for which he had been sent.

The nation mourned Nelson as no other warrior of the nineteenth century. Following the Battle of Trafalgar his body was brought back to London and given a state funeral in St Paul's Cathedral. Twenty-four years later, in 1829, work began on a lasting memorial to the Battle of Trafalgar in what was to become London's pre-eminent square. The original design for this was drawn up by John Nash, a close friend of the former Prince Regent, now King George IV. Prior to this time the land now occupied by Trafalgar Square was part of the Royal Mews. Nash's plan was modified by Charles Barry, who in 1840, besides putting in the terrace and steps at the northern end of the square, set about erecting a suitable monument to Britain's most famous admiral. Thus, nearly forty years after the Battle of Trafalgar, when most of those who had served with him were dead, Nelson was commemorated with what is probably London's most famous monument: Nelson's Column.

Nelson's statue, sculpted by Edward Baily, is 17 feet high and stands on a column and plinth that together are 185 feet high. Around the base of the column are four large-scale bronze reliefs that tell the story of the Battle of Trafalgar. Four enormous bronze lions by Edwin Landseer seem to guard the column from the four quarters, north-east, south-east, south-west and north-west, and echo the four lions which support the coronation chair of the United Kingdom. They are clearly intended to give voice to the belief that Britain, as the lion kingdom par excellence, had inherited the blessings given to Judah by his father Israel in the Old Testament: 'Judah is a lion's whelp: from the prey, my son, thou art gone up: he stooped down, he couched as a lion, and as an old lion; who shall rouse him up? The sceptre shall not part from Judah, nor a lawgiver from between his feet, until Shiloh come; and unto him shall the gathering of the people be' (Gen. 49: 9–10). Landseer's lions were set up at Trafalgar Square in 1868, by which time the teachings of Wilson, Hine and others were gathering increasing recognition. To British Israelites at least, the inherent symbolism of the British lion as that of Judah needed no proving.

Nelson's column itself, in many ways reminiscent of those raised by Roman emperors, dominates the area of Trafalgar Square; it dwarfs the nearby equestrian statues of Charles I and George IV, and even the pillar-mounted statue of the duke of York (later King William IV) that stands around the corner at the end of Waterloo Place. Granted, he was a hero; but why, one asks, was Lord Nelson so honoured, over and above even monarchs? It is a difficult question. There can be little doubt that John Nash was a Freemason, and so was his principal patron, King George IV. We must ask, therefore, whether Nelson too was a Freemason – perhaps a very senior one – and whether this was the reason for his being commemorated with London's premier monument. As in the case of Sir Christopher Wren, this seems to have been a subject that has created considerable interest among masons themselves. In a pamphlet entitled *Was Nelson a Mason?* Brother F. W. Seal-Coon gives details of how, when and where Nelson may have been recruited into Freemasonry and of how he was remembered by other masons after his death. Though the evidence is not conclusive, it is at least suggestive.

Horatio (later Viscount) Nelson was born at Burnham Thorpe in Norfolk in 1758. The son of the rector, it might have been more expected that he would go into the church rather than to sea. His mother, Catherine née Suckling, was a grand-niece of Sir Robert Walpole, England's first prime minister. This connection might have offered him the chance of some preferment had the elder man still been alive; but Walpole had died in 1745, some thirteen years before Nelson's birth. His successors, such as his eldest son and Nelson's namesake, Horatio Walpole, do not seem to have been of much use in helping Nelson's career either, though Horatio Walpole, who lived in London and was a man of letters rather than politics, may well have been a Freemason.

Of more practical use to the young Nelson was his uncle, Captain Maurice Suckling; later to become comptroller of the navy, Suckling obtained a naval commission for Horatio. After various postings, in 1779 Nelson found himself in the West Indies as a lieutenant on the flagship of Sir Peter Parker. Here he was taken violently ill and spent time convalescing in the home of Sir Peter and his wife. They were to become lifelong friends and offered Nelson the sort of patronage that had been so lacking from the Walpoles. When Nelson recovered from his illness Sir Peter, who was governor of Jamaica, promoted him to the rank of captain. Nelson was put in command of first the *Badger*, a brig, and then the *Hinchinbrook*, a frigate.

Why a young and as yet undistinguished lieutenant should be so honoured by the governor of Jamaica and his wife as to be personally looked after by them when sick is a mystery – unless, that is, there were other, more subtle reasons. According to the author of the pamphlet *Was Nelson a Mason?*, Sir Peter Parker was then Provincial Grand Master of the Jamaica Lodge of Freemasons. It follows that if the young Nelson were himself already a Freemason by that time, this gentleman may have felt honour bound to help his 'brother in the craft'. It is possible, of course, that Sir Peter himself might have recruited Nelson into Freemasonry; but other evidence suggests that it is more likely that he joined in his native Norfolk, quite possibly through the auspices of his own uncle, Maurice Suckling. Evidence from the county points to this being the most likely scenario.

Burnham Thorpe, Nelson's home town, lies in the

north-west of the county of Norfolk. As a young sailor, Nelson would naturally have gravitated to Great Yarmouth, on the east coast, which as well as being an important fishing port was a station of the Royal Navy. In 1552 Queen Elizabeth had granted it to the admiralty under a charter. This had been confirmed in 1668 by Charles II, who was largely responsible for rebuilding the British navy after the Civil Wars. At that time England and the Netherlands were in contention for supremacy over the North Sea, and Yarmouth and its fellow Lowestoft, the two most easterly British ports, would have been very important in this connection.

For Nelson, as a sailor in the Royal Navy, Great Yarmouth would have been his home port. This is very important, for the aforementioned pamphlet by F. W. Seal-Coon links him with a masonic lodge there.

Among the furniture now in possession of the Lodge of Friendship No. 100 at Yarmouth, is a stone bearing an inscription to Nelson: it is an oblong polished block of white marble about the size of a large brick; on the top is a small aperture for the insertion of a Lewis, so that it evidently was intended for use as a 'perfect ashlar'. On each of the long sides is an incised inscription: that on one side commemorates the foundation of the Lodge of United Friends, and runs as follows:

Lodge of United Friends, No. 564
Constituted on Friday, 11th August, A.D. 1797
(a groove is marked here on the stone)
JAMES DAVY, Senr Warden
WILLm MADISON, Junr Warden
JOHN GREEN, Junr Secretary

The names of the Wardens . . . are those contained in the warrant of the Lodge, but for some reason, which I [Bro. F. W. Seal-Coon] conjecture, the name of the W. M. [Worshipful Master] (James Fromaw), has been deliberately erased by cutting a deep groove in the marble where the name must have stood; the groove is polished throughout so as to look as little unsightly as possible.

On the opposite side of the stone is cut the following:

In Memory of Bro[r] Vt NELSON
of the Nile, & of Burnham Thorpe, in
Norfolk, who lost his life in the arms
of Victory, in an engagement with
ye Combin'd Fleets of France & Spain,
off Cape Trafalgar, Oct 21, 1805
Proposed by Bro[r] John Cutlove.

Most unfortunately the minute books of the Lodge belonging to this period have all disappeared; they might have supplied corroboration of the inference from the above description, that Nelson was initiated in or became a member of the Lodge of United Friends. It is at all events extremely unlikely that, in a place where Nelson was so well known as he was at Yarmouth, the members of the Lodge would have dared to place on the Stone, commemorative of their own constitution, an inscription claiming him as a brother, which, if untrue, would have exposed them to ridicule and contradiction from many who also knew the facts.[3]

It is interesting to note in this connection that a 'Lewis' refers both to a mechanical contrivance used for lifting up heavy blocks of stone and to the son of a practising mason who joins the craft. The 'perfect ashlar' is one of the pieces of furniture in a masonic temple. It symbolizes a developed mason: one made smooth by his experience of Freemasonry. If Horatio Nelson had been introduced to the craft by his uncle, Maurice Suckling, then he might have been regarded as the latter's 'Lewis': he 'who bears the heat and burden of the day, from which his aged parents . . . ought to be exempt'.[4] According to this stone, the 'Lodge of Friends No. 564' was constituted on 11 August 1797. This was twenty years after Nelson first met Sir Peter Parker, so he cannot have been initiated here before journeying to the West Indies in 1777. However, in July 1797 he was wounded in action during an engagement on Santa Cruz de Tenerife. He lost an arm in this battle and was sent home to recuperate. As home meant Norfolk, it is not at all unlikely that if he were already a practising Freemason, he should have enrolled at a new lodge that was just being founded in his home port of Yarmouth. In any case, even if he were not already a Freemason, as he spent nine months in convalescence he may well have joined the Lodge of Friends to distract himself from the boredom of shore leave.

The second piece of Brother Seal-Coon's evidence also comes from Yarmouth. This concerns a snuff-box that Nelson is said to have given to a John Harcourt.

Bro. Robert Elliott Thorns of Norwich, has in his possession a round black papier maché snuff-box, with gilt Freemasons' emblems on the lid which was given to his relative, John Harcourt, by Lord Nelson, when they dined together at Yarmouth. Its history is authenticated by a letter written by John Harcourt's daughter, who was present on the occasion; she could not recollect the date, but says; 'My father took me with him to Yarmouth and we met Horace Nelson and had dinner together . . . I don't know the name of the Inn but I sate at the window and looked at the ships on the river whilst Horace and my father chatted, and he gave the box after dinner to my father . . . we always called him Horace, he was not Lord then, I think he was captain.'[5]

Nelson was raised to the peerage as a baron after his victory at the Battle of the Nile in 1798. Thus the gift of the snuff-box must have been made before this date. At the time he lost his arm, in July 1797, he was already a rear-admiral by seniority. So if he was a captain at the time of the gift the dinner must have been before this date, probably during the ten years between the ending of the American War of Independence in 1783 and the outbreak of the war with revolutionary France in 1793. By this time he had already met and impressed a number of senior Freemasons, including the duke of Clarence (afterwards King William IV), who was himself later a Grand Master by Royal Prerogative. He therefore had had ample opportunity to have been invited to become a mason himself. The story concerning the gift of the snuff-box therefore supports the theory that Nelson was a Freemason before the formation of the Lodge of Friends in Yarmouth. Indeed, it may have been on his inspiration that the lodge was founded in the first place.

The third piece of evidence marshalled by Brother Seal-Coon concerns a banner preserved not in Yarmouth but in the city of York. He cites an article, published in Volume 12 of A. Q. C., by 'W. Bro. Alfred Proctor, I. P. M. of the York Lodge No. 236'. This banner has written on it: 'England expects every Man to do his Duty. In memory of HORATIO VISCOUNT NELSON Who fell in the Moment of Victory off Cape Trafalgar Octr 21 1805.' Below this inscription are various masonic devices. These, says Brother Seal-Coon, are 'the Sun, the Square and compasses on the V. S. L. and the Moon' and they are followed by the words: 'We rejoice with our Country But mourn for our Brother.' All of this evidence, while not absolutely conclusive, would seem to indicate that Nelson was indeed a Freemason – and probably quite a senior one at that.

Freemason or not, the statue of Nelson on top of the Corinthian column of Trafalgar Square was clearly intended to be more than an epitaph for the admiral himself. The height of the column, 185 feet, is said to be the average depth of the English Channel. However, as this would be impossible to work out and in any case varies with the tides, this cannot be the true reason for selecting this height. The real reason becomes apparent when the extra 17 feet of the statue are added to it. We come then to a rather remarkable height for the monument as a whole of 202 feet. This is, of course, the same height as the Monument on Fish Street to the Great Fire of London and it means that the same geometry applies to Nelson's column as applies to the earlier monument. Thus, just as the Monument suggests that Christopher Wren had in mind the geometry of the *vesica piscis*, so too does Nelson's column. Like the Monument, at midsummer Nelson's Column will cast a shadow giving the proportions of $1:\sqrt{3}$. This means that the sun will be seen to shine around Nelson's head as it crosses the eastern sky in the morning and the western sky in the afternoon of the summer solstice (see plate 42). The afternoon shadow cast by Nelson's statue as the sun crosses in the west at an altitude of

30° reaches exactly to the edge of the square.

Like the Monument in Fish Street, Nelson's column also implies an invisible pyramid with a side of 550 feet – large enough to cover the entire square. Throughout the eighteenth and nineteenth centuries, from the vantage point of London, the sun would still be positioned in the sign of Leo the lion at the time of year when it culminated in the southern sky at an altitude of 51° 51′ – the same as the slope of the Great Pyramid. Thus there is a geometrical link between Nelson's Column, the invisible pyramid that it implies, and the sign of Leo in the sky.

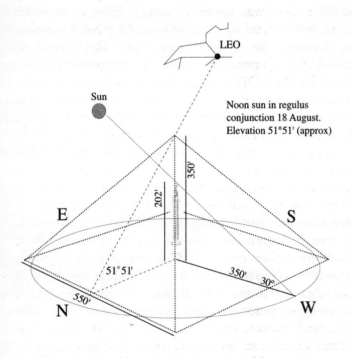

Fig. 43. Invisible pyramid around Trafalgar Square.

As we have seen, after Nelson died at the Battle of Trafalgar his body was brought back to London and buried in St Paul's Cathedral. However, this was no ordinary burial, not even by the standards of a national hero. His tomb lies at the very heart of the church, exactly under the crossing of the aisles and beneath the centre of the great dome. This is the point that Christopher Wren is said to have marked on the ground with a piece of an old tombstone carrying the Latin legend *Resurgam*. In a curious way, Nelson's tomb echoes this theme. Above his sarcophagus, which like that of a pharaoh contains four coffins, one inside the other, is another, elaborate sarcophagus of black marble. This was orginally prepared for, though not used by, Cardinal Wolsey. On the side of Nelson's tomb is written the simple legend: HORATIO VISC NELSON. Curiously, this is an anagram for HIS COVENANT OR SOIL, a fitting epithet for a hero buried at the very centre of a cathedral connected with the legendary phoenix.

From all the above it can be seen that, consciously or unconsciously, the builders of Trafalgar Square constructed a monument that brought together the twin streams of Freemasonry and British Israelitism in a grand patriotic gesture. The monument to Nelson at the southern end of the square carries reliefs on its northern, eastern and western sides that tell the story of Nelson's earlier victories at Copenhagen and Cape St Vincent. The southern relief is reserved for the Battle of Trafalgar itself and the admiral-martyr's death at the moment of victory. It also records the famous words: 'England expects every man will do his duty.' This theme of duty, so beloved of Victorians, is what seems to have made Nelson particularly special in the eyes of his contemporaries: he was Everyman doing his duty by establishing the British empire.

Nelson's statue, 185 feet above the roar of the traffic below, faces resolutely down Whitehall towards what has always been the sacred heart of England: Westminster Abbey. Here, in the shrine of St Edward the Confessor, stands the coronation seat, the epitome of royal power. For seven hundred years, until 1996, this housed the Stone believed by British Israelites and Freemasons alike to be the very pillar raised by Jacob at Bethel in honour of his covenant with God. Nelson's statue, therefore, was designed to face reverently towards the Stone of Destiny, the mystic keepsake that underpins the very throne of Britain. This being identified with the 'lion-throne' of Judah, it is not without consequence that on the day when the sun is at the pyramid angle of 51° 51′, as seen from Trafalgar Square, it culminates exactly over Westminster Abbey in the royal sign of Leo.

Nelson's column at Trafalgar Square also acts as a junction between the Strand running west–east, and Whitehall, running north–south. Thus in a mystic way it links St Paul's Cathedral, Wren's Temple of the New Jerusalem, which stands more or less directly to the east at the other end of the Strand and Fleet Street, with the royal shrine of Westminster Abbey to the south. This would seem to have been its intended purpose.

In 1911 the Admiralty Archway was built by Austin Webb. It was originally intended to be the entry point to a processional way leading to the Victoria Monument in front of Buckingham Palace. Because of the outbreak of the First World War, the scheme of which this was to be but a part was never completed. Though with American help the war was eventually won, the cost to Britain was enormous, in terms of both resources and lives lost. In these circumstances it would have been inappropriate to carry on with a building scheme that drew further attention to the exalted role of the monarchy when the ordinary people of the country had lost so much. Yet, paradoxically, it was during the First World War that the British Israel movement reached the height of its popularity. In part this was because, during this time of great suffering, people were attracted to a system of ideas that 'proved' they were God's chosen people; it gave reassurance that in the end things would turn out well.

There were, however, more specific reasons for thinking that 'Shiloh' was soon to come and that the sceptre, held in trust by Britain for so many centuries, would soon be returned to its true owner: Jesus Christ the Messiah. In November 1914, the Ottoman empire entered the war on the side of Germany and Austria-Hungary and against the allied powers: Britain, France, Serbia, Russia and Italy. At that time the Ottoman empire, though for long regarded as the 'sick man of Europe' and much reduced from its greatest power some three centuries earlier, still controlled large tracts of the Middle East, including what are now Iraq, Saudi Arabia, Jordan, Syria, Lebanon – and Israel. For Britain and France, the entry of the Ottoman Turks into the war posed a real threat to trade, as a Turkish advance from Palestine into Egypt would jeopardize the shipping route via the Suez Canal. To counter this threat, in 1916 the British launched offensives in Arabia, Mesopotamia and Syria. At the urging of T. E. Lawrence – 'Lawrence of Arabia' – the nomadic Arabs were armed and urged to rebel against Turkish occupation. The climax of these events came on 11

December 1917 when General Allenby, the field marshal in charge of the British expeditionary forces, received the surrender of the keys of Jerusalem. This took place at the Citadel, next to the Jaffa Gate, which stands on the spot where King Herod had his palace and Jesus was tried before his crucifixion. Allenby was a devout man and a British Israel sympathizer; his nephew, the present Viscount Allenby of Megiddo, is not only president of the Anglo-Israeli Archaeological Society but also patron of the British-Israel World Federation. As a mark of respect to the city of Jerusalem, which he regarded himself as having delivered rather than conquered, the first Viscount Allenby dismounted from his horse when he came to the city gates. As he entered the city on foot he is said to have remarked: 'Where the King of kings has walked, it is not meet that I should ride.'

For British Israelites the delivery of Jerusalem seemed prophetic in the extreme. Jerusalem had been under the rule of non-Israelite, Gentile powers ever since the destruction of King Herod's temple in AD 70. With the surrender of the city to British forces, it was now back under 'Israelite' (i.e. British) control. As it had been prophesied in the Bible that this would only occur in the 'latter days', shortly before the last judgement, it seemed to many to indicate that the end was nigh. As further confirmation that this was so, according to a number of prophecies in the Bible, prior to the return of the Messiah there would be a great battle fought at 'Armageddon', the Hill of Megiddo in the Jezreel valley. Allenby's victory in a battle fought at this very site – for which he was awarded the title Viscount Allenby of Megiddo – seemed further evidence that prophecies for the end of days were being fulfilled.

In 1918, with the Great War over, there was a widespread feeling that the end-days were about to begin. Jerusalem was now in British hands, and so too (or so it was believed by British Israelites the world over) was the throne of David and Solomon – safely ensconced inside the coronation throne at Westminster. This was seen as a preparation for the imminent return of Jesus Christ, who could be expected to sit on the throne of David, either ruling the world from its present location in 'New Jerusalem' (London) or, if he preferred, moving it back to 'Old Jerusalem' in Palestine. In preparation for this momentous event, in 1919 a number of independent 'identity' groups amalgamated to form the 'British-Israel World Federation'. Patroness of this new society was Princess Alice, countess of Athlone, who was herself a grand-daughter of Queen Victoria and thus a descendant of the royal house of Great Britain.[6]

Princess Alice, like everyone else involved with the British Israel movement at the time, must have imagined that the period of waiting would be short; that within her own lifetime 'all these things would be accomplished'. However, this was not to be. As the 1910s gave way to the 1920s and the Messiah failed to put in an appearance, so it became increasingly difficult to assert that the First World War was the Armageddon prophesied in the Bible. Not only that, but it was not long before it was obvious that Britain after the First World War was not the same country as it had been before. Too many men had died needlessly in the trenches, ordered over the top by senior officers dangerously out of touch with ordinary sentiments. Gone for ever was the belief, nurtured for centuries, that a God-fearing aristocracy knew how to govern the country for the good of the people. In its place arose a new labour movement that, rejecting biblical prophecies of a New Jerusalem, sought its inspiration in the philosophy of Karl Marx.

Cracks were also beginning to appear in the British empire. At the same time that workers in Britain were demanding better wages and working conditions, the imperial ideal was being challenged by secessionist movements. The most important of these, if only because it was closest to home, was in Ireland. The Dublin Easter uprising of 1916 had been put down with force and fifteen of the rebels hanged as traitors. However, though the troubles in Ireland seemed to have been contained, this had been done at great cost: 106 British troops had been killed in the fighting and a further 271 wounded. Casualties on the rebel side had been considerably lighter, but even so, those who had either died in the fighting itself or been executed in its aftermath became martyrs. Now all attempts at restoring stability were viewed as further repression. The rebel cause, which initially had been little more than a fringe movement to be treated with derision, was now gaining an unstoppable momentum. In 1920, in an attempt to reach a peaceful settlement that might be acceptable to all, a Home Rule Act was passed through Parliament. This split the island of Ireland into two parts, with considerable autonomy given to each. However, this was not enough as far as the republicans were concerned, and the following year twenty-six counties seceded from the Union of Great Britain altogether to become the Irish Free State.

For British Israelites, who believed that the Stone of Destiny had been brought to Ireland by Jeremiah the prophet prior to its removal to Scotland, this was incomprehensible. How could the United Kingdom of Great Britain and Ireland be split up in this way at the very moment when it should be celebrating Christ's imminent return as king over Israel? What strange twist of fate was it that would separate the Israelites of Ireland from the rest of the Holy Kingdom of Britain? No answer could be found to this question at the time, and it still hangs in the air today.

As if the loss of Eire were not enough, during the 1930s independence movements began to grow elsewhere in the British empire, notably in India and Palestine. These developments were slowed for a time by the onset of the Second World War but, as in Ireland, they could not be halted for ever. Still in a state of shock following the Second World War, Britain lacked the will as well as the money to hold together what remained of its vast empire. On 14 August 1947 India and Pakistan received their independence. The following year Britain quit Palestine, the bulk of which became the embryonic Jewish state of Israel. What began as a trickle now became a flood, as one by one Britain lost the remaining territories that made up its empire. Within two decades, though British pride was somewhat assuaged by the creation of a much looser federation, the British Commonwealth, the empire was no more than history, virtually all that remained a few island dependencies too small to be self-sufficient.

Thus it was that by 1970 Britain, which in 1900 had been far and away the most powerful nation on earth, was reduced to an insignificant backwater on the fringes of Europe. Barely able to keep itself afloat economically, it was now almost entirely dependent on the United States militarily. Even this, however, was not the end of the story of British decline. For fifty years following the defection of the counties making up the Irish Republic the United Kingdom itself had remained stable; but the centrifugal forces had not really abated, and during the 1970s civil war broke out again in the six counties of Northern Ireland. It became evident that, in this far-off corner of Europe, the religious divide between Catholics and Protestants was still as wide as at the time of James II and William III. For Catholics, north and south of the border, there was a sense of grievance that Ireland had been partitioned at all. On the other hand, many Protestants were British Israelites and regarded allegiance to the crown as not just a political matter but one of faith. These two views of Ireland's destiny were and are incompatible, and though this is never mentioned publicly by politicians of either side, it is this clash that is the real dynamic behind the present-day troubles.

In the 1970s nationalism of a different sort also began to make itself felt in Scotland and Wales. At the same time, in 1973, Britain joined the European Economic Community. Unknown to the majority of British voters, those running this society – later known as the European Community (EC) and now as the European Union (EU) – had hidden ambitions that it would itself one day become a fully fledged state: a United States of Europe. Within this new superstate Britain would be divided into several smaller provinces, as it had once been in the Roman empire. Politically speaking, London, far from being a 'New Jerusalem', the capital of the world, would be a mere satellite of Brussels where the real power lay.

By now the British Israel movement, which had been in sharp decline for decades, almost disappeared from sight. Any notion of Britain as 'God's awin Israel' seemed as quaint as the Edwardian furnishings of their headquarters in Buckingham Gate. As if to confirm the end of any claim England might have to being the long-lost Israel, in 1996 the British Prime Minister, John Major, sought to appease nationalist feelings north of the England–Scotland border by ordering the return to Scotland of the Stone of Scone. This was duly accomplished on St Andrew's Day, 30 November 1996. To the sound of wailing bagpipes, the coronation stone, a rough block of sandstone that for seven hundred years had sat within its purpose-built throne in Westminster Abbey, was delivered to Edinburgh Castle. The suggestion that the stone could be brought back to London for coronations did nothing to calm unease in England that the government was taking a massive gamble in thinking that the Scots would ever be willing to allow the stone to leave Scotland again, even temporarily. This posed the question as to whether the next king or queen of England would have to be crowned twice: once in Westminster and a second time in Edinburgh. With the removal from London of this powerful symbol of national unity, the concept of Britain as a United Kingdom received a further heavy blow.

The facts of power were soon to follow this symbolic transfer of sovereignty. John Major's Conservative Party went on to lose the 1997 general election and almost immediately the new Labour government elected in its place set in motion the process that has given birth to the first Scottish Parliament since the Act of Union of 1707. This new Parliament met in Edinburgh for the first time on 12 May 1999. To many commentators looking on from outside, the establishment of this new devolved legislature seems likely to be but the first step towards the final break-up of the United Kingdom into its constituent nations. It looks increasingly likely that Northern Ireland will cease to be a province of Great Britain and be forced into an unwilling union with the Republic of Eire. Scotland almost certainly and Wales quite probably will become mini-nation-states under the umbrella of the European Union. Thus, whatever the truth may be concerning the legends surrounding the Stone of Scone, it cannot be denied that its return to Scotland has coincided with events that would not have been foreseen even five years earlier. Where this leaves England is the unanswered question of our times. Will it, as many of its politicians seem to hope, abandon independence and enter into ever deeper union with a federalist Europe? Or will it now, under its own solitary flag of St George, rise like the phoenix out of the ashes of its old self? Only time will tell.

EPILOGUE

When I began this investigation into London as representative of the archetypal sacred city of 'New Jerusalem', I had no idea where it would lead. Still less could I have imagined, nearly thirty years ago, that we would one day be contemplating the break-up of the United Kingdom and the incorporation of Britain into a United States of Europe. Yet, like it or loathe it, this seems to be the direction in which the current of history is sweeping us.

To us, living as we do in a cynical age, the idea that intelligent men should dream of rebuilding London as a version of the New Jerusalem seems laughably strange. However, it has to be remembered that our ancestors lived in a different world: one in which the words contained in the Bible were considered to be absolute truth. The Bible prophesied that before the Second Coming the erring tribes of Israel would be reunited with their brethren the Jews. Through analysis of biblical prophecy many people believed that the 'lost tribes', having escaped westwards after their displacement from the Holy Land by the Assyrians, had regathered in Britain. As Britain was the foremost colonizing power of Europe, had been responsible for taking the Bible to the four corners of the world and had a throne which contained a stone traditionally believed to have been 'Jacob's Pillow', it was natural that nineteenth-century Britons should want to believe that their nation was indeed lost Israel. While such ideas excite only ridicule among intellectuals today, within the context of Victorian England there were steps of logic all along the way that brought people to this conclusion. Given this situation, it was also logical that the British should identify their capital city with Jerusalem and that this identification should be marked by the building of suitable monuments.

Yet London is not a new city. It would seem that from even before the times of the Romans there was a city on the north bank of the Thames believed by many to have been called Trinovantum or 'New Troy'. Indeed, the legend of Trinovantum was accepted as historical fact up until about 1700. An unbiased reading of ancient records, especially the works of Julius Caesar, leads indisputably to the fact that the ancient British were not the savages of modern fantasy. In his book *De bello gallica*, Caesar describes Britain as being a triangular land. Analysis of the dimensions of the triangle he describes shows that the Britons of his period (the first century AD) had a knowledge of sacred geometry. They clearly knew about the relationship of $1:\sqrt{3}$ and in a very ingenious way related this to the practical business of squaring the circle. Thus it can be seen that Caesar's description of the triangle land, no doubt given to him by Druids, was nothing less than a practical mnemonic. It is worth recapping on how, as I believe, it came about in recent centuries that the Trojan link was forgotten and London was rebuilt to represent the New Jerusalem.

Prior to the Anglo-Saxon invasions of Britain in the fifth century AD there was a native, British church. This church, known as the Culdee or Chaldean, claimed an apostolic foundation. According to Gildas, a monk living in the sixth century, Christianity had first been brought to Britain in 36 AD. Though Gildas does not mention it, legend has it that at this time Joseph of Arimathea and twelve companions came to Britain with the Holy Grail. We may guess that even at this early period, when Gildas was writing, there was a conception that the British were at least in part descended from the lost tribes of Israel; for Gildas' book is very much in the style of Jeremiah's Lamentations over the fall of Jerusalem and seems to equate the Britons with the Old Testament Israelites.

King Henry VII, who came on to the throne of England in 1485, was half-Welsh. He was in fact the first Welsh king to sit on the throne of Britain since the death of Cadwallader in AD 689. His direct claim to the throne was decidedly weak, but he was able to legitimize his position by pointing to his Welsh lineage, which went back through King Arthur to the legendary Brutus, founder of Britain. He was therefore able to claim that far from usurping the throne of England from the Plantagenets, he was restoring it to its rightful owners: the descendants of the ancient kings of Britain. Though himself of the house of Lancaster, Henry VII further legitimized his rule by marrying Elizabeth of York, the daughter of King Edward IV. This brought together the houses of York and Lancaster and, to celebrate this union, Henry made use of the symbol of the Tudor rose: part red and part white. His son, King Henry VIII, remodelled the Order of the Garter, originally founded by Edward III in emulation of King

Arthur's Round Table. He had the Round Table which now hangs in Winchester Great Hall repainted and a Tudor rose painted at its centre. From this time onwards the rose became a major emblem signifying both the mysteries of England and the Order of the Garter.

Henry VIII also rebelled against the authority of the Roman Catholic Church. He was well aware that the native British church traced its origins back to long before the arrival of Augustine in Kent in AD 697. He well knew the legend that the Britons had been converted to Christianity by Joseph of Arimathea in AD 36, prior to the establishment of the first church in Rome. Accordingly, it followed that the British church was senior to the Roman and that he, as king, was the true defender of the Christian faith: a title still claimed by British sovereigns to this day. This was the legal basis for the position of his reformed Church of England and his justification for dissolving the monasteries.

Queen Elizabeth I, who came to the throne in 1558, took her father's reforms further. Threatened by Spain and the risk of Catholic insurrection, she drew comfort from a belief that the British were in reality God's Israel. She also drew strength from her family connections with the line of Brutus and in particular the kings who ruled in London prior to the Roman invasions. Accordingly, she had statues of King Lud and his sons placed in niches on her rebuilt Ludgate. Henry VIII had reorganized the Order of the Garter better to support his political and religious aims; during Elizabeth's reign, strenuous attempts were made to develop a network of alliances with the other Protestant kings and princes of Europe. She used the offer of membership of the Order of the Garter as both a carrot and a reward for those sympathetic to the cause. At this time, too, certain influential people in England (notably Dr John Dee and his circle of admirers) began dreaming of an overseas empire. The voyages to America of the Gilbert brothers, of their half-brother Sir Walter Raleigh and of Sir Francis Drake laid the foundations of what was to become the British empire.

In 1603 Elizabeth died and was succeeded by King James I, who was (according to James Anderson) a 'Grand Master by Royal Prerogative' of the Freemasons. Coming from Scotland (though still through Henry VII of the Tudor–Brutus bloodline), he brought a fresh impetus to the idea of British Israel. It had long been believed by the Scots that they, like the English and Welsh, were descended from the lost tribes of Israel and that their kings sat on the throne of David. Because of this the early Stuarts believed absolutely in the divine right of kings. To emphasize his lineage and place as a 'king of Israel', James had Aldersgate, the northern entrance to the City of London, rebuilt. In niches either side of his own equestrian statue he placed figures of the prophets Jeremiah and Samuel. These were accompanied with suitable texts implying that not only was he, James, a king of Israel but his capital city of London was the analogue of Jerusalem. This seems to have been the beginning of a conscious attempt to transform England's capital into a utopian city: the New Jerusalem.

Meanwhile, on the continent of Europe religious divisions were becoming ever more deeply entrenched. For a time Prague, the capital of Bohemia, acted as a beacon of hope in a darkening world. Under the rule of a relatively benign emperor, Rudolf II, Rosicrucianism was able to flourish. At the core of this philosophy was a belief that knowledge could be gained by studying nature and that through such knowledge life could be improved. When, in 1620, religious strife broke out in Europe and the Protestant intelligentsia of Bohemia and Germany were driven into exile, London became the new centre for this 'natural philosophy' or, as we would call it today, science. During the 1640s, when Britain was at war with itself, a group of scientists formed themselves into a secret college. After the Restoration of 1660 they were able to come out of the shadows and form a new scientific body: the Royal Society.

By 1700, perhaps in response to the 'New Jerusalem' idea, the belief that London pre-dated the Romans and had once been called Trinovantum had fallen out of fashion. During the previous century English Freemasonry, which prior to this date had been something of an elite club, gradually came out into the open. This process was completed with the formation of the United Grand Lodge of London in 1717. The earliest recorded Freemasons of whom we have record are Sir Christopher Wren, Elias Ashmole and Sir Robert Moray – all founder members of the Royal Society. The Freemasons of the seventeenth century looked upon the 'Augustan style' of ancient Rome as the architectural ideal. Following the Great Fire of London in 1666, Wren and his friends had the opportunity to carry out some rudimentary archaeological research. Below the rubble of the burnt city they found remains of Roman London. When they set about rebuilding the city it was with a vision that it should become a 'New Jerusalem' – but dressed in the fashionable garb of ancient Rome.

The Monument to the Fire that was put up in Fish

Street was in effect the foundation stone of the new city – the New Jerusalem – that Wren built. While paying lip-service to an earlier (perhaps mythical) tower that may once have stood nearby at Billingsgate, it was designed to demonstrate that London was especially blessed by the heavens. For, like the obelisk at Heliopolis in Egypt, it cast at the solstice a shadow from which could be generated the *vesica piscis*. From this, other meaningful sacred geometry could be deduced. This must have been well understood by Sir Christopher Wren, who as well as being highly skilled as a geometer was one of the world's foremost astronomers of his day and had been making sundials since the age of fourteen.

Wren rebuilt St Paul's Cathedral in the fashionable Augustan style but re-orientated its axis so that it aligned with the Temple Church. It was clearly intended that, just as the Temple Church was an analogue of the Jerusalem Church of the Holy Sepulchre, so the new St Paul's should represent the Temple of Solomon. In this way London was secretly consecrated as the New Jerusalem, which was thus indeed, as the poet William Blake surmised, built in England's green and pleasant land.

In the two centuries that followed, the British empire grew and London prospered. For reasons that are not obvious, Admiral Lord Nelson (who was also almost certainly a Freemason) was buried beneath the crossing of St Paul's Cathedral. During the 1840s Trafalgar Square was laid out with Nelson's Column as its principal feature. This column does, in a sense, stand similarly at the crossroads of London and therefore of the empire. To its south, in the direction faced by the statue of Nelson, lies Westminster, home to Parliament and the famous Abbey of St Peter's. To its east lie the Strand, Aldwych, Fleet Street and St Paul's. As the, so to speak, pivot of London, Trafalgar Square quite naturally attracts attention: it is the equivalent of the Place de la Concorde in Paris. Intentionally, the builders of Nelson's Column, who were undoubtedly also Freemasons, gave it (if you include the height of the statue) the exact same height as the Monument in Fish Street: 202 feet. Thus the solar-generated geometry that pertains to the earlier memorial put up by Sir Christopher Wren also applies to Nelson's Column. At the summer solstice, the afternoon shadow reaches to the edge of the square to the east of the column. The square that could be drawn using this length as the radius of an equal perimeter circle was clearly the size of the original Trafalgar Square before it was modified by later architects. In this way Nelson's Column can be understood as the successor to the Monument in Fish Street: the foundation stone of Victorian London.

During the course of the 1950s and 1960s London, which had been heavily bombed during the Second World War, was rebuilt piecemeal in a modernist fashion. The architects involved were not schooled in anything as arcane as the 'Augustan style' and were, so it would seem, completely oblivious of any idea that the city should reflect the pattern of a 'New Jerusalem'. St Paul's Cathedral, which at the time of its reconstruction by Wren had stood out as far and away the largest, most impressive building in the City, was now to be surrounded by ugly shops and office blocks. The myriad of Wren churches – those which had survived – were now mostly similarly obscured by high-rise buildings.

This is the city of London that confronts visitors

today: a vast metropolis of sprawling suburbs, a mish-mash of architectural styles from Elizabethan through Victorian to Edwardian and modern. The London of today is, in a sense, a microcosm of the whole world, for it contains communities of people from every part of Europe, the old empire and even other parts of the world that never were British colonies. It is a vibrant city: the most economically dynamic in Europe, a vast emporium where anything and everything can be bought or sold. Indeed, so important is London to world trade that every international company of any size has to have an office there. It is also the world centre for banking and finance, where currencies, bonds and shares are traded as nowhere else.

London is also the world capital for the arts. The British Museum contains the largest and most complete collection of antiquities in the world; the National Gallery has one of the finest collections of art to be seen anywhere. There are at least three world-class orchestras based in London. For shops, theatres, opera houses, cinemas, restaurants, pubs, parks and concert halls, there are few if any cities that can begin to compete in number, quality and variety. Yet nothing stays static for long; and, like the River Thames that laves the same shores it has for centuries, London has to flow with the times. For even if today's London seems more 'New Babylon' than 'New Jerusalem', yet the British Israel legacy lies only just below the surface. You do not have to travel far in London to see a stone lion or some other monument to an all but forgotten vision: an empire founded on the Bible preparing the way for the Messiah. It is not a bad legacy, and one of which Christopher Wren would not be ashamed.

GEOMETRICAL CONSTRUCTS BASED ON CAESAR'S DESCRIPTION OF BRITAIN

In his *Commentarii de bello gallico* Julius Caesar writes that the island of Britain is triangular:

> The island is triangular, with one side facing Gaul. One corner of this side, on the coast of Kent, is the landing-place for nearly all the ships from Gaul, and points east; the lower corner points south. The length of this side is about 475 miles. Another side faces west, towards Spain. In this direction is Ireland, which is supposed to be half the size of Britain, and lies at the same distance from it as Gaul . . . This side of Britain, according to the natives' estimate, is 665 miles long. The third side faces north, no land lies opposite it, but its eastern corner points roughly in the direction of Germany. Its length is estimated at 760 miles. Thus the whole island is 1,900 miles in circumference.[1]

Caesar himself only ever visited the south-east corner of the island and he tells us that even Gallic traders knew next to nothing about Britain except for its south coast. It follows, then, that he received the information that Britain was shaped like a triangle from certain of

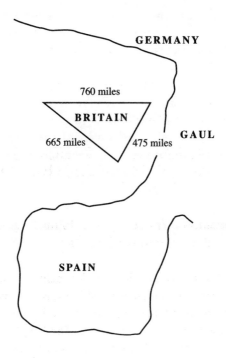

Fig. 44. Caesar's map of Britain.

the Britons themselves. However, even a casual look at a map of Britain reveals that this information was erroneous. Only in the most general terms can the island be described as triangular in shape, and even then the dimensions Caesar gives for the lengths of the coasts are wrong. At first sight, therefore, his map of Britain – if such we may call it – is all but useless.

The Britain that Caesar had had described to him may have been the ideal form in the minds of the Britons, but it approximates only very slightly to the real geography of the island. However, closer analysis of Caesar's figures reveals that they are based on a geometrical figure with extraordinary properties. Although the dimensions of the island as given to Caesar are at first sight unpromising, if the lengths are each divided by 95, we see that the proportions of the sides of the triangle are 5: 7: 8. When drawn, the triangle looks like the one shown in figure 45.

If you know the relative lengths of the sides of any triangle, then it is only a matter of simple trigonometry to ascertain its angles. Using the cosine rule we find that:

$$CosA = (b^2 + c^2 - a^2) / 2bc$$

Thus

$$CosA = (8^2 + 5^2 - 7^2) / 2 \times 8 \times 5$$
$$= (64 + 25 - 49) / 80$$
$$= 40/80 = 0.5$$

Reference to cosine tables or a calculator with mathematical functions quickly reveals that angle A is 60°.

If we now drop a perpendicular from C to D, we get a right-angled triangle ACD. Since angle A is 60°, angle ACD has to be 30°. Cos 60° = AD/AC = 0.5. Since AC = 8, AD = 4. Thus D divides AB in such a way that DA = 4 units and BD = 1 unit. Thus the triangle ACD is half of an equilateral triangle of side 8 units.

The geometry of Caesar's map does not stop here. If we drop a perpendicular from B to E it creates another 30°:60°:90° triangle: ABE. The angle ABE is 30°, and as AE has to be half the length of AB, it must be 2.5 units in length. If we subtract this length from AC we get the length of CE, which comes out at 5.5 units.

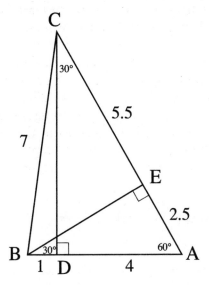

Fig. 45. Proportions of the triangle of Britain.

Using double this length, we can construct the square FGHI of side 11 units (see figure 46). The length CB is 7 units long, and if we draw a circle using this as its radius it will have the same perimeter as the square FGHI. In other words, the dimensions of the figurative island of Britain as revealed to Caesar are based on a diagram that enables the circle to be squared.

This diagram bears within it the proportionate relationships of the Great Pyramid of Giza, where the radius of the equivalent circle is the height of the pyramid and the sides also have an equal perimeter length. The relative dimensions of the square and the circle are implicit in British units of measure to this day: for a circle with a diameter of seven yards will have a perimeter of 22 yards, i.e. 1 chain. The chain of 22 yards is not a measure much used these days, but it is

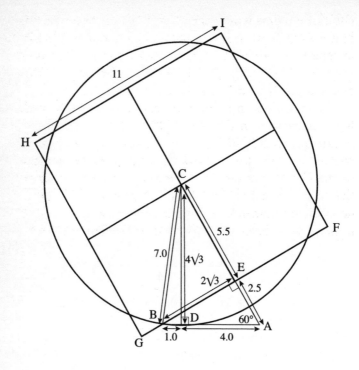

Fig. 46. Squaring the circle with Caesar's map of Britain.

still the length of a cricket pitch. More commonly used is the furlong of 220 yards or 10 chains. The British mile is 8 furlongs or 80 chains in length.

How or when this knowledge was imported into Britain is not known for sure. However, ancient British units of measure show close parallels with Egyptian units of measure, and it was established as long ago as the 1960s by the late Professor Alexander Thom that stone circles in Britain were based on complex geometry. The royal cubit of Egypt, 7 'palms' in length, is very close to being 21 British inches in length (20.62). The standard cubit of 6 palms would therefore be 18 inches, which is half a yard. Thus a British chain is 44 standard cubits in length. A circle of 7 yards diameter therefore produces a square of perimeter 44 Egyptian cubits. This seems unlikely to be a coincidence.

The megaliths in Britain indicate a connection with high civilization in the period 3100–2100 BC, contemporaneous with 'Old Kingdom' Egypt. The description of Britain as an idealized triangle that gives the measure of the Great Pyramid may therefore either go back to the time when Stonehenge, Avebury and other neolithic monuments were built – the Pyramid Age – or it may have been the work of later 'Trojans', who

Fig. 47. The triangle land of Troy.

according to traditional British history sought refuge in the island of Britain two generations after the Trojan war.

The ancient city of Troy – or Ilium as it is more properly called – was the capital of a province called the Troad. This formed the north-western peninsula of Anatolia from which the Britons claimed to have originally come. The Troad is an almost perfect equilateral triangle of sides roughly 50 miles that stretches from the ancient city of Dardanus (on the Dardanelles) along the Aegean coast to Cape Lekton, from there along the Gulf of Edremit to Adromittium, and finally back overland to Dardanus. The Troad is said by the Greeks to have been so named after an ancestor of the Trojans called Troas. However, inspection of the map would suggest otherwise: that Troad really meant 'triangle land' in the language of the Trojans.

This has relevance to our study of Britain. According to Nennius, the ninth-century historian, Caesar fought his 'Battle of the Ford' outside 'Trinovantum'. Caesar himself refers to the tribe of Britons living in the region of what we now call London as the 'Trinovantes'. According to all traditional histories Trinovantum is the ancient name of London. It is said to mean 'New Troy'. Now, as we have seen, Caesar describes the island of Britain as being triangular. It is therefore tempting to think that the name Trinovantum originally applied to Britain as a whole and was later transferred to London as the capital city in the same way that Ilium, the capital of the Troad, came to be known simply as Troy.

NOTES

PROLOGUE

1 John Michell, *City of Revelation*, Garnstone Press, London, 1972. Now revised and renamed *Dimensions of Paradise*, Thames & Hudson, London, 1988.

2 John Michell, *New Light on the Ancient Mystery of Glastonbury*, Gothic Image, Glastonbury, 1990, p. 101.

CHAPTER 1

1 In some histories and genealogies Brwt is sometimes called Prydain.

2 Geoffrey of Monmouth, *History of the Kings of Britain*, trans. Lewis Thorpe, Penguin, London, 1996, pp. 73–4.

3 The story of Aeneas is, of course, a Roman epic and the subject of Virgil's *Aeneid*.

4 According to some Welsh authors this etymology is wrong. The true derivation of the name London, they say, is from Llan-dein, meaning 'Town on the Thames'. See e.g. *The Chronicles of the Kings of Britain*, translated from the Welsh copy attributed to Tysilio by Revd Peter Roberts, E. Williams, London, 1811.

5 For further details of a possible connection between Britain and Troy, see Appendix.

6 *Caesar: The Conquest of Gaul*, trans. S.A. Handford, Book Club Associates, London, 1993, pp. 110–11.

7 St Swithin's Church was bombed during the Second World War. It was excavated in 1960–1 by a team led by Professor W.S. Grimes.

8 Geoffrey of Monmouth, *History of the Kings of Britain*, p. 106.

9 See *Evening Standard*, 5 February 1999.

10 See report in *Evening Standard*, 18 December 1998.

11 *Tacitus, The Annals*, trans. Michael Grant, London, Book Club Associates, 1990, p. 331.

12 Geoffrey of Monmouth, *History of the Kings of Britain*, p. 100.

13 Revd J. Williams ab Ithel, *Barddas*, Welsh Manuscript Society/ Longman & Co., London, 1862, p. 41.

14 What may well be King Arthur's gravestone was found in 1990 at a lonely church in South Wales by Alan Wilson and Baram Blackett. For details see Adrian Gilbert, Alan Wilson and Baram Blackett, *The Holy Kingdom*, Bantam Press, London, 1998.

15 *The Anglo-Saxon Chronicles*, trans. Anne Savage, Macmillan, London, 1984, p. 41.

16 Geoffrey of Monmouth, *History of the Kings of Britain*, p. 280.

CHAPTER 2

1 *Iolo MSS*, comp. and trans. Taliesin Williams, Foulkes, Liverpool, 1888, pp. 416–17.

2 For a detailed discussion of this whole subject area, see Gilbert et al., *The Holy Kingdom*, ch. 18.

3 Frances A. Yates, *The Occult Philosophy in the Elizabethan Age*, Ark, London, 1983, p. 85.

4 Other commentators derive the name London from the

Welsh Caer Lliant Dain, meaning 'fortress on the strand of the Thames'. *Lud Dinas* or 'city of Lud' has to be another contender, though, for the root from which was derived the Latin name *Londinium*.

5   Taken from G.B. Harrison, *The Letters of Queen Elizabeth*.

6   *Anglo-Saxon Chronicles*, p. 34.

7   The best of the later versions of Hardynge's Chronicle is preserved in the British Library as Harleian MS 661.

8   Gildas, *De excidio et conquestu britanniae*.

9   Ibid.

10   Ibid.

11   James Melville

12   Yates, *The Occult Philosophy*, p. 85.

CHAPTER 3

1   In 1584 Humphrey Lhoyd published his *History of Cambria* (Wales). This included a list of the kings of Brittany. Two kings by the name of Alan are mentioned, the second living at the time of Cadwallader (d. AD 689). The last king of Brittany was Saloman III. He was succeeded by Alan, first duke of Brittany, who was probably a near relative. This was about the time of the Norse invasions and the establishment of Normandy. It seems very likely, therefore, that the male Stewart line went back to this duke.

2   The last king of Scotland to be crowned at Scone was Charles II in 1651.

3   The elder sister of Queen Elizabeth I, not to be confused with Mary Queen of Scots, Mary Tudor was a devout Catholic and refused to be crowned on the coronation seat used by her brother Edward V. Instead she sat on a gilded chair blessed and sent over by the pope especially for the purpose.

4   In 1996, presumably as a sop to Scottish nationalism, the

British prime minister John Major had the Stone of Scone shipped back to Scotland. It is currently in Edinburgh.

5 C. Mageoghagan (translator), *Annals of Clonmacnoise*, edited by Denis Murphy, University Press, Dublin, 1896, pp. 26–7.

6 See R. Bauval and A. Gilbert, *The Orion Mystery*, London, 1994, ch. 11, where it is explained how the Benben stone was regarded as the seed of the phoenix.

7 Knight and Lomas. They claim to have obtained this information from the *Year Book of the Grand Lodge of Ancient Free and Accepted Masons of Scotland 1995*. See C. Knight and R. Lomas, *The Hiram Key*, Arrow, London, 1997, p. 427.

8 The City of Edessa, now called Sanliurfa, lies in south-eastern Turkey. Muslims in the area believe it to have been the birthplace of Abraham, making it a premier shrine. It also has many, later, Christian traditions associated with it. From 1099 to 1145, when it was retaken by the Muslim Turks, it was the capital of an important Frankish principality, the County of Edessa.

9 After the fall of Jerusalem in October 1187 his residence was moved to Cyprus.

10 The Stone of Scone as such was already in London at this time.

11 The *History of Britain* by Nennius was almost certainly compiled *c.*AD 800. It therefore pre-dates Geoffrey of Monmouth's *History of the Kings of Britain* by some three centuries. Nennius' sources are clearly much older than this.

12 Christopher Knight and Robert Lomas, *The Hiram Key*, Arrow, London, 1997, p. 391.

CHAPTER 4

1 For a detailed discussion of these themes see Frances Yates, Astraea, Pimlico, London, 1993.

2   While still a young man Zizka had lost one eye in a duel. Later he lost the sight of his other as well. However, even when completely blind he continued to lead his army, still winning victory after victory.

3   Robert Hooke, *The Posthumous Works of Robert Hooke*, Frank Cass, London, 1971, p. 206.

CHAPTER 5

1   This date is not given directly in the document but can be inferred.

2   *Fama Fraternitatis*, trans. A.E. Waite, in *The Real History of the Rosicrucians*, repr. Black Books, 1996, p. 77.

3   While Damcar and Damascus are frequently confused in the German text, it would appear that they are not meant to be taken as one and the same. From the context it seems that Damcar is intended to be some other place – perhaps Mecca. On the other hand, it may be an entirely imaginary creation of the author.

4   Ibid. (*Fama*), pp. 68–9.

5   Ibid. (*Fama*), p. 73.

6   Ibid. (*Confessio*), p. 92.

7   Ibid. (*Confessio*), p. 93.

8   Michael Maier, *Atalanta Fugiens*, trans. Joscelyn Godwin, Frankfurt, 1617.

9   *Confessio*, in *The Real History of the Rosicrucians*, p. 94.

10   Ibid. pp. 83–4.

11   Joscelyn Godwin, *Robert Fludd*, Thames & Hudson, London, 1979, p. 11.

CHAPTER 6

1   Prolegomena to Elias Ashmole, *Theatrum Chemicum Britannicum*, London, 1652, repr. Kessinger Publishing.

2   William Gilbert, *De Magnete*, trans. P. Fleury Mottelay, Dover, New York, 1958.

3   The site where Gresham House once stood is now occupied by the Natwest Tower.

4   Charles Piazzi Smyth, *The Great Pyramid* (first publ. as *Our Inheritance in the Great Pyramid*, London, 1864), repr. Grammercy Books, New York, 1978, pp. 137–8.

5   Ibid., p. 138.

CHAPTER 7

1   For informed arguments in favour of these theses, and even that Francis Bacon was a secret love-child of Queen Elizabeth I, see Peter Dawkins, *Francis Bacon, Herald of the New Age*, Francis Bacon Research Trust, Warwickshire, 1991.

2   Brian Vickers (ed.), *Francis Bacon* (The Oxford Authors), Oxford University Press, Oxford, 1996, p. 126.

3   Ibid., p. 169.

4   Ibid., p. 172.

5   *The Works of Francis Bacon*, ed. and trans. Basil Montague, vol. 3, Parry & MacMillan, Philadelphia, 1854, p. 333.

6   Ibid., pp. 334–5.

7   Ibid., pp. 334–6.

8   Vickers (ed.), *Francis Bacon*, p. 471.

9   Knight and Lomas, *The Hiram Key*, pp. 402–3.

10 Ibid.

11 Ibid., p. 396.

CHAPTER 8

1   He later moved on to Poland, where he established a school for the exiled Bohemian Brethren.

2   *Hermetica*, trans. Walter Scott, Solos Press, Shaftesbury, 1992, pp. 202–3.

3   See Knight and Lomas, *The Hiram Key*, p. 446.

4   See Frances Yates, *The Rosicrucian Enlightenment*, Routledge & Kegan Paul, London, 1972, p. 182.

5   Christopher Wren (jun.), *Parentalia*, London, 1741.

6   Ibid.

7   Ibid.

8   R. Chartres and D. Vermont, *A Brief History of Gresham College 1597–1997*, Gresham College, London, 1997, p. 31.

9   This was the miracle in 2 Kgs 20: 8–11, whereby the shadow on a sundial was seen to go backwards by ten degrees.

10 R. Chartres and D. Vermont, *A Brief History of Gresham College*, p. 31.

11 The bulk of the Arundel collection of books and manuscripts is now held by the British Library.

CHAPTER 9

1   Wren (jun.), *Parentalia*.

2   Michael White, *Isaac Newton*, Fourth Estate, London, 1998, p. 172.

3   Alexander Piatigorsky, *Freemasonry*, Harvill Press, London, 1997, pp. 207–8.

4   Yates, *The Rosicrucian Enlightenment*, p. 210.

5   For a convincing argument as to how the Templars were behind the Gothic explosion of the twelfth and thirteenth centuries, see Louis Charpentier, *The Mysteries of Chartres Cathedral*, Research into Lost Knowledge Organization, London, 1972.

6   See Gen. 22.

7   As Knight and Lomas point out in *The Hiram Key*, the ruins the Templars would actually have been excavating were not in fact those of Solomon's Temple but rather of King Herod's.

8   Charpentier, *The Mysteries of Chartres Cathedral*, p. 55.

9   *Hermetica*, p. 191.

CHAPTER 10

1 Anderson's *Royal Genealogies*, which lists royal pedigrees from around the world, is still regarded as the definitive volume of its kind.

2 James Anderson, *Constitutions of the Freemasons*, London, 1738.

3 Wren (jun.), *Parentalia*.

4 Brother the Revd F. de P. Castells, AKC, *Was Sir Christopher Wren a Mason?*, Kenning & Son, London, 1917, pp. 7–8.

5 Anderson, *Constitutions*, 1738 edn, p. 8.

6 Margaret Whiney, *Wren*, Thames & Hudson, London, 1971, p. 197.

7 William Stirling, *The Canon* (facs. repr.), Garnstone Press, London, 1971, pp. 238–40.

CHAPTER 11

1 *Sepher Yetzirah*, trans. Revd Dr Isidor Kalisch, L.H. Frank & Co., New York, 1877.

2 In December 1992 Robert Bauval sent me a synopsis for a proposed book entitled *Cities for the Second Coming*. Included with this synopsis was a folio of plates indicating how the principles of Hermetic-Kabbalah had found practical application in the designs for the New London as submitted by Christopher Wren and John Evelyn on the 11th and 13th of September 1666 respectively. According to Bauval, the New Jerusalem idea was expressed in Evelyn's 'Tree of Life' plan for the new city, whereby important intersections were to be placed according to the *sephiroth*. Bauval's plates also showed how the central, octagonal area of Wren's redesigned St. Paul's could have been modelled on the Dome of the Rock Mosque of 'Old Jerusalem', thereby symbolising that the cathedral was then being visualised as a new Solomon's

Temple for a 'New Jerusalem'. These ideas were to be included in a book entitled *The New Jerusalem of the West*. This was one of four books that we contracted to write together in 1993. In the event only one of them, *The Orion Mystery*, reached fruition and we abandoned the other three projects.

3 Today that distinction is held by Winchester Cathedral, whose total length is a mere 556 feet.

4 According to Stow the tower was 260 feet high with a spire of 260 feet, making 520 feet in all. According to Camden the combined total was 534 feet. Dugdale reports the tower to have been 260 feet and the spire 274 feet, again giving 534 feet as the total.

5 19 Charles II, ch. 3, section 29; see *The Official Guide to the Monument*, Corporation of London, 1994.

6 Vitruvius, *The Ten Books on Architecture*, trans. Morris Hicky Morgan, Dover, New York, 1960, p. 15.

7 *The Official Guide to the Monument*, p. 11.

8 Ibid., p. 13.

9 Ibid., p. 15.

CHAPTER 12

1 For details about the meteoritic cults of Egypt, see Bauval and Gilbert, *The Orion Mystery*.

2 For further details on this subject see Adrian Gilbert, *Signs in the Sky*, Bantam, London, 2000.

3 See Michael Baigent et al., *The Holy Blood and the Holy Grail*, Jonathan Cape, London, 1982, p. 204.

4 Geoffrey of Monmouth, *The History of the Kings of Britain*, p. 65.

5 The altitude of the sun will actually be about half a degree higher, but as the sun's diameter is itself half a degree, it will be close enough to 30° for the difference to be insignificant.

6 Vitruvius, *The Four Books of Architecture*, trans. Morgan, pp. 13–14.

7   William Lethaby, *Architecture, Mysticism and Myth*, Solos Press, Shaftesbury, 1994, p. 14.

8   Ibid., pp. 184–5.

9   For further details on this subject see Gilbert, *Signs in the Sky*.

10 The sun still culminates at 51° 51′ on 18 August, but because of precession, although it is still in the sign of Leo at this time, it is no longer conjunct with Regulus.

11 Vitruvius, *The Four Books of Architecture*, trans. Morgan, p. 114.

CHAPTER 13

1   Figures from *Encyclopaedia Britannica*, 1951 edn, vol. 14, p. 356.

2   Smyth, *The Great Pyramid*, p. 558.

3   Pamphlet by Brother F. W. Seal-Coon, archives of Grand Lodge, London.

4   Piatigorsky, *Freemasonry*, p. 246.

5   Pamphlet by Seal-Coon.

6   She continued in this role until her death in 1981.

APPENDIX

1   Caesar: *The Conquest of Gaul*, trans. Handford, p. 111.

BIBLIOGRAPHY

Anderson, James, *Constitutions*, London, 1738.

Ashmole, Elias, *Theatrum Chemicum Britannicum*, originally London, 1652, reprinted by Kessinger Publishing Co., Montana, 1990.

Ashmole, Elias, *The History of the Most Noble Order of the Garter*, first published London, 1715, reprinted by Kessinger Publishing Co., Montana, 1998.

Baigent, Michael, Richard Leigh and Henry Lincoln, *The Holy Blood and Holy Grail*, Jonathan Cape, London, 1982.

Bligh Bond, Frederick, *An Architectural Handbook of Glastonbury Abbey*, originally London 1909, reprinted by Research into Lost Knowledge Organization, London, 1981.

Caesar; S.A. Handford (trans.), *The Conquest of Gaul*, Book Club Associates, London, 1993.

Charpentier, Louis; Ronald Fraser (trans.), *The Mysteries of Chartres Cathedral*, Research into Lost Knowledge

Organization, London, 1972.

Chartres, Bishop Richard and David Vermont, A *Brief History of Gresham College 1597–1997*, Gresham College, London, 1997.

Dawkins, Peter, *Francis Bacon, Herald of the New Age*, Francis Bacon Research Trust, Warwickshire, 1997.

Geoffrey of Monmouth; Lewis Thorpe (trans.), *History of the Kings of Britain*, Penguin Books, London, 1996.

Gilbert, Adrian, Alan Wilson and Baram Blackett, *The Holy Kingdom*, Bantam Press, London, 1998.

Gilbert, Adrian, *Signs in the Sky*, Bantam Press, London, 2000.

Gilbert, William; P. Fleury Mottelay (trans.), *De Magnete*, originally London 1893, republished by Dover Publications, New York, 1958.

Godwin, Joscelyn, *Robert Fludd*, Thames & Hudson, London, 1979.

Harrison, G.B., *The Letters of Queen Elizabeth*, Funk & Wagnall, New York, 1935, reprinted 1968.

Hooke, Robert, *The Posthumous Works of Robert Hooke*, Frank Cass & Co. Ltd, London, 1971.

Kalisch, Isidor (trans.), *Sepher Yezirah*, L. H. Frank & Co., New York, 1877.

Lethaby, William, *Architecture, Mysticism and Myth*, Solos Press, Dorset, 1994.

Lhoyd, Humphrey, *History of Cambria*, London, 1584.

Maier, Michael; Joscelyn Godwin (trans.), *Atalanta Fugiens*, Phanes Press, Grand Rapids, 1989.

Mendoza, Ramon, *The Acentric Labyrinth, Giordano Bruno's Prelude to Contemporary Cosmology*, Element Books, Shaftesbury, 1995.

Michell, John, *New Light on the Ancient Mystery of Glastonbury*, Gothic Image, Glastonbury, 1990.

Michell, John, *Dimensions of Paradise* (formerly *City of*

Revelation), Thames & Hudson, London, 1988.

Montague, Basil (ed. & trans.), *The Works of Francis Bacon*, Parry & MacMillan, Philadelphia, 1854.

Morgan, Morris Hicky (trans.), Vitruvius, *The Ten Books on Architecture*, originally Harvard University Press, 1914, reprinted by Dover Publications, New York, 1960.

Pennick, Nigel, *Sacred Geometry*, Thorsons, Wellingborough, 1980.

Piatigorsky, Alexander, *Freemasonry*, The Harvill Press, London, 1997.

Roberts, Peter (trans.), *The Chronicles of the Kings of Britain*, translated from the Welsh copy attributed to Tysilio, E. Williams, London, 1811.

Savage, Anne (trans.) *The Anglo-Saxon Chronicles*, Papermac, London, 1984.

Scott, Walter (trans.), *Hermetica*, Solos Press, Dorset, 1992.

Smyth, Charles Piazzi, *The Great Pyramid*, originally published as *Our Inheritance in the Great Pyramid*, London, 1880, reprinted by Grammercy Books, New York, 1978.

Stirling, William, *The Canon*, originally London, 1897, reprinted by Garnstone Press, London, 1971.

Tacitus, *The Annals of Imperial Rome*, translated by Michael Grant, Book Club Associates, London, 1990.

Vickers, Brian (ed.), *The Oxford Authors, Francis Bacon*, Oxford University Press, Oxford, 1996.

Waite, Arthur Edward (trans.), *The Real History of the Rosicrucians*, first published London 1887, reprinted by Black Books, USA, 1996.

Whiney, Margaret, *Wren*, Thames & Hudson, London, 1971.

White, Michael, *Isaac Newton*, Fourth Estate, London, 1998.

Williams, Taliesin (comp. and trans.), *Iolo MSS*, Foulkes, Liverpool, 1888.

Williams, Revd. J. ab Ithel, *Barddas*, Welsh Manuscript Society, Longman & Co., London, 1862.

Yates, Dame Frances A., *Astraea*, Pimlico, London, 1975.

Yates, Dame Frances A., *Giordano Bruno and the Hermetic Tradition*, Routledge, London, 1978.

Yates, Dame Frances A., *The Occult Philosophy*, Ark, London, 1983.

Yates, Dame Frances A., *The Rosicrucian Enlightenment*, Routledge, London, 1993.

INDEX

NOTE: rulers of England have the title 'king' or 'queen'; those of other countries have the title and name of country. Page numbers in *italics* denote illustrations; those in **bold** are plates.

413

417

428

SIGNS IN THE SKY
Prophecies for the birth of a new age
by Adrian Gilbert

In this riveting archaeological detective story, bestselling author Adrian Gilbert reveals the true meaning of the prophecies of the Old and New Testaments, prophecies that have an enormous significance for our own age.

The prophets of the ancient world, in their search for a fixed calendar on which to inscribe the dates of events far into the future, looked to the skies. In a world before electric light, the revolution of the stars and progression of the constellations of the zodiac were an accurate and lasting means of measuring the passage of time. The astrologically aligned monuments – such as the pyramids – were placed to record the progress of the years, counting down to the end of an age.

The constellation of Orion, the figure of Man set in stars, has now arrived at its northernmost point – a journey that has taken nearly 13,000 years. At the same time, the summer-solstice sun, in the hand of Orion, is due to cross the eastern and western sky exactly over the Khafre pyramid. The belt of Orion is now rising over the Mount of Olives in Jerusalem; and on either side of the Orion constellation will be visible the seven planets of the ancients – the seven angels of prophecy. Could this be the Sign of the Son of Man in Heaven, described in the Book of Revelation as marking the beginning of the Apocalypse? It will not be long before we find out.

0 552 14710 9

A SELECTED LIST OF NON-FICTION TITLES AVAILABLE FROM CORGI BOOKS

THE PRICES SHOWN BELOW WERE CORRECT AT THE TIME OF GOING TO PRESS. HOWEVER
TRANSWORLD PUBLISHERS RESERVE THE RIGHT TO SHOW NEW RETAIL PRICES ON COVERS
WHICH MAY DIFFER FROM THOSE PREVIOUSLY ADVERTISED IN THE TEXT OR ELSEWHERE.

All Transworld titles are available by post from:
Bookpost, PO Box 29, Douglas, Isle of Man, IM99 1BQ
Credit cards accepted. Please telephone 01624 836000,
fax 01624 837033, Internet http://www.bookpost.co.uk
or e-mail: bookshop@enterprise.net for details.
Free postage and packing in the UK. Overseas customers: allow
£1 per book (paperbacks) and £3 per book (hardbacks).